I0795708

IMAGES
of America

BROOME COUNTY 1850–1940

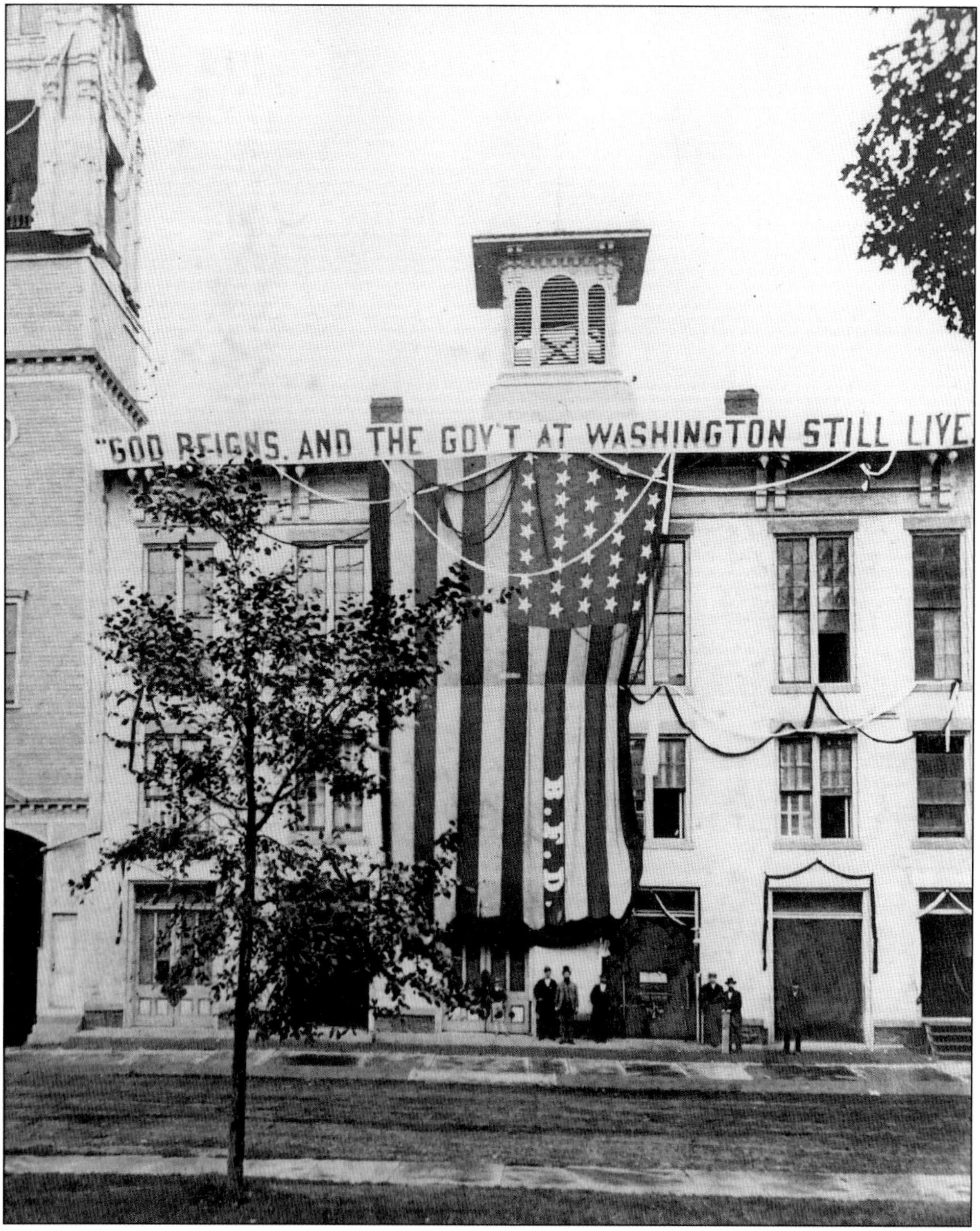

The Binghamton Fire Department, built in 1857, is draped in bunting to celebrate the end of the Civil War.

IMAGES
of America

BROOME COUNTY 1850–1940

Ed Aswad and Suzanne M. Meredith
Foreword by David Rossie

ARCADIA
PUBLISHING

ISBN 978-0-7385-1075-0

Published by Arcadia Publishing
Charleston, South Carolina

Printed in the United States of America

Library of Congress Catalog Card Number: 2002106715

For all general information contact Arcadia Publishing at:
Telephone 843-853-2070
Fax 843-853-0044
E-mail sales@arcadiapublishing.com
For customer service and orders:
Toll-Free 1-888-313-2665

Visit us on the Internet at www.arcadiapublishing.com

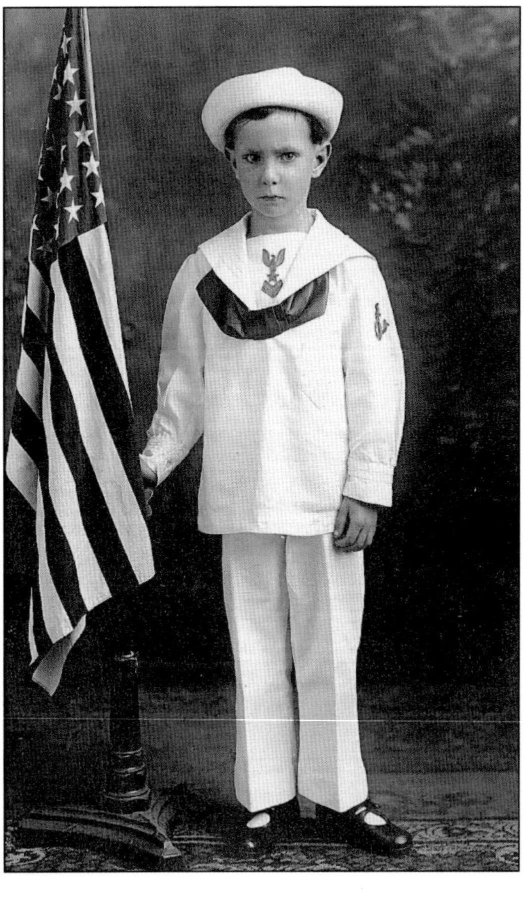

A seven-year-old boy exhibits patriotism prior to World War I.

Contents

ACKNOWLEDGMENTS

The authors are grateful to the many people who contributed time, advice, photographs and friendship. Without the help of the following, this book would not have been possible: the Amos Patterson Museum, Betty Bartlow, Robert Barber, Patty Blishak (deputy commissioner), the Town of Union Parks Department, Charles J. Brown, the Broome County Historical Society, the Broome County Library History Center, Alfred Eno, John Green, Charlotte Harrington, Pam and Glen Hicks, Thomas Hipp, Don Jordon, Robert Keller, Maureen Kimble, Janice Mangan, Ruth Mcadon, Wayne Meyers, Dr. Thomas Nytch, Robert and Betty Palmer, Leonard and Evelyn Robenolt, Alice Ruby, Ralph Sheehy, Gerald Smith, Hope Spicer, Jacqueline Tedesco, the Town of Union Parks Department staff, Laddie Vana, Mary Wilson, Paul Youngs, Dorothy Hatounian, and John Simon of Skipperwood Music.

Special thanks go to David Rossie for the foreword, Rev. Cynthia Kimler for the introduction; and Pearl Webb for editing the book.

FOREWORD

If my grandparents, who lived most of their lives in Broome County, could by some happy circumstance return, they would, I fear, find little that looked familiar. "Whatever became of the Boston Store?" my grandmother might ask. The Boston Store was what she called the department store that stood at the corner of Court and Water Streets long after it stopped being the Boston Store and became Fowler Dick and Walker, which, of course, is now Boscov's. What, for that matter, became of Water Street?

Ah, but hand them a copy of this book of photographs that recall life here in the late 19th and early 20th century and I suspect they would smile and say, "Yes, yes, I remember. That is how it was."

Change is unrelenting. Time passes; so do generations. Memories fade, and our ties to history, once personal, are reduced to yellowed newspaper clippings, letters, and family albums. That is what Ed Aswad and Sue Meredith have put together in these pages, a family album of sorts; the family being those who made what was grandly if incorrectly called "the Triple Cities" into a vibrant industrial community that was a model of diversity long before sociologists put a name to it.

Women and children no longer roll cigars or stitch fabrics in sweatshops for pennies an hour, and that is a good thing. Men and women no longer make shoes in a dozen EJ factories that reached from Endicott to Binghamton, and that is not good. The work has gone, not just from our communities but from our shores. The empty factories, their windows broken, remain as silent reminders of a once vibrant era.

If past is prologue, as Shakespeare wrote, perhaps we may someday see a return of the hop fields, a local brewery or two, and maybe even a renewal of passenger rail service, but not, if I get to choose, the Great Bend rattlesnake farm).

Until then, we have these photographs to keep the memories alive.

—David Rossie

INTRODUCTION

From somewhere in my childhood memories, a song takes flight whenever I see the name Broome County. I hear gentle acoustic guitar music, the sincere voice of a friend, and words that so many people have come to understand and associate with their lives.

A few phrases from a song by John Simon bring to mind why we live in this beautiful valley:

> For better or worse I ended here—
> But now I'm home in Broome County,
> I'm at home with all of you;
> and even when I don't know what to do;
> I've got new friends like you to help see me through.

The history of Broome County is the story of people who, searching for a better life, came to the valley of opportunity and, for better or worse, found themselves at home. In this fascinating new book, Aswad and Meredith look into the lives of these ordinary and extraordinary people. The photographs and stories included in the collection offer glimpses at life in all its fullness: the good, the cads, and the weird—everything from mobsters to sea monsters, wild pigs running amok to a beer-guzzling firehorse. There are legends of lost treasure, shadows of previous cultures, otherworldly spirits and spirits distilled, caves and secret rooms, ruffians and holy hoppers, remedies, marital advice, and many practical uses for road dust. The images and words open to us a portal not to another world, but to our world—the people and events that helped fashion who we are as a community today. Broome County continues to be a place where people end up, and are all the better for it, as they, and we, find ourselves truly at home.

These stories are indeed the byways of Broome, where humor and character will always survive. An ancient Indian oration says, "Our names and spirits are on the waters and will never wash away." All the names before and after us join those spirits on the waters and wind, making us a part of the timeless cycle of Broome County.

—Rev. Cynthia Kimler

One

Early Broome

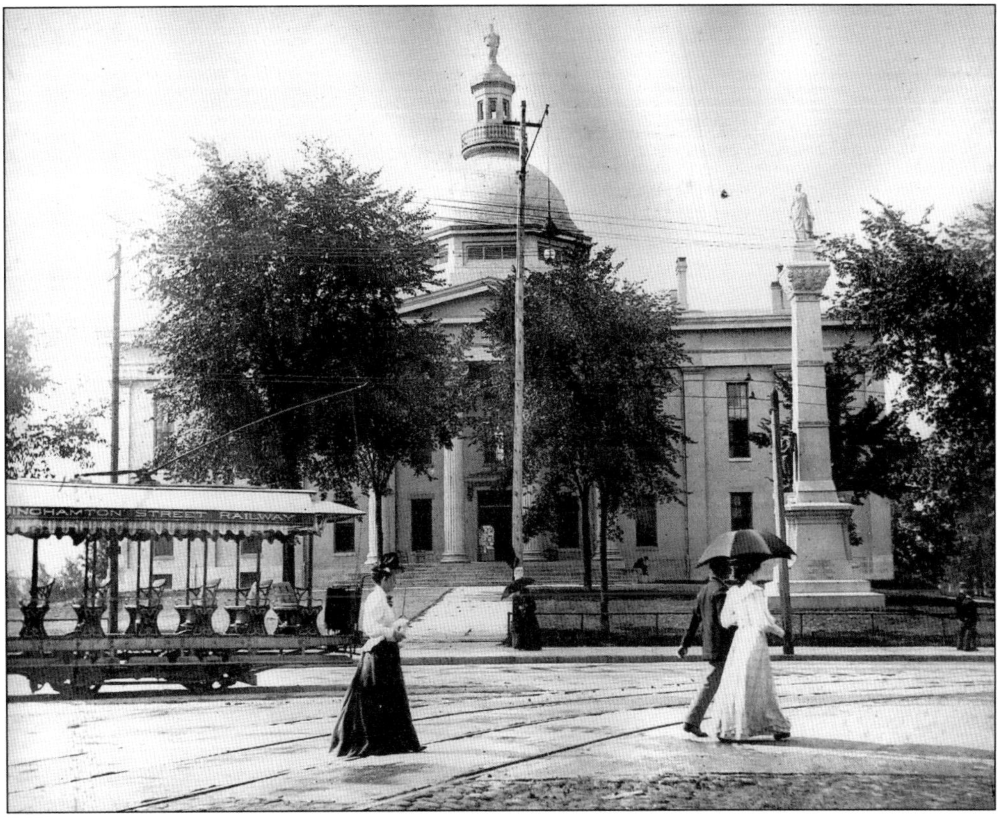

Broome County is the heart of the southern tier of New York. Binghamton is the seat of its government and symbol of welcome to a community rich in heritage and promise for the future, ready to meet the challenges of a new day. It is a valley of merging waterways embowered in hills of dramatically changing foliage, a vista holding a symphony of memories and an area in transition from industrial dominance to the unlimited potential of tomorrow.

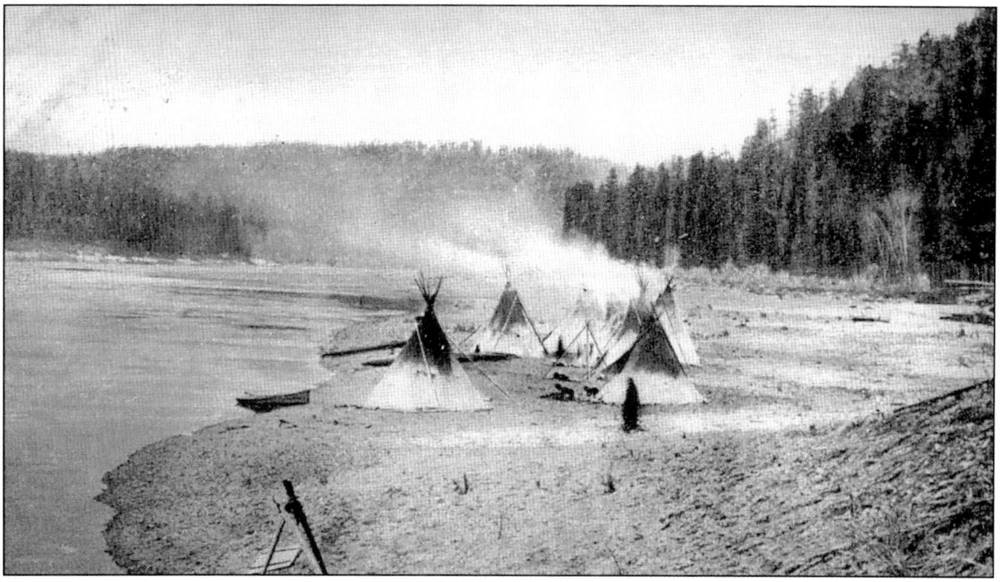

Broome County was Iroquois territory when European explorers arrived, and there is documented evidence of Native American settlements dating from 2000 B.C. The people hunted prehistoric beasts, fished, and farmed using stone tools and points similar to those pictured below, all collected regionally. Many of their settlements were eliminated during the Clinton-Sullivan campaign of the Revolutionary War, but evidence of their life can still be found along the rivers and mountains. The photograph above is a re-creation of a temporary Native American settlement on the bank of the river.

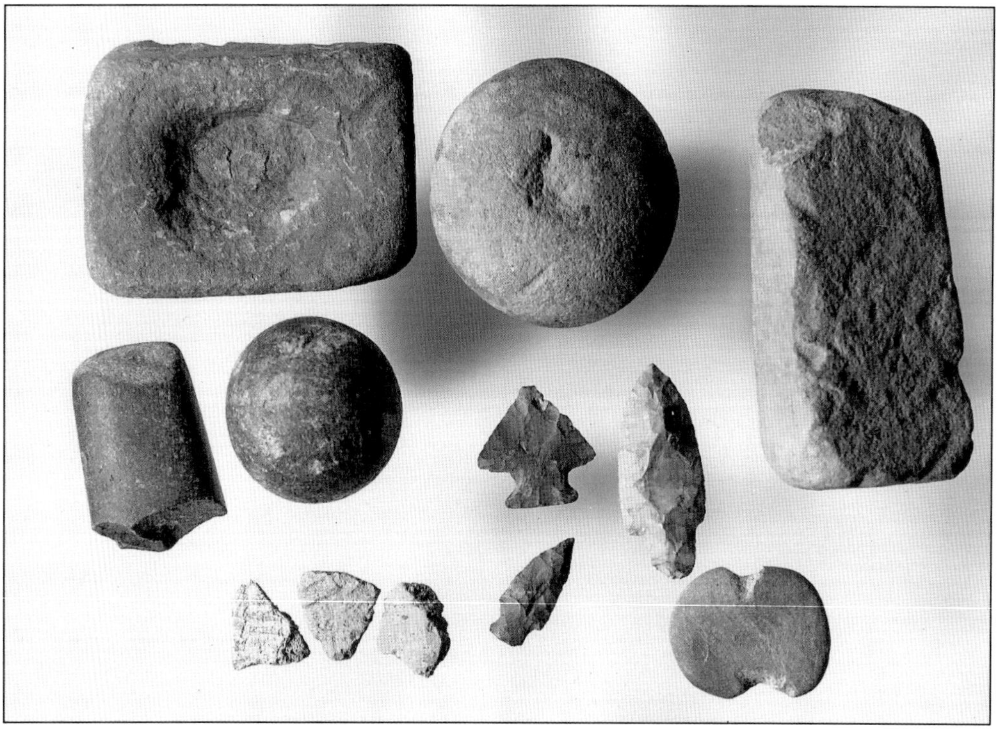

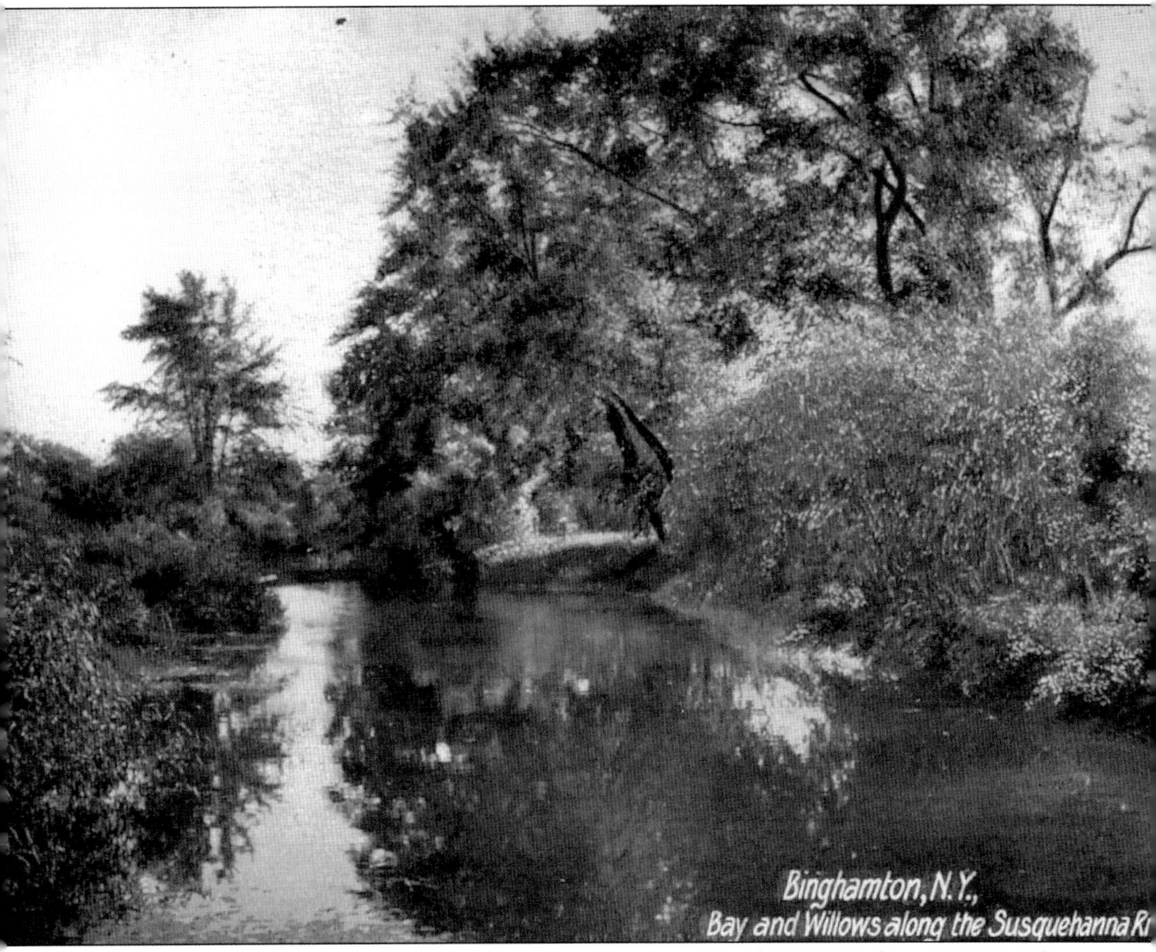

At the "willows" on the Susquehanna River, Native Americans began a trek to retrieve salt from a secret source. Within 12 hours they returned with buckets of the still-warm salt. Because salt was a valuable trade item, homesteaders tried to follow the natives and discover the secret location, but were always unsuccessful. Thong trees dotted the landscape; however, the new settlers did not understand the significance of the living signals. Bent as saplings and held in place with leather thongs, the angled trees pointed toward springs or salt pits.

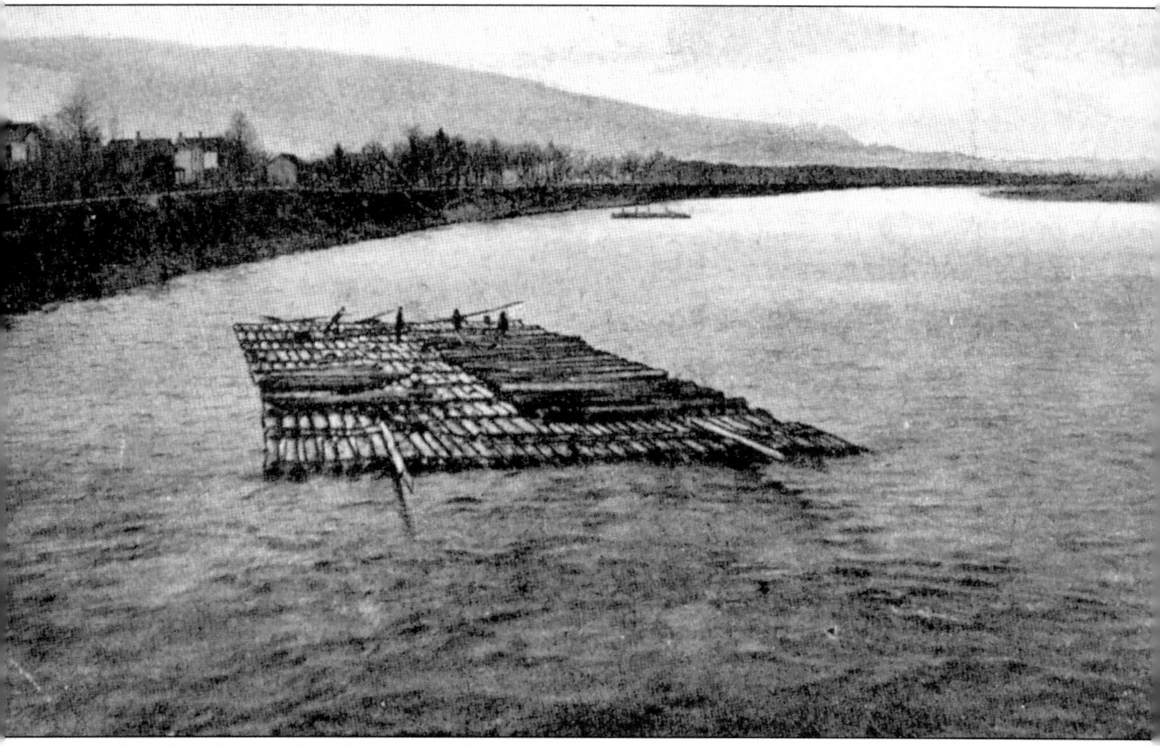

Abundant forests played a major role in pioneer economy, inspiring a thriving lumber industry. In the spring, logs were floated downstream in huge rafts to distant markets. A Vestal man left a diary recording events of a raft trip in 1881:

> 4/25—got stuck on a rock above Skinners at Rocky Forest Mountain in attempting to land. Tried for an hour to get off but got dark and waited until morn, pushed the raft off with a Yankee windlass.
> 4/26—got up at 4:15 & got on river again.
> 4/27—went through Nanticoke shoot, two feet of water in the shoot, our spring pole broke and let the forward platform hang up on the bottom of the shoot and broke ends of two runners before getting on stern first.
> 4/30—reached Harrisburg and had an offer of $15.00.
> 5/5—Hirtaud made an offer but not enough, Cassillo looked at the raft.
> 5/6—sold the raft to Mr. Small. EXPENSES: shaving 10 cents—paid cartage 75 cents—steak 15 cents—postcards 5 cents.

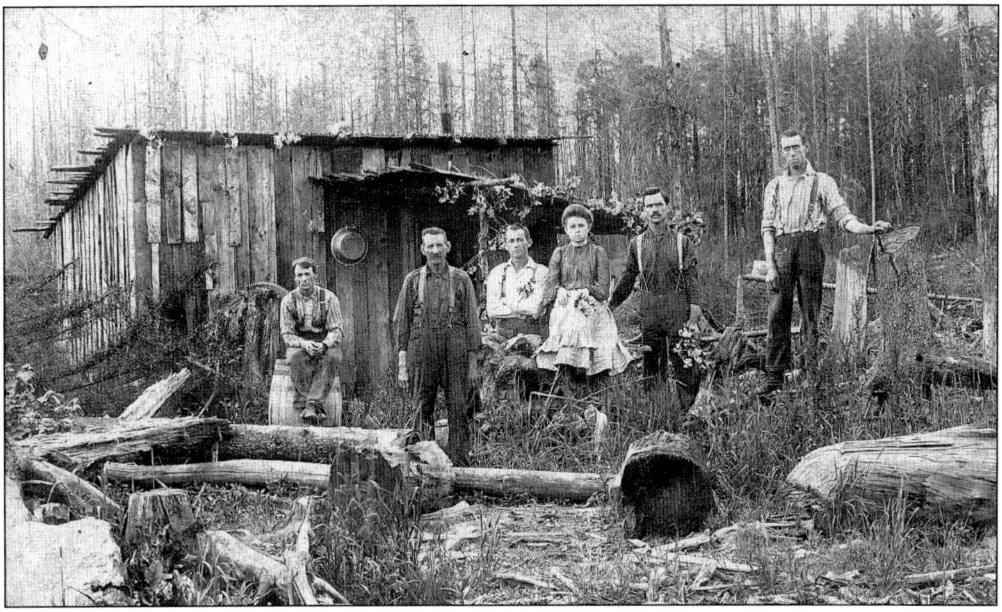

In 1876, a writer described a slowly developing area: "During the process of getting off lumber, agriculture was sadly neglected and Broome County had a most slovenly appearance. When the last tree fell, then attention was paid to cultivating the land and homestead surroundings." This cabin is probably from the slovenly era.

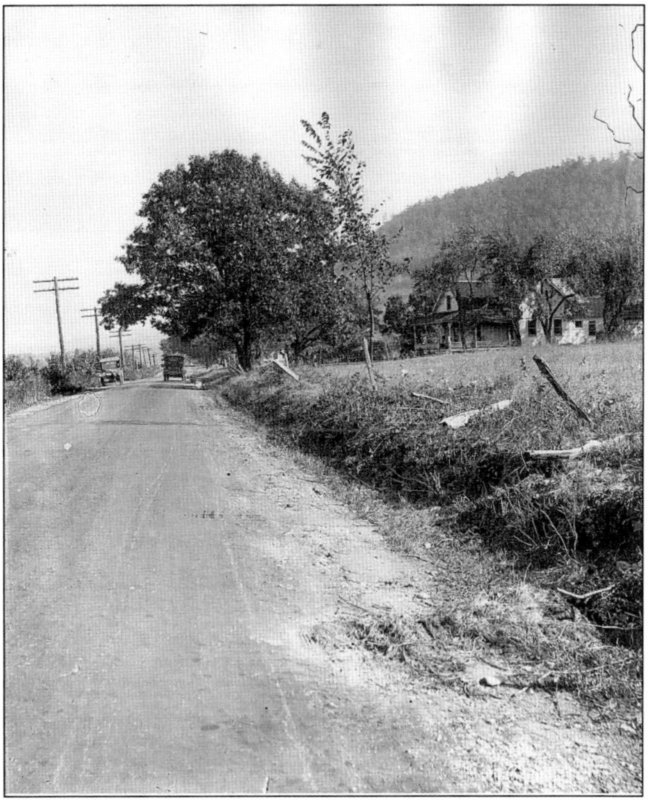

Settlers Col. William Rose and Leonard and Amos Draper built cabins near this site on what is now Front Street in Binghamton. They purchased land from the Native Americans for one barrel of corn a year, plus part of the game killed. The lease was later voided by New York, as law prohibited individuals from "dickering with the natives." In more recent years, the county poor farm was constructed in this area.

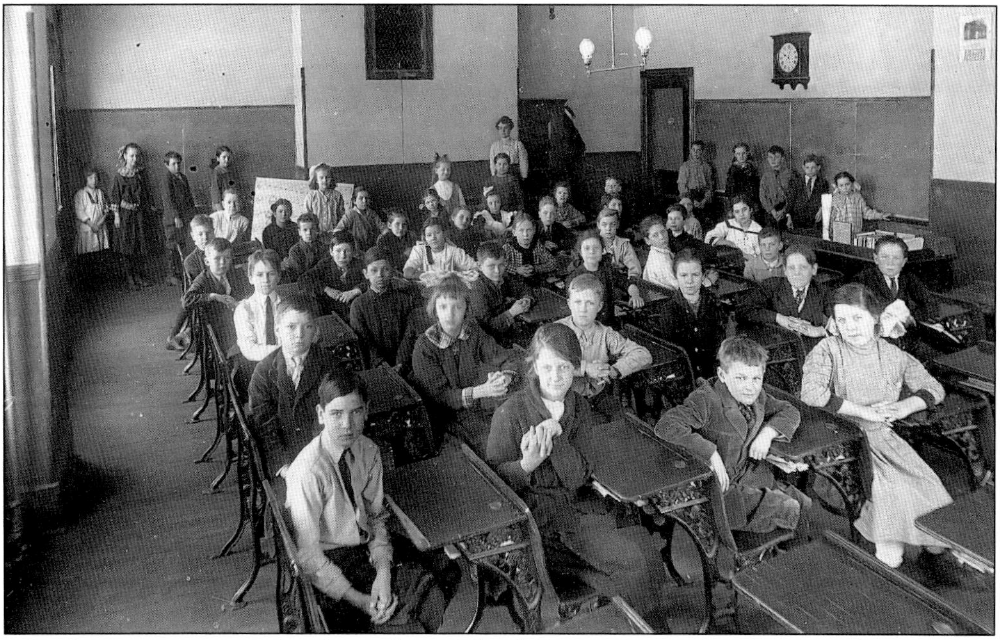

Schools were a priority of early residents. The following letters from local teachers describe their situations:

> 1849—My small charges are running and laughing, some busily employed adorning the walls with maple boughs and scattering leaves all over the floor that I must keep clean. My school house is furnished with all the necessary apparatus, Mitchells outline maps, a globe, a large blackboard, brooms, dippers, a ruler and a bed for the small ones to rest upon. My scholars number about 30 and are as pretty as any children I ever saw. I am to provide the fuel for winter and the parents bring in books. They are building an academy here and it will be a fine place for the young ladies.
> 1925—I have about 60 pupils all the time and I am almost a frazzling when work is done.
> The certificate is for a local teacher in 1865, who had to be qualified in moral character as well as learning. The photograph is a 1916 class of respectful, well-dressed children.

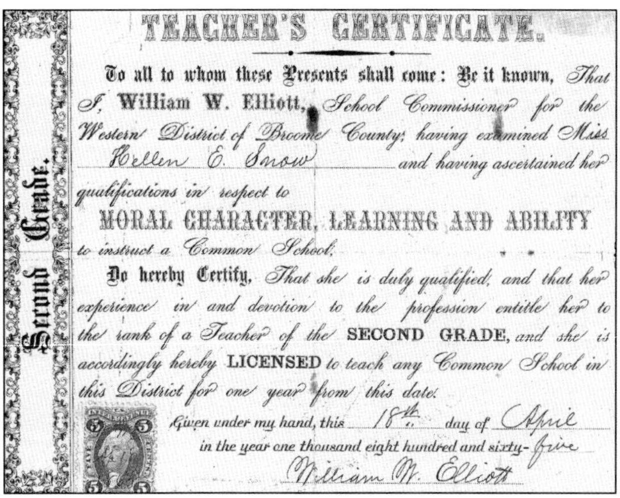

Second Grade.

TEACHER'S CERTIFICATE.

To all to whom these Presents shall come: Be it known, That I, William W. Elliott, School Commissioner for the Western District of Broome County; having examined Miss Hellen E. Snow and having ascertained her qualifications in respect to

MORAL CHARACTER, LEARNING AND ABILITY

to instruct a Common School,

Do hereby Certify, That she is duly qualified, and that her experience in and devotion to the profession entitle her to the rank of a Teacher of the SECOND GRADE, and she is accordingly hereby LICENSED to teach any Common School in this District for one year from this date.

Given under my hand, this 18th day of April in the year one thousand eight hundred and sixty-five

William W. Elliott

Long ago it was not unusual for several generations of a family to live together. The elderly contributed to the household by performing less-demanding tasks. A loom was standard equipment in early homes, when all the material for clothes, blankets, sheets, and towels was homespun. Working the loom was the perfect occupation for Grandma Bolles in 1900.

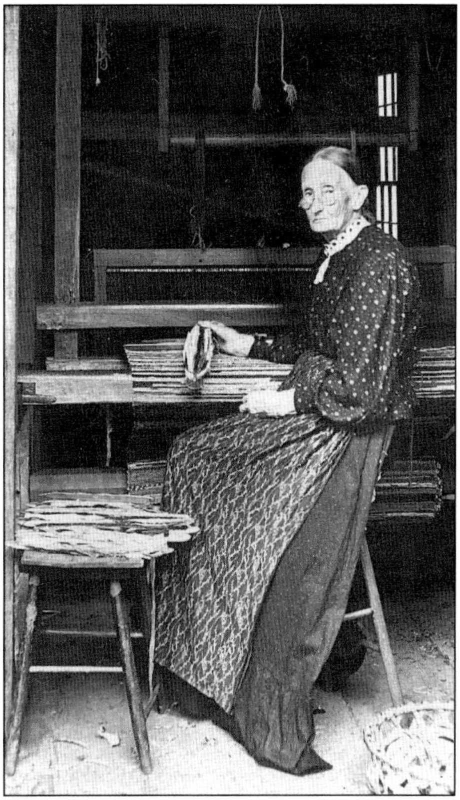

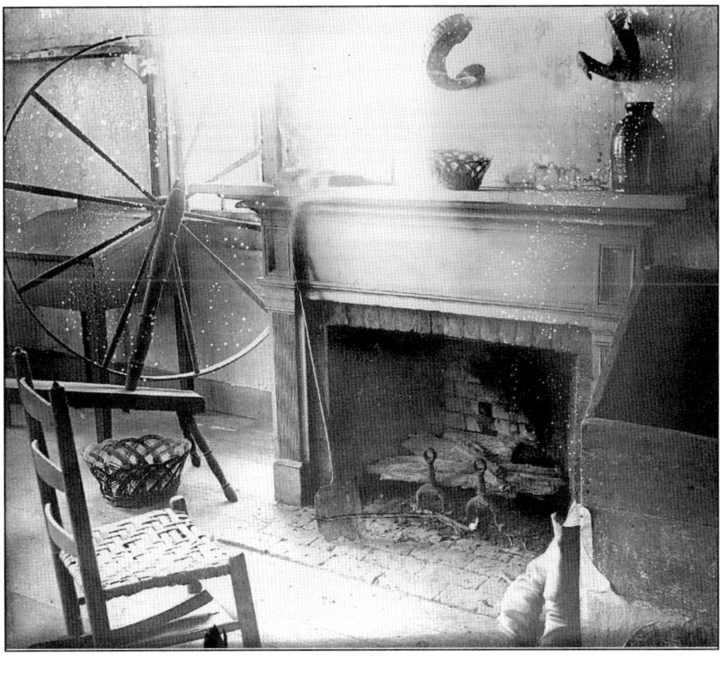

Nearly every cabin had a spinning wheel near the fireplace. Most homesteaders had neither the cash nor the opportunity to purchase ready-made items from stores. Spinning and weaving were often the occupations for the elderly lady or the live-in "spinster." Work was accomplished by the faint glow of the fire or oil lamps.

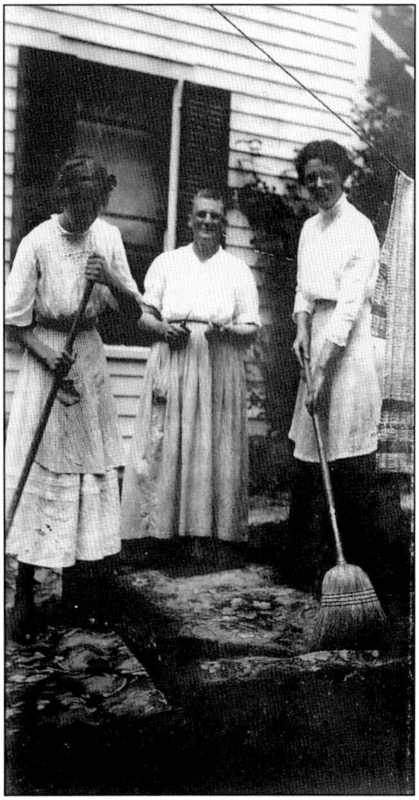

Women used whisk brooms to clean carpets in 1910. The need for brooms and accessories inspired several local businesses (none remain). Working life was documented in a 1845 letter: "I am to work for Wm. Green making broom machines and the pay is steady." In 1905, Doolittle and Son produced a "Broome and Towel Holder" guaranteed to make a broom last longer and keep its shape, using the spelling of the county to promote products.

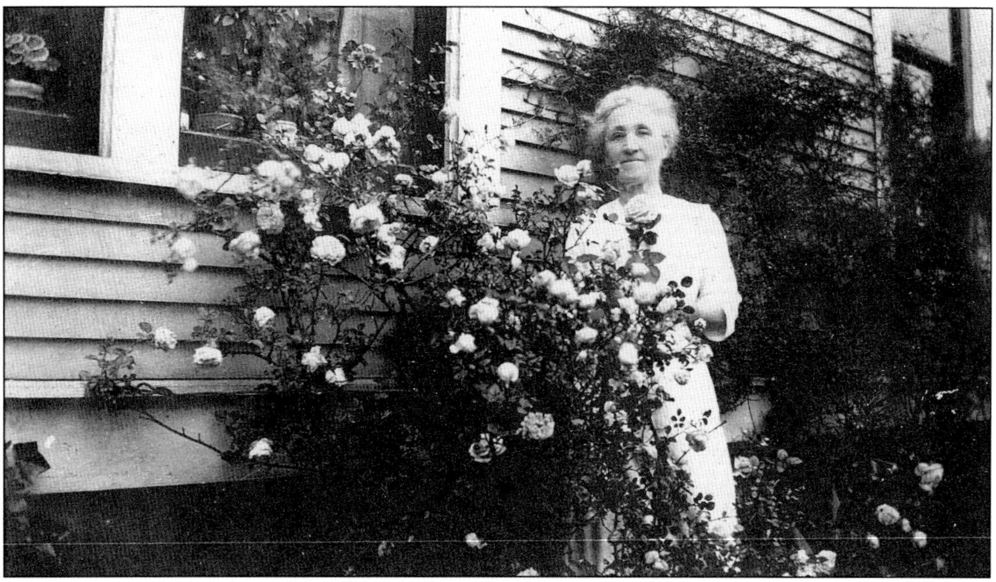

The lady pictured received this letter in 1870: "Helen, I must tell you what I was afraid to say when I was there. I love you will you be my wife. I have not got much to call my own but I think poor folks take as much comfort as the rich. I can support you if I have my health thou perhaps not in such style as you would like."

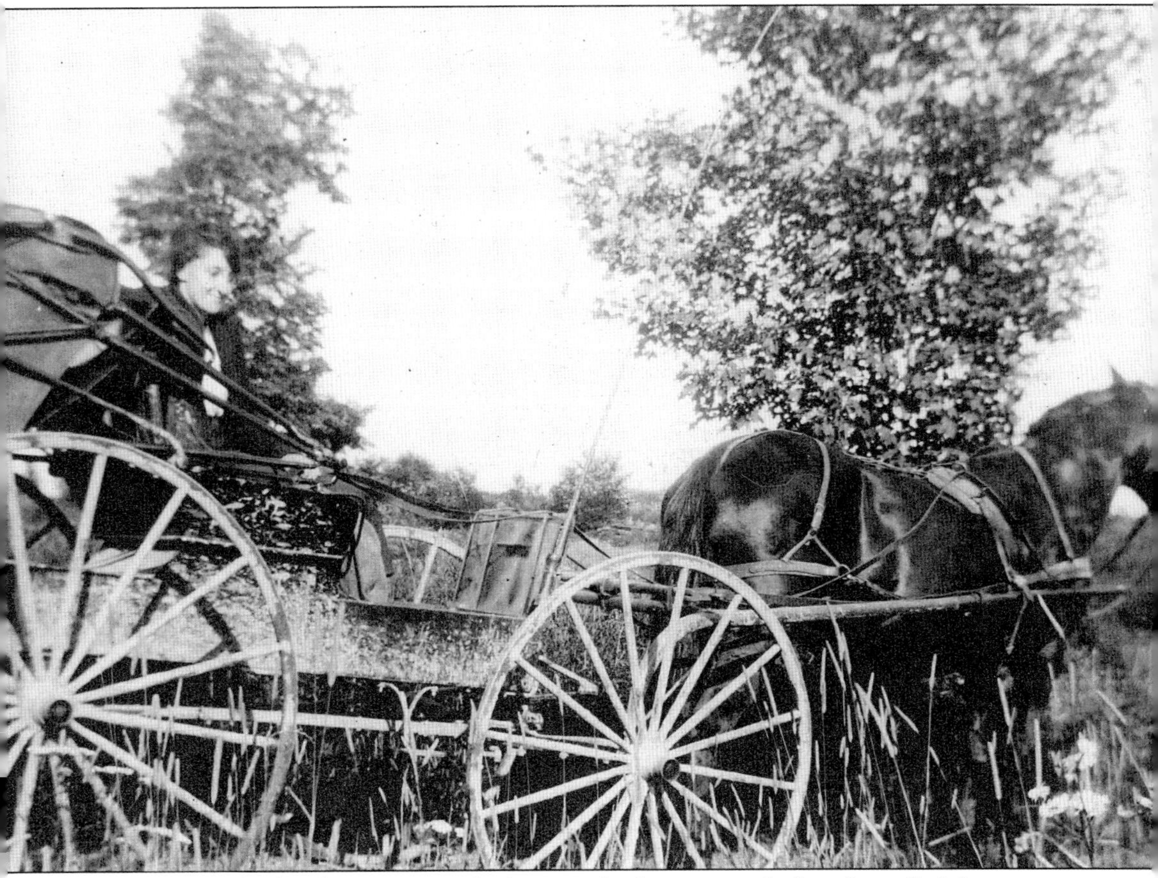

Each year after the last harvest moon had set, at the beginning of what she called the posset season, Grandma Harriet would hitch the buggy and pack it with bolts of red flannel and the secret ingredients for her infamous asafetida bags. She journeyed to all the relatives to make sure they would survive harsh winter elements and ill humors. Each of her progeny was fitted with a double layer of long red flannel underwear. The victims, as they regarded themselves, were securely sewn into a union suit and given instructions to remain so covered until spring. Around every neck Grandma hung her specialty, a small pungent sack of herbs. The family has a record of members living to "ripe" old ages, perhaps attributable to the asafetida bags' ability to repel both germs and humans. Considering what the aroma must have been by spring, the wonder may be that anyone got close enough to have descendants.

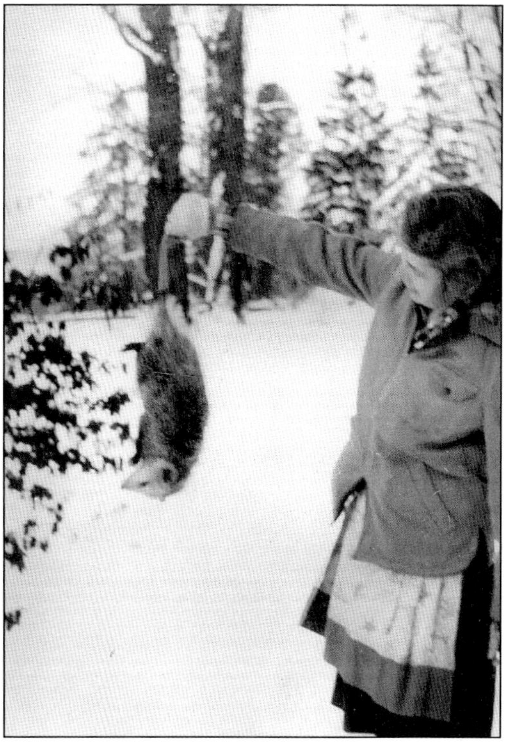

A recipe was included with this photograph: "Use freshly got opossum. Clean it like a pig, scrape, not skin it. Chop liver very fine and mix with bread crumbs and such, onion, and spices and bind it with an egg and stuff the body with this. Sew up opening, roast and baste. Make crispy by rubbing with a rag dipped in its own grease. Also makes a very palatable stew."

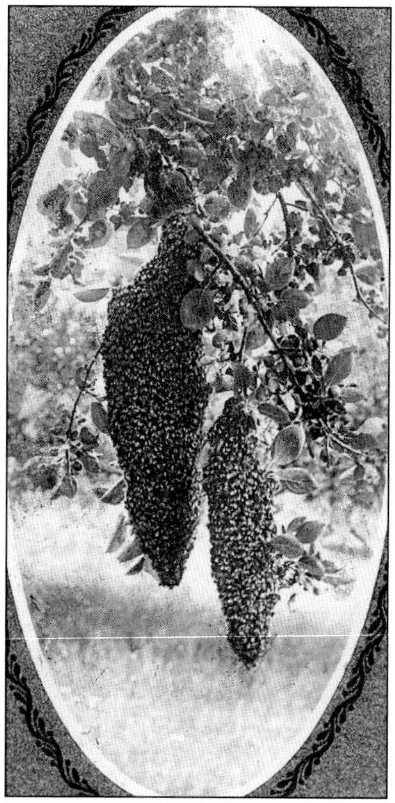

A photographer with a good eye captured this artistic swarm of bees in 1900. Bees were considered part of the early household, and hives were draped in black crepe at the death of a family member. Honey was used as food and as a cure for ulcers, rheumatism, catarrh, croup, and sore throat. It was also used to make mead.

The Rounds family was among the earliest settlers in Vestal. Heila Rounds, born in 1905, managed the Rounds Coal Company and lived on the family estate until her death in 2001. In this photograph she is five years old.

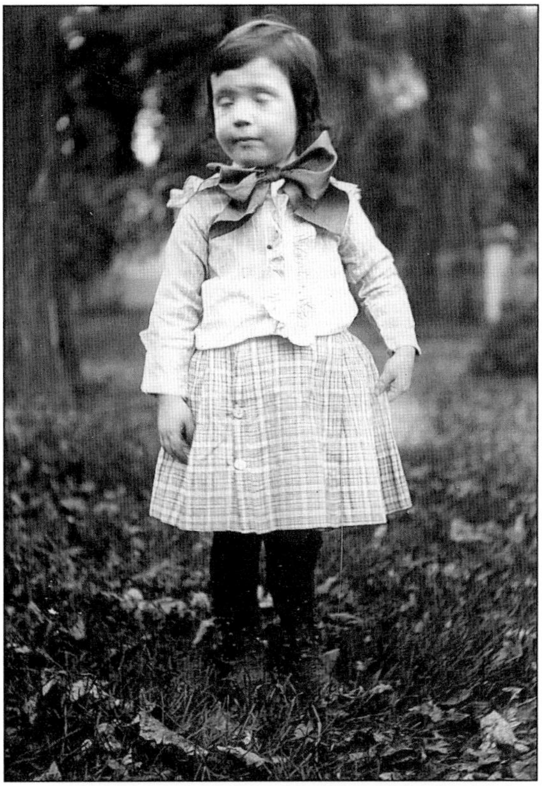

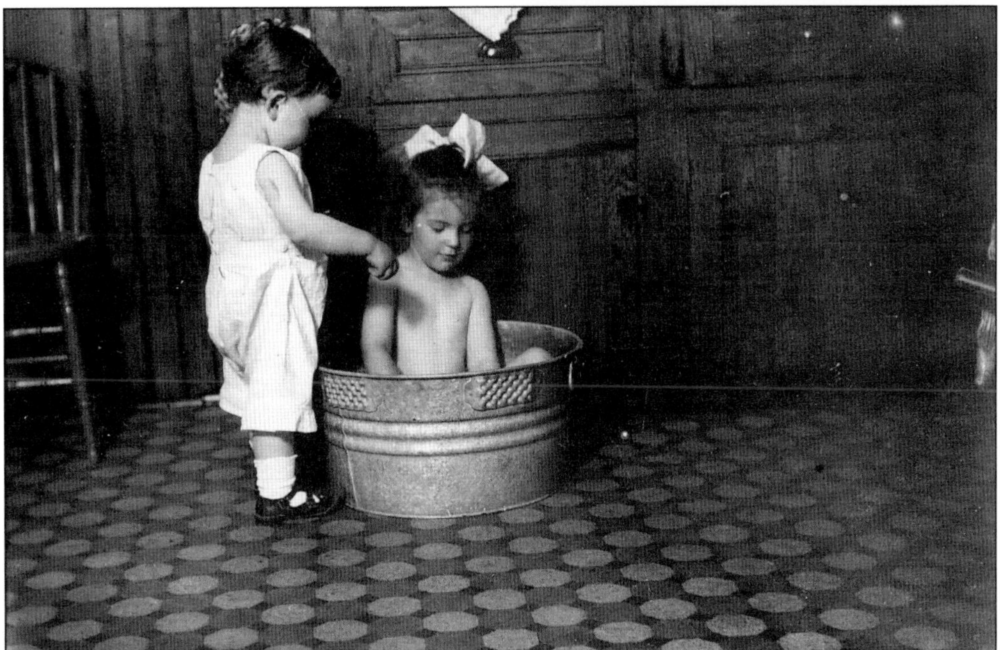

When this photograph was taken in 1897, approximately eight percent of the country had running water and bathroom facilities in the house. A galvanized tub in the kitchen was standard equipment for the occasional bath.

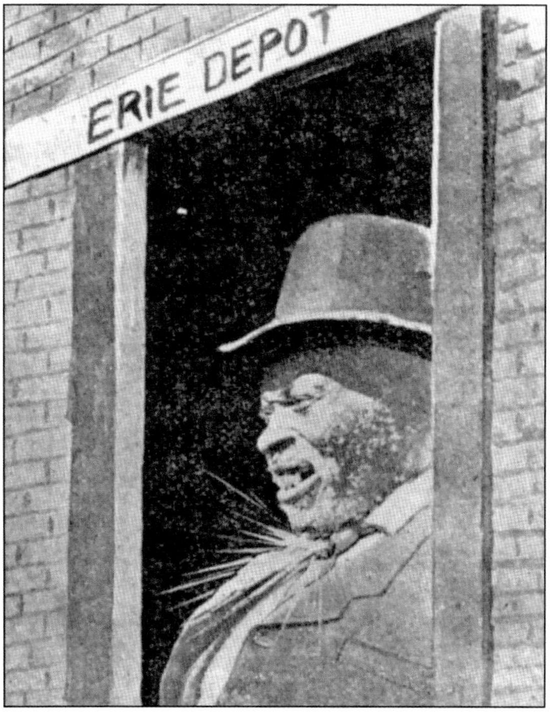

Born into slavery in Dixie, "Laughing Charlie" escaped to the North by traveling to freedom on the Underground Railroad. He ran a barbershop in Union in 1901 and later worked as a bootblack in the Binghamton Erie Train Station. His philosophy was, "Have all the fun in this here world you can, don't never cry and don't get mad, laugh and the Lord will hear you."

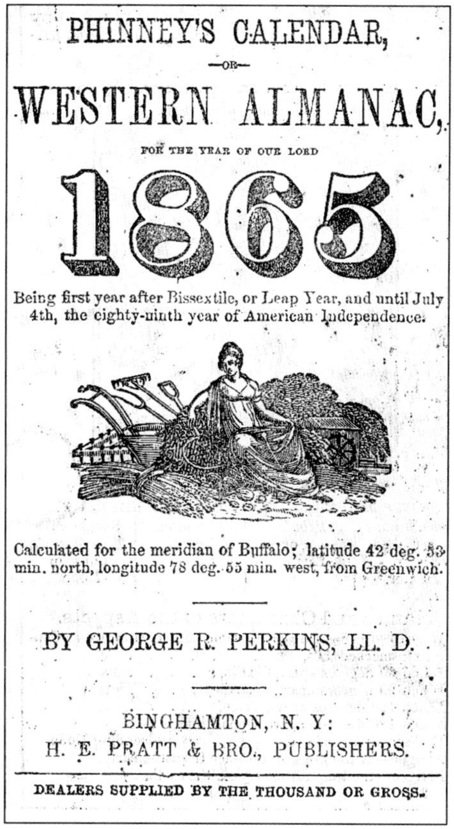
PHINNEY'S CALENDAR,

—OR—

WESTERN ALMANAC,

FOR THE YEAR OF OUR LORD

1865

Being first year after Bissextile, or Leap Year, and until July 4th, the eighty-ninth year of American Independence.

Calculated for the meridian of Buffalo; latitude 42 deg. 53 min. north, longitude 78 deg. 55 min. west, from Greenwich.

BY GEORGE R. PERKINS, LL. D.

BINGHAMTON, N. Y:
H. E. PRATT & BRO., PUBLISHERS.

DEALERS SUPPLIED BY THE THOUSAND OR GROSS.

H. Pratt and Brothers was in business in Binghamton prior to 1858, selling books, stationery, and paper hangings. That year, they paid a wholesaler 12 cents each for 8 rolls of ordinary wallpaper and obtained 10 strips of border for 90 cents. By 1865, publishing was added to the list of services and this almanac was printed.

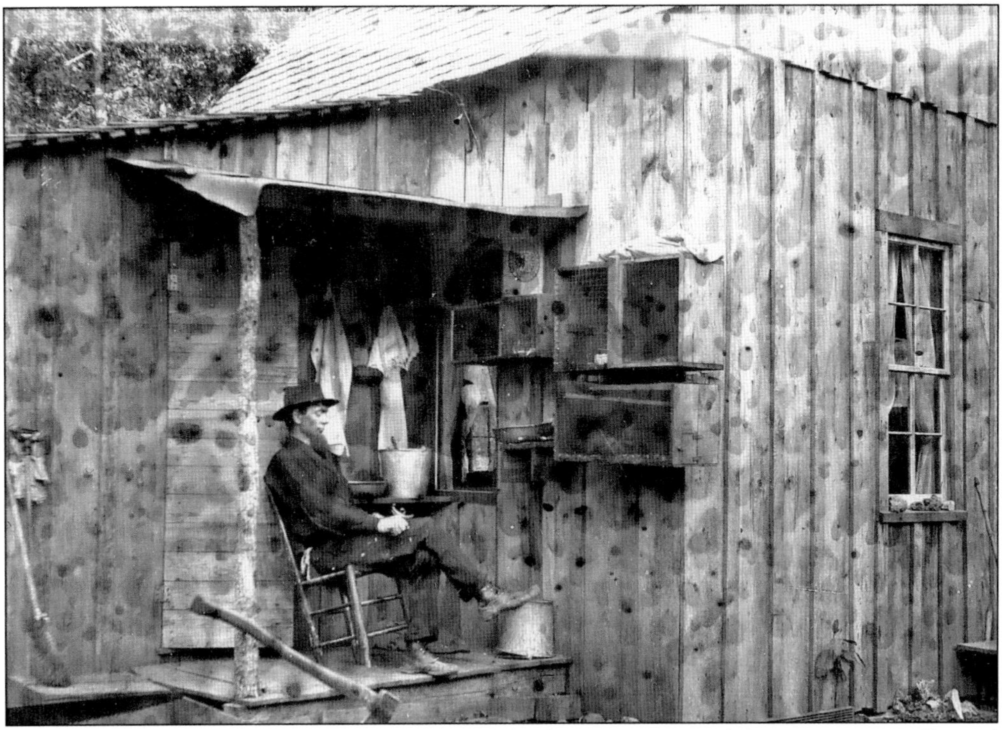

When the day's work was done, the men of the house got to indulge in more intellectual pursuits, such as whittling on the front porch.

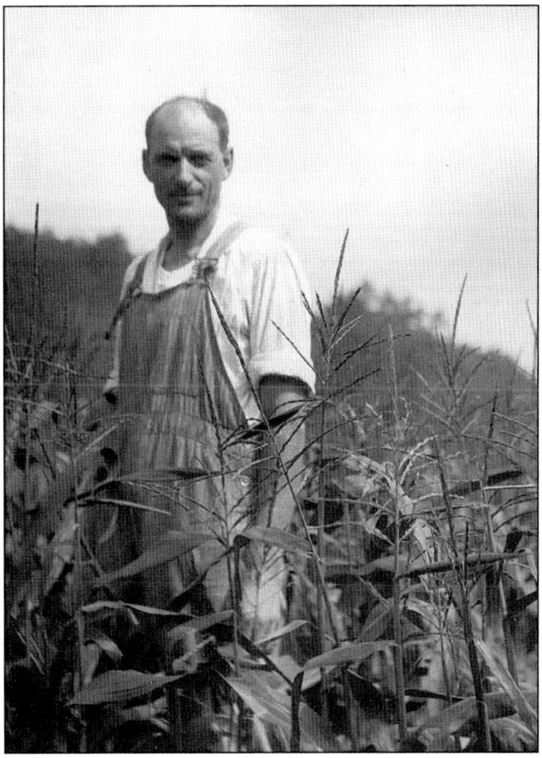

As agriculture began to replace logging, laws were passed to protect crops. In 1833, the town of Union voted that "any man who has Canadian bull thistles growing on his land shall cut them down before they go to seed or forfeit the sum of five dollars, one half to go to the town and one half to his neighbor." A farmer *c.* 1898 admires his corn, free of thistles.

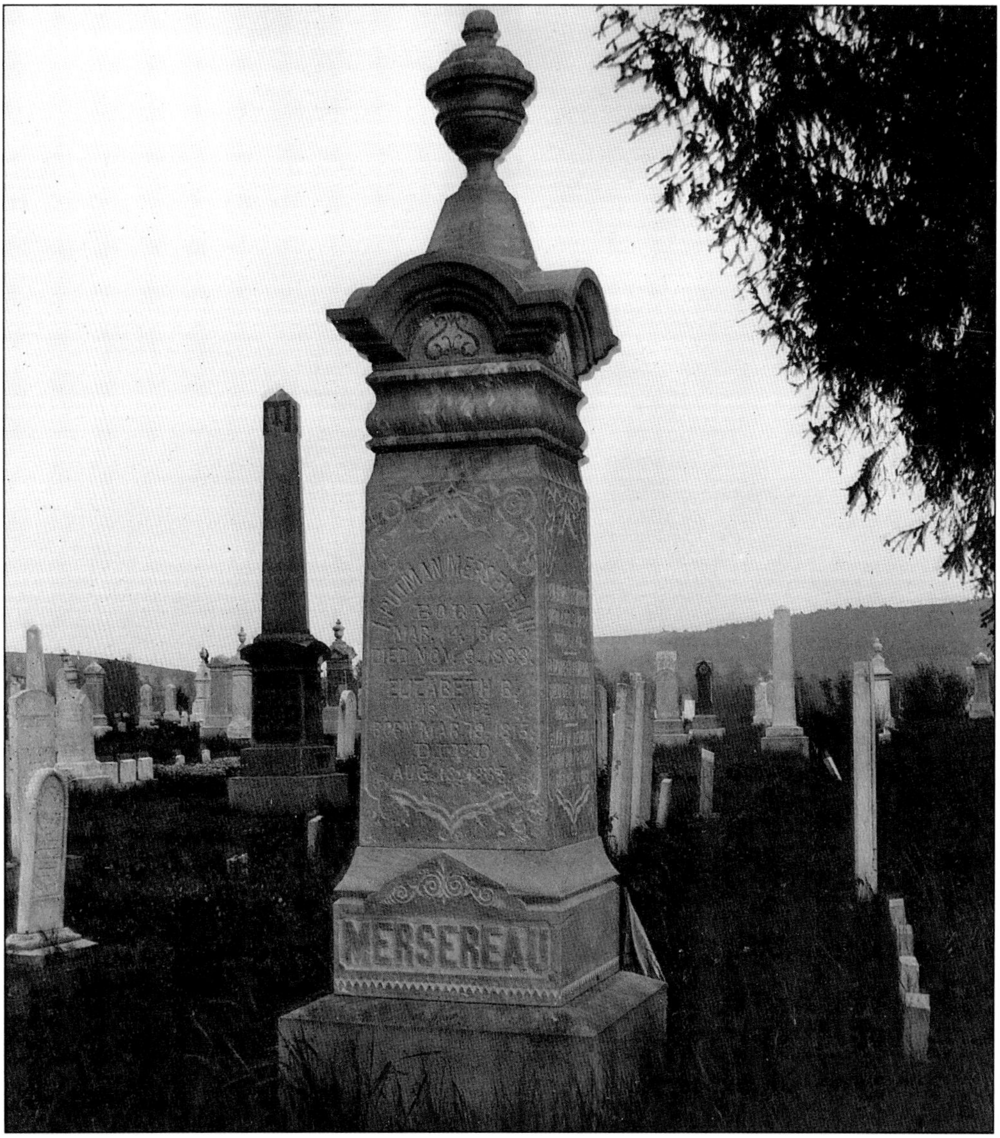

In 1859, Union resident Israel P. Mersereau joined the Pike's Peak gold diggings. He operated a trading post, worked a gold claim, and sent frequent letters home. The following is one of his letters:

> Dear sister and friends in Union, There are 300 sluices in this gulch yielding from $20, to $80 per day per man (gold is selling for $18 an ounce). One pan got me $200 on a branch of the Chicago Creek. I will winter in Golden City where I bought a 100 foot square lot from an Arapaho Indian for a bridle and two and one half gallons of whiskey. Last winter there was suffering & starvation but I think there is no danger now. We are in Utah territory & I am a state man politically, because there is no government now, no laws except revolver & bowie knife.

Members of the Mersereau family were prominent settlers in Union. No photograph of Israel Mersereau has survived, but many members of the family are buried in this Endicott cemetery.

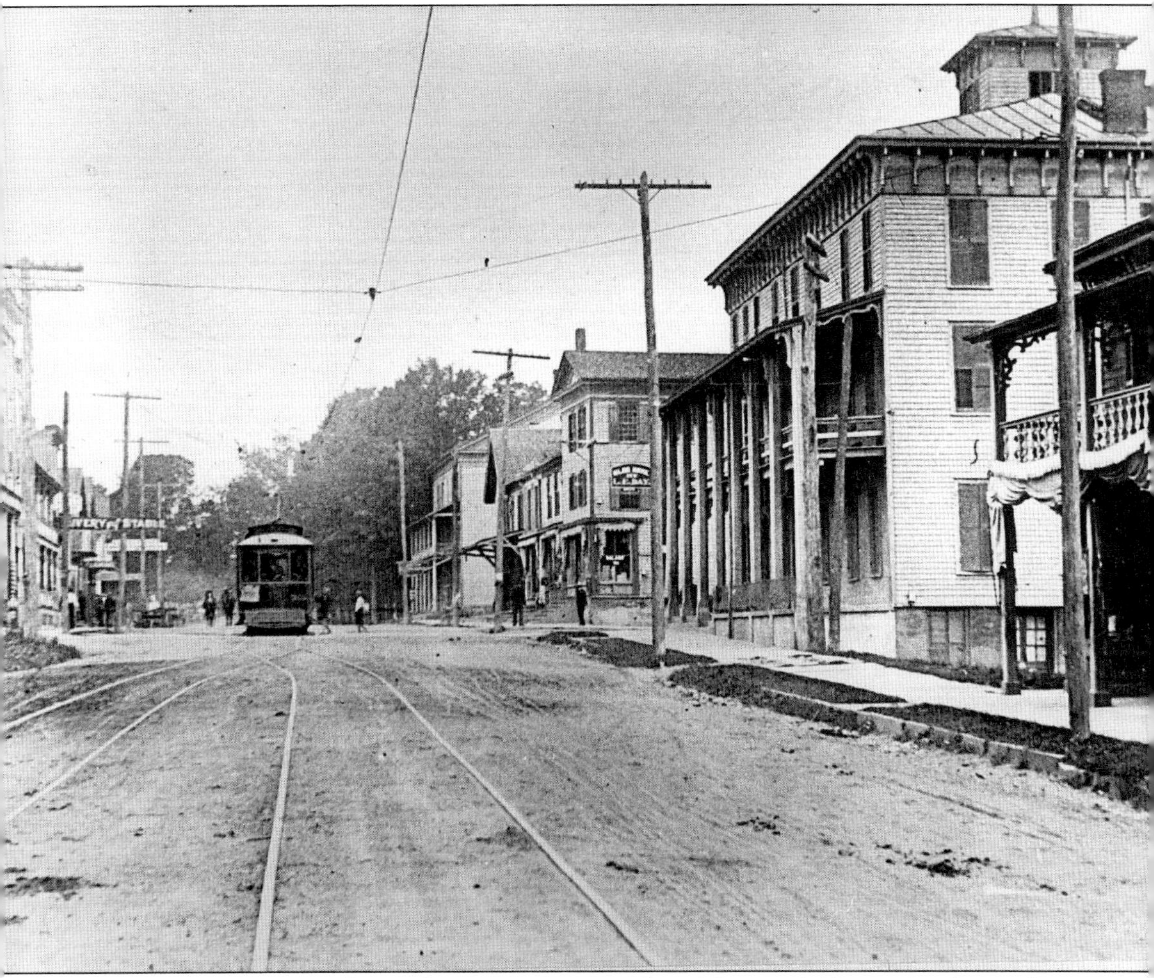

The first hotel in the village of Union was erected at Main and Nanticoke Streets by Lewis Keeler. It moved to a nearby site and was later replaced by the Major House. Keeler paid for much of his stock by bartering rum because cash was scarce. Most of the shopping in the 1850s was done by men, so spirits flowed from the saloon and store in amazing quantities, much more quickly than the toothbrushes. Keeler was a member of the local Liberty Men, who believed in abolition. An 1853 news report said Keeler's generosity to an escaping slave was "unkindly used." Henry Wilson came to him claiming to be a fugitive slave and accepted gifts and assistance for an escape to Canada. The "fugitive" repaid Keeler's kindness by stealing a valuable pair of gold spectacles. Constables found Wilson had made a business of fraudulently soliciting help. He was apprehended and brought to justice. This scene shows Main Street in Union c. 1890. The Major House is the large building on the right, where Keeler's tavern once stood.

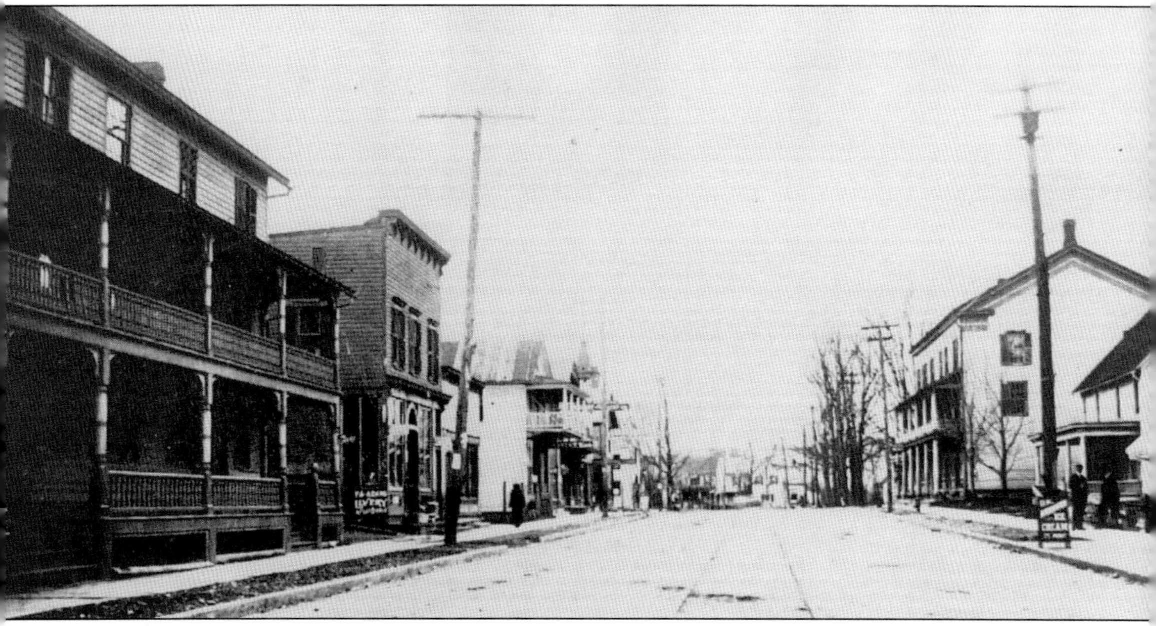

This view of Main Street in Old Union *c.* 1915 shows the Red Men's Hall and the old Cottage Hotel on the left. The hotel was built *c.* 1851 on the ashes of the earlier Union Hotel. The Red Men was founded in Baltimore in 1834 as a fraternal, social, political, and insurance society, but the club roots may extend as far back as 1816. Prior to the 1830s, it was also a drinking club, but soon transformed into a pro-temperance group. The Red Men maintained a purpose of emulating and perpetuating the culture of the American Indian, but in 1899, the membership voted to ban any person with Native American blood from joining the organization. Membership was high in the Union area until the mid-1900s, when secret fraternal organizations began to lose popularity. There is still a Red Men building on Main Street in Union.

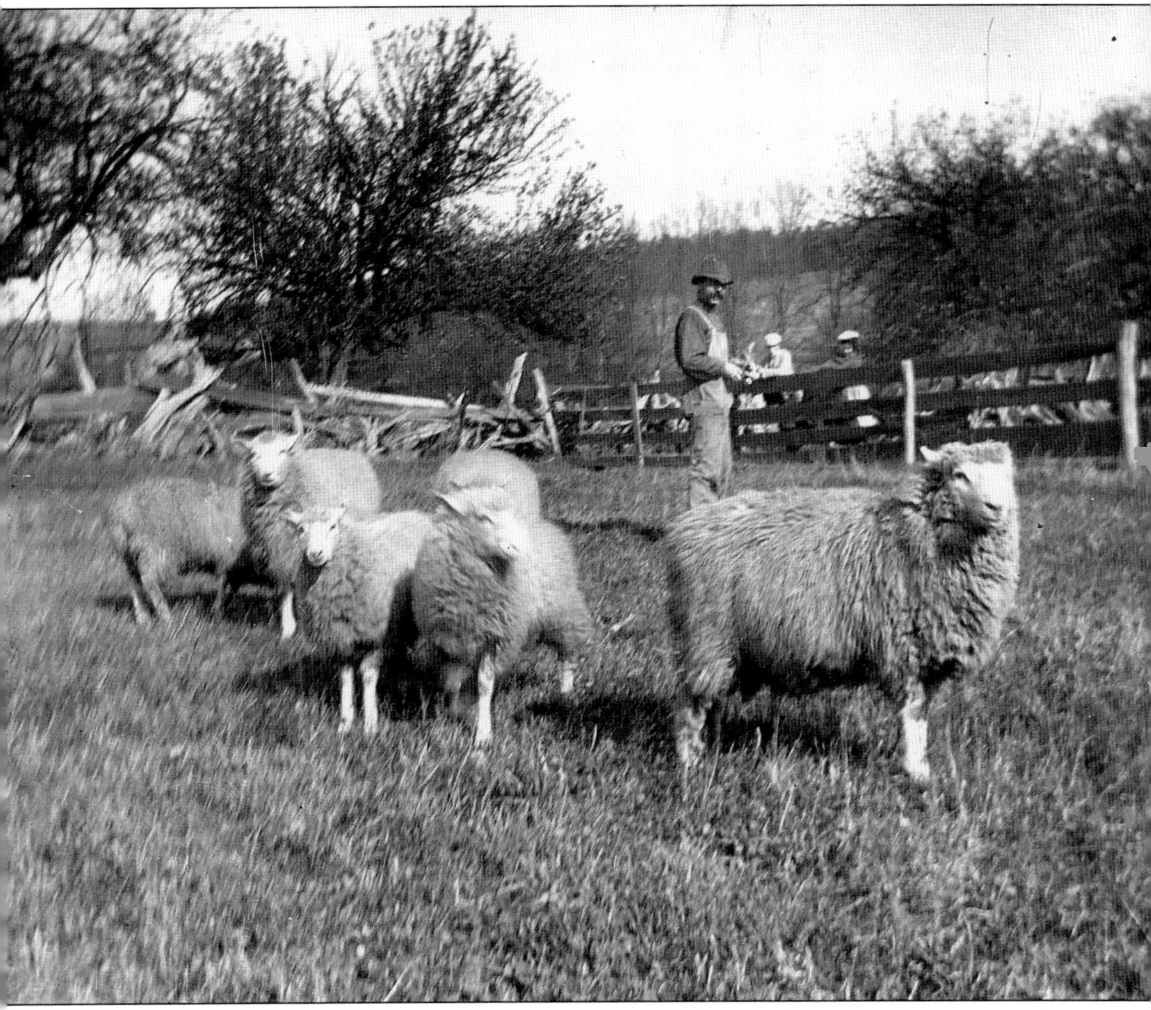

Sheep were protected in 1790 by this law: "Any ram at large and getting into any man's enclosure among his sheep the owner must pay 8 shillings damages for illegal propagation or forfeit the ram." In 1860, the *Binghamton Daily Republican* carried this story about a Fourth of July celebration in 1817:

> Amos, a shoemaker and sheep farmer, set to have a celebration in a becoming manner. He dressed his best lamb for the occasion and at 2 o'clock: "my self, my wife, my old maiden sister on the wrong side of 50, and my old Negro man Dick all sat down. After benediction and a goblet of Clark's best Ale we toasted, as I hate the profusion of wasting gunpowder for a salute, Dick cheered the toasts. After thirteen toasts we found our beer was exhausted and were compelled to omit a few. By the by, I would mention that none in my family ever drink ardent spirits, wine or whisky which is the reason why we sustain such excellent health in the decline of life."

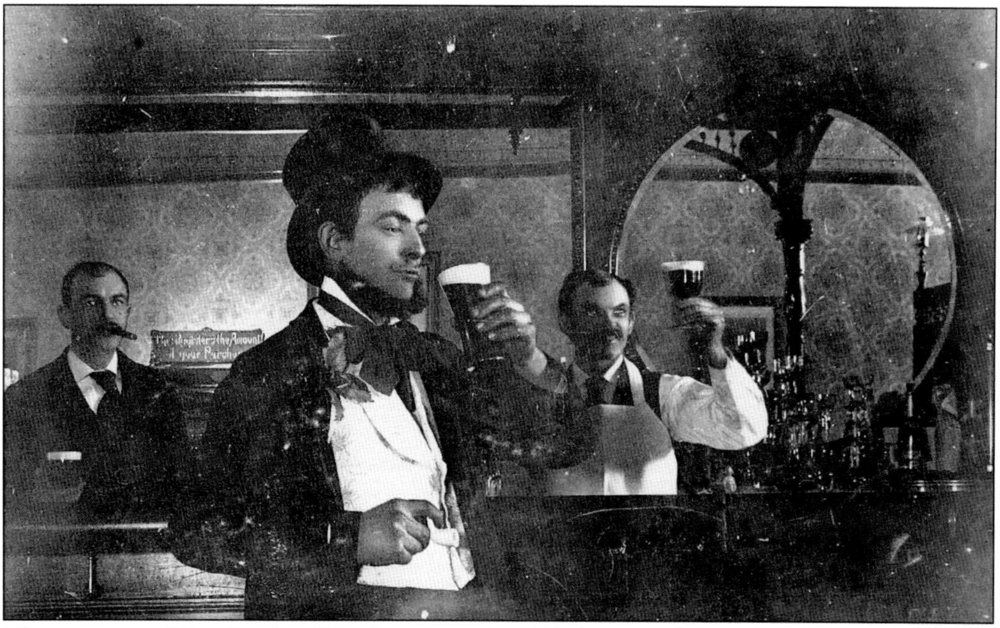

The prominent West family of Binghamton owned a brewery and, eventually, a pub. This is the interior of the West Bar in 1895, located on the corner of Main and Front Streets.

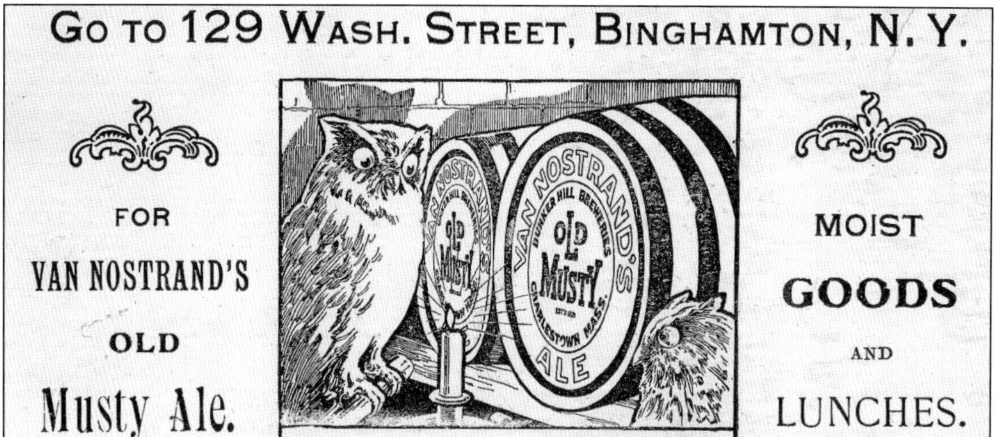

Drinking establishments abounded in the late 1800s. This advertisement was handed out by the Owl Pub, at 129 Washington Street, as evidence of its sociability. "Moist Goods" were the specialty of the house, although lunches were also provided. Another advertisement posted inside the bar read "Bier for sale," so the owner was either spelling in German or humorously offering transport to the grave (maybe both).

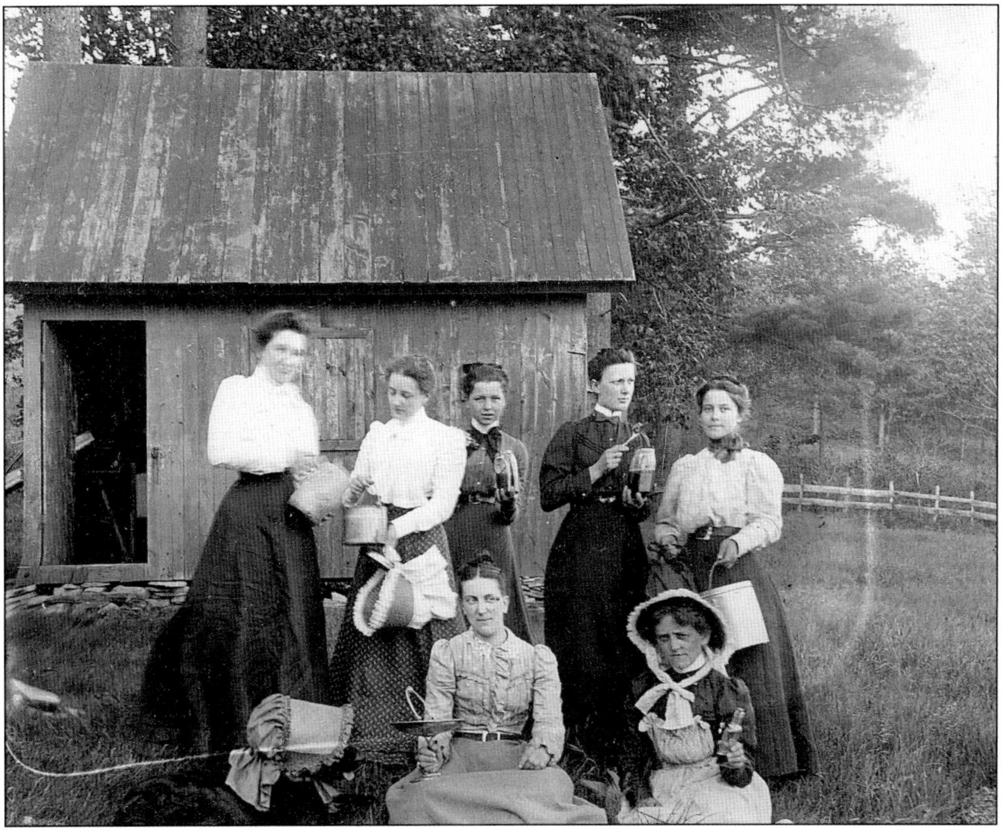

At this picnic for the ladies, flasks of brew, bonnets, and berry buckets were the ingredients for a successful day at the family cabin in the woods *c.* 1898.

The 18th Amendment, instituting Prohibition in 1919, made alcohol illegal and satisfied the legions of people in the temperance movement. When it became obvious the law was unsuccessful, Prohibition ended in 1932. Many organizations encouraged voluntary abstinence by suggesting members sign "Temperance Pledges." This flag was created by temperance cards from members of a local Methodist church.

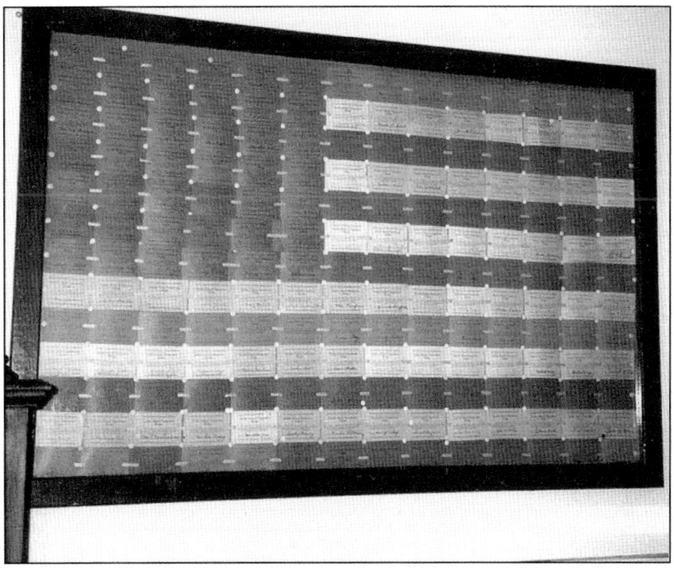

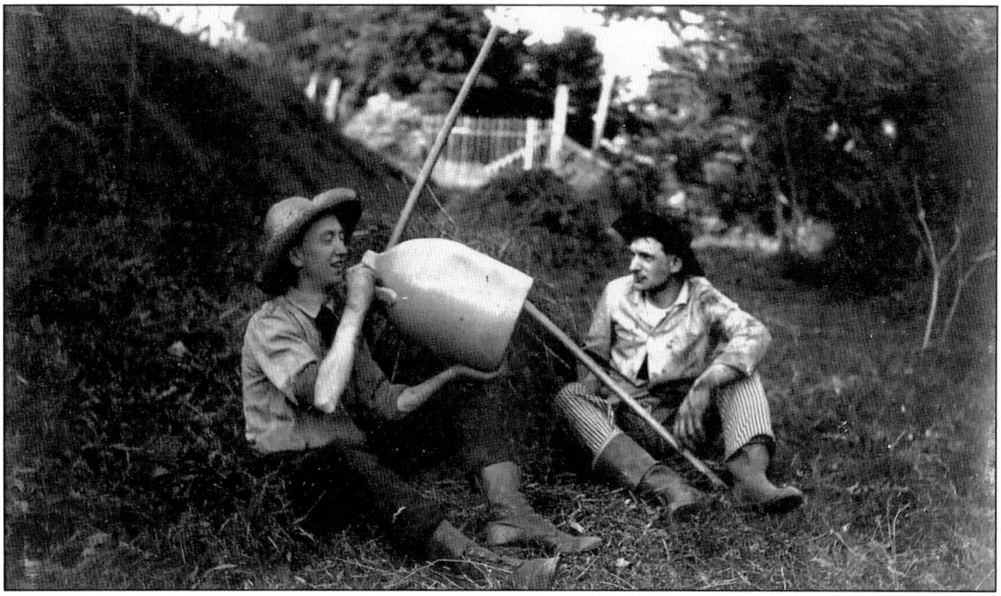

In early America, whiskey was as good as currency. Corn squeezings, moonshine, and hard cider were made as a cash producer on many homesteads. Whiskey was also considered a medication and preventative for fever, ague, rheumatism, and nagging. "Pass the jug" takes on a whole new meaning with a container as large as the one in this photograph.

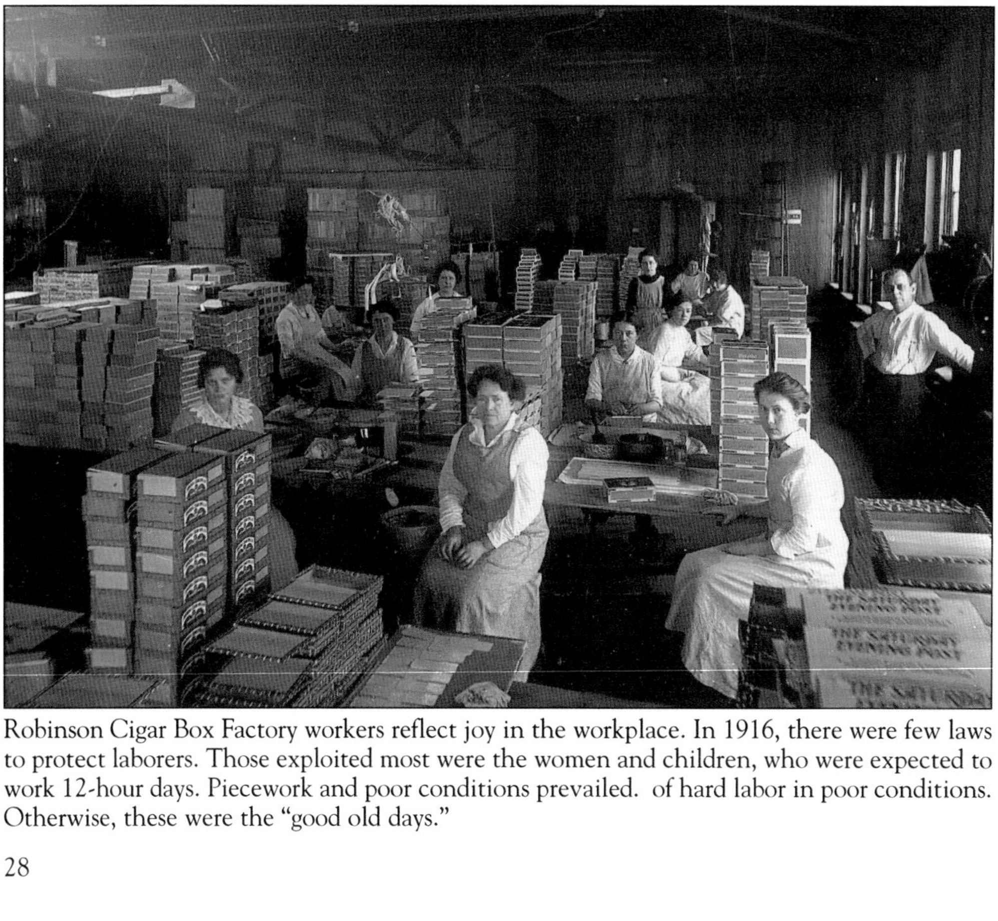

Robinson Cigar Box Factory workers reflect joy in the workplace. In 1916, there were few laws to protect laborers. Those exploited most were the women and children, who were expected to work 12-hour days. Piecework and poor conditions prevailed. of hard labor in poor conditions. Otherwise, these were the "good old days."

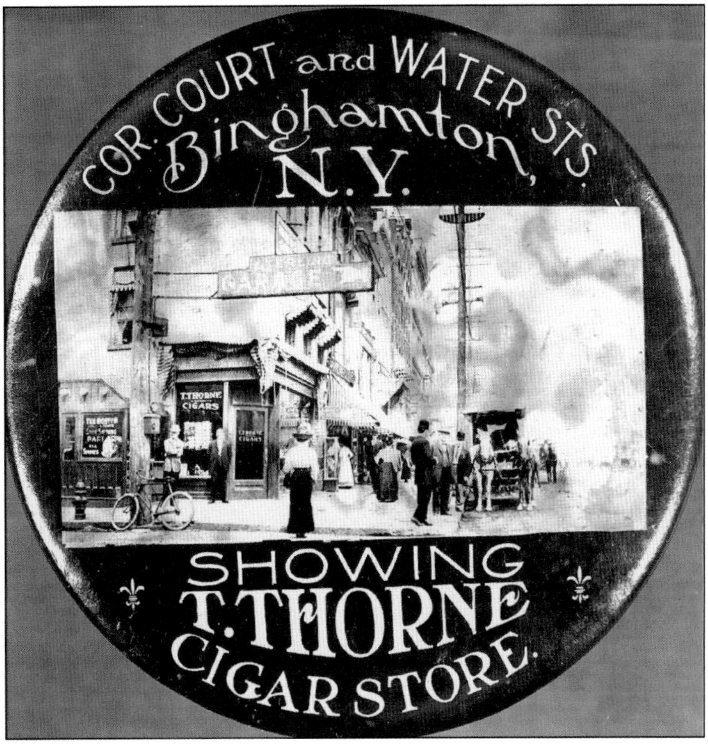

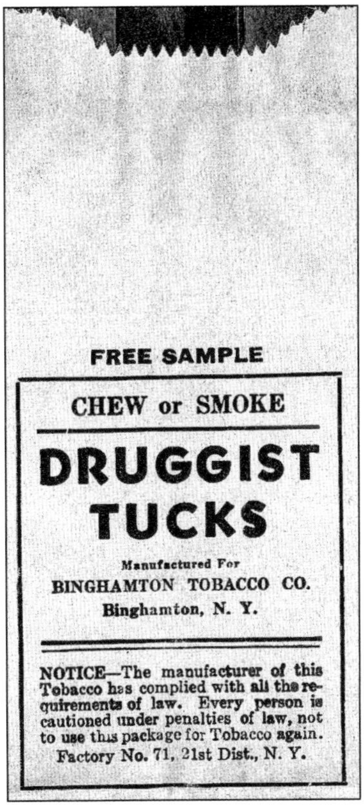

Cigar production in Broome County started small in 1850 with three or four shops making just enough cigars for the local market. By the 1860s, the cigar tax helped finance the Union army during the Civil War. The year 1888 saw 47 businesses manufacturing cigars. In the 1920s, Binghamton was the fifth-largest producer in the nation, employing at least 5,000 people. The photographs show an advertising button for a Binghamton store specializing in tobacco products and a typical free sample to chew or smoke.

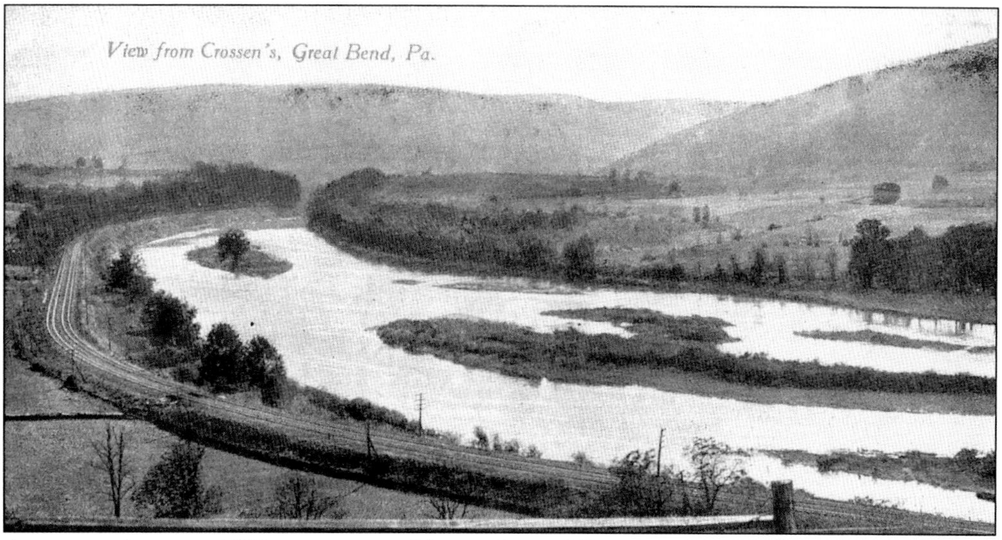

As reported in an 1897 newspaper, "A number of Broome County denizens are helping establish a rattlesnake farm in the Deep Hallow section of Great Bend, Pa. Each snake is worth a whopping $2.75 to a medical company for use in a rheumatism cure. Snakes on the property are also better than cats as mousers. Without fangs they could even be pets. High boots are a necessity."

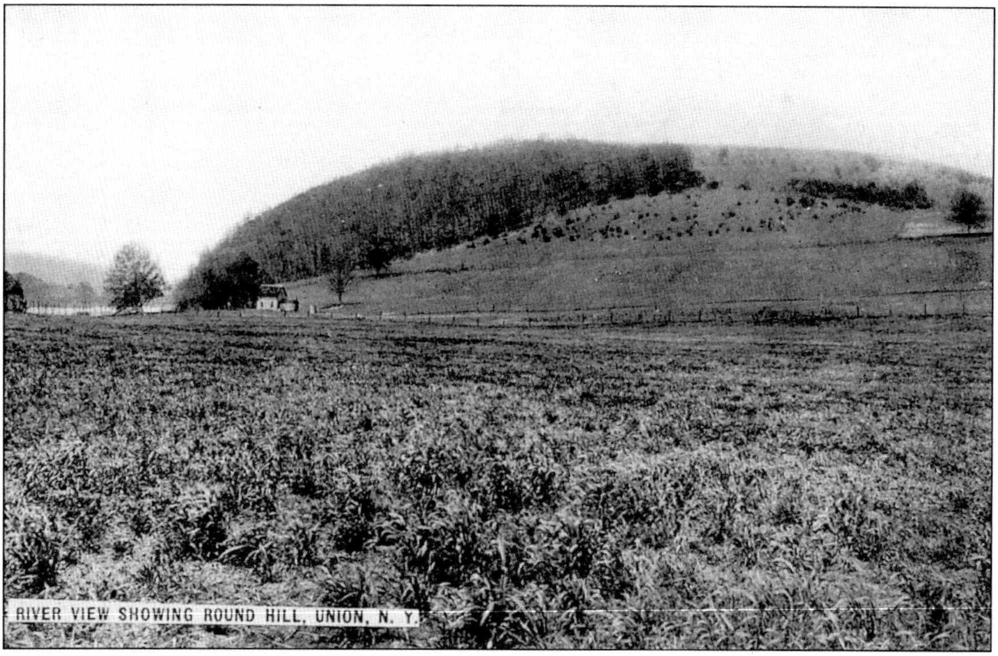

Before hospitals were built, other accommodations had to be made for people with contagious diseases. During an 1852 smallpox scare, the Broome County Board of Health required Union to build a pesthouse on the south side of Round Hill near the river on land owned by Peter Mersereau. People afflicted were quarantined from the public until recovery or otherwise.

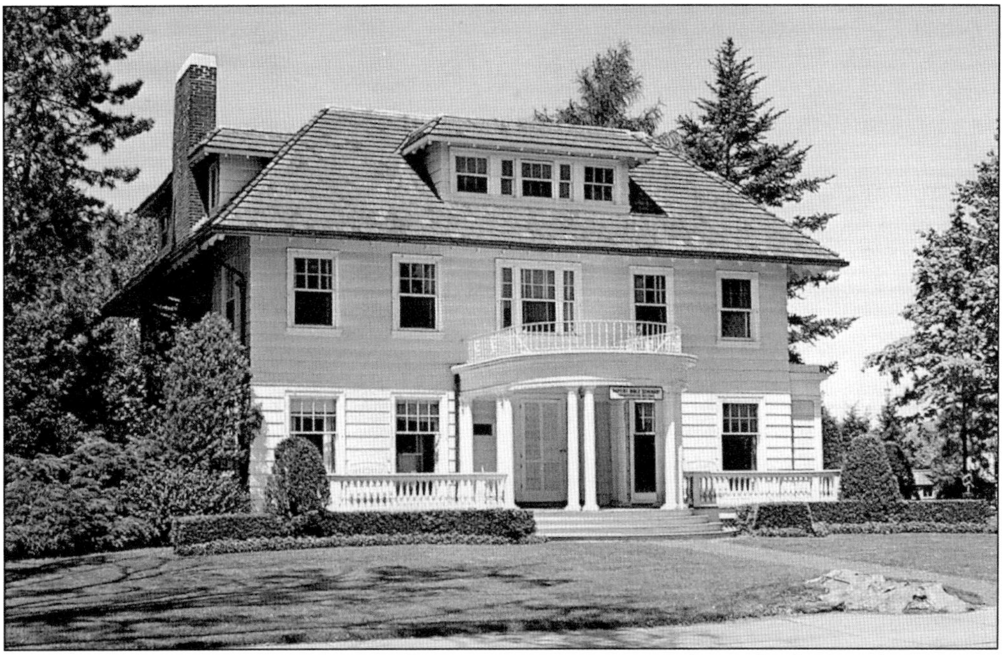

The house at 335 Main Street in Johnson City was presented to Charles F. Johnson as a wedding present in 1919 by his uncle George F. Johnson. For many years "Mrs. Charlie," as she was known, was a supporter of the Wilson School of Nursing, hosting elaborate garden party graduation ceremonies on the extensive grounds behind this home. The photograph below is of a 1933 nursing class. Note the portrait of Mrs. Johnson over the fireplace in the nurses' residence. The home has been preserved and is now the headquarters for the Broome County Federation of Labor.

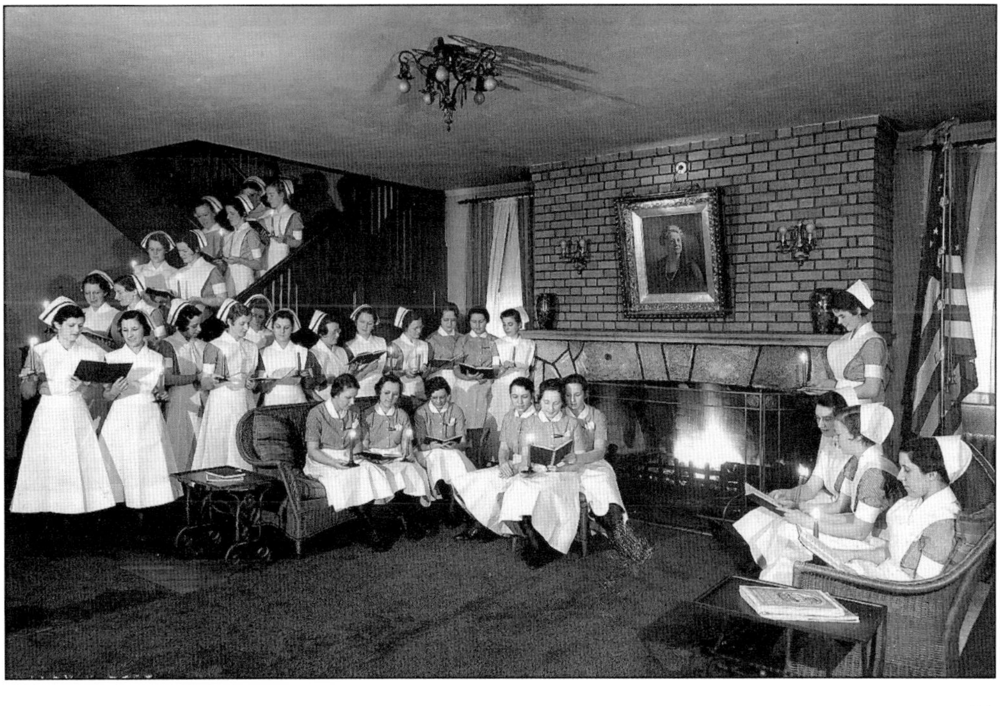

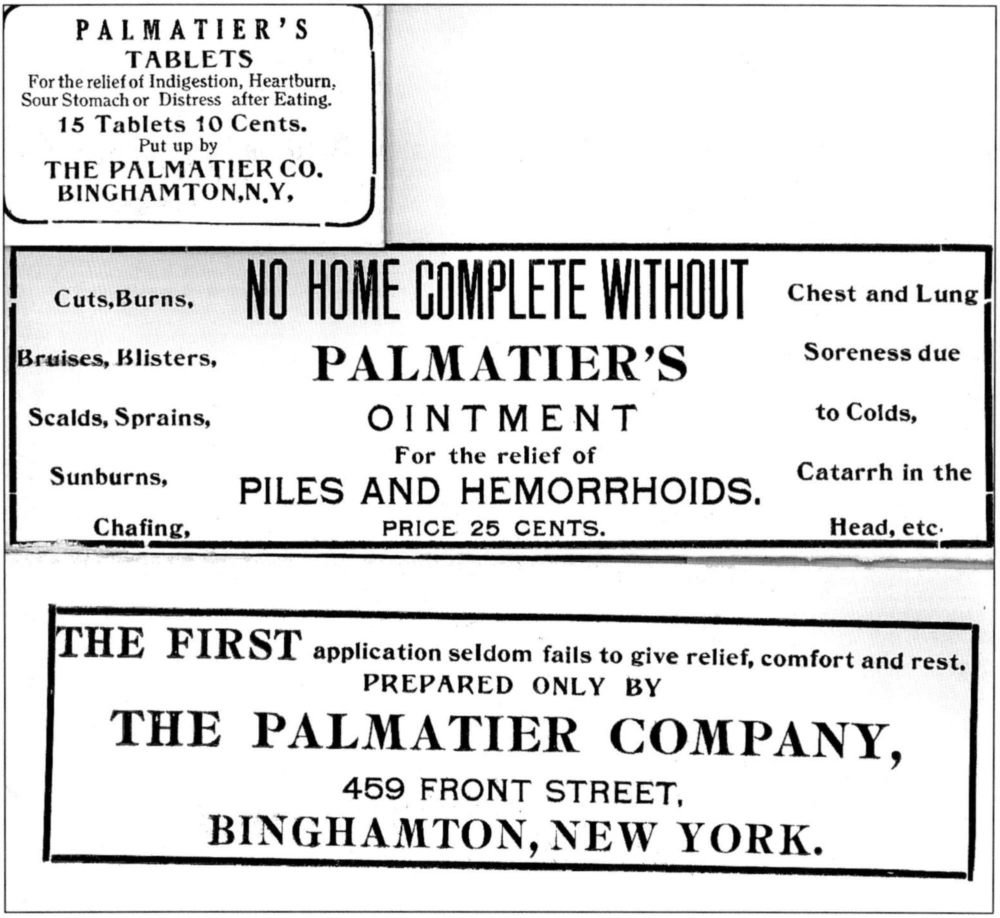

The Palmatiers were contemporaries of Willis S. Kilmer and, like the Kilmers, produced patent medicine products. All ointments and tablets were guaranteed to cure the ills of life. Pictured is a box of the certain cure. The Palmatier farm, on Front Street in Binghamton, had a famous boarder for a few months—the great race horse Exterminator. The Palmatier estate is the site of the future Dickinson Town Hall.

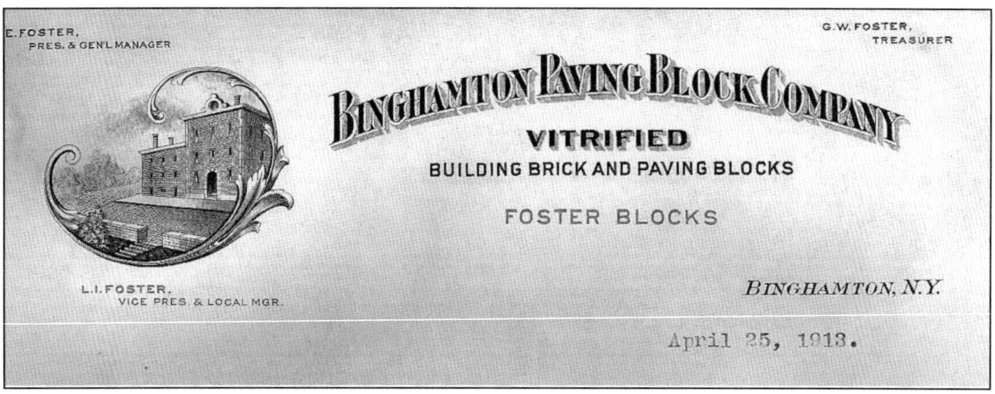

The Binghamton Paving Block Company was in business in 1913, providing bricks and paving blocks to make roads. A newspaper article in the late 1850s noted, "The good plank road all the way from Union to Nanticoke Springs make[s] the stage trip eminently comfortable."

The Pleasant Mountain House was in Sanitaria Springs, a locale noted for unusual natural springs. Water cures were the rage from 1850 to the 1920s, each spring claiming healing properties. A "sulpho-phosphate" spring located near this house was said to splash sparkling white lights into the air. Scientists believed it was the only spring of its kind in the world. A spring on Mount Prospect caused excitement in 1872. "The Saline-chalybeate waters have valuable qualities that will prove to be the great desideratum of Binghamton!" There were also water cures in Vallonia Springs, Colesville, and Nanticoke Springs.

In 1852, a Nanticoke resort offered a "domestic watering place for health and retiracy amid romantic groves where visitors can chew the cud of fancy." The sulfur and iron springs were declared an invigorating tonic for drinking and bathing. By 1865, the last Nanticoke resort had burned and "the area was doomed to decay." As a final comment on the healing waters, an old epitaph reads, "Here I be with my two daughters all from drinking saline chalybeate waters. If we had stuck to Epsom salts we would not be laying in these here vaults."

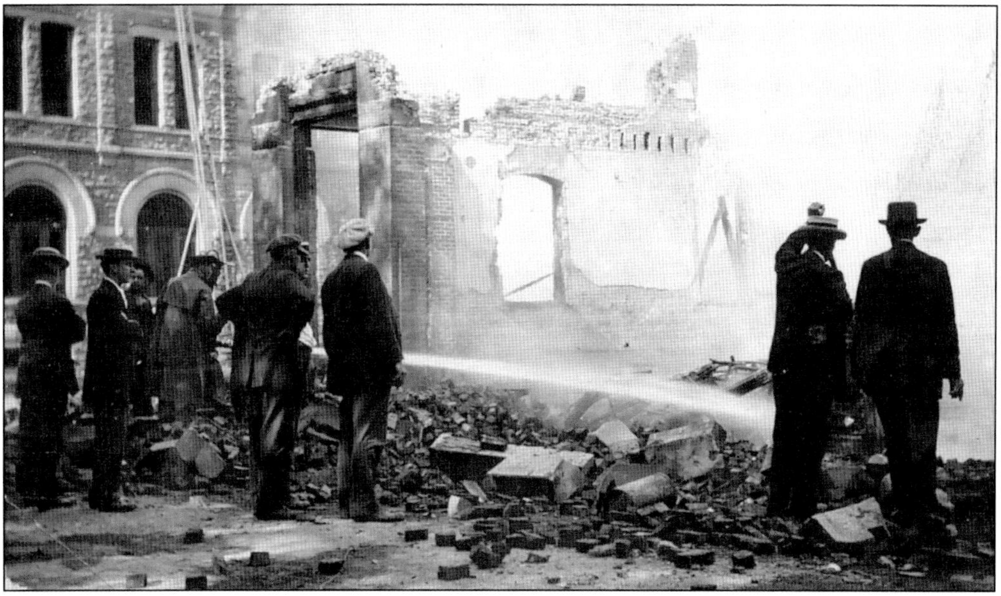

The Binghamton Clothing Company burst into flames on July 22, 1913, dooming 31 workers to death. Until that day, 100 people had worked in the "overall factory" owned by Reed Freeman. Five days later, a funeral cortege was organized, and caskets were placed on flatcars on the trolley tracks. Most of the victims were unidentifiable and were buried in a circular plot in Spring Forest Cemetery. The photograph above is of the fire; the one below is of the funeral procession through the city. Thousands of mourners lined the streets, paying respect to those lost in the largest factory tragedy in the state.

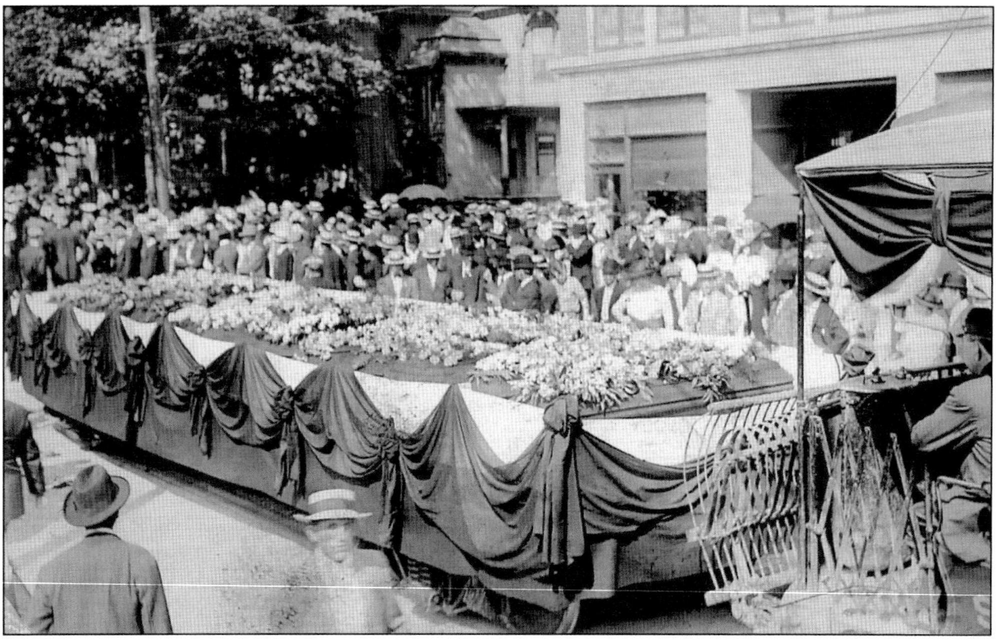

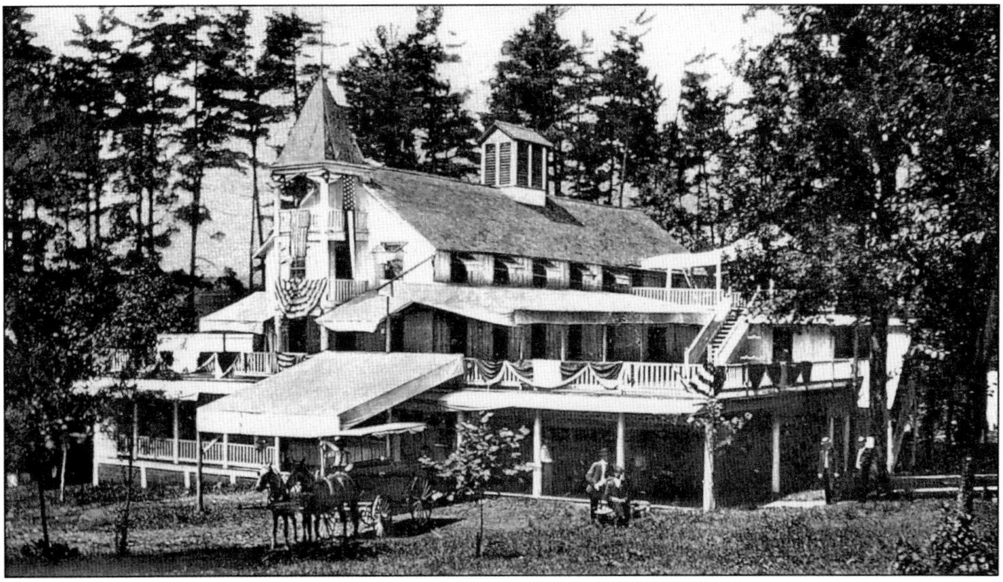

Reed Freeman was a founder of the Chautauqua Assembly at Carmel Grove. Freeman donated great sums of money earned from his Binghamton Clothing Company to this Methodist campgrounds in Endwell. A typhoid epidemic caused by contaminated river ice used at Carmel Grove killed dozens, including Reed's daughter-in-law. In 1914, the year after his business burned, a cyclone destroyed Carmel Grove. It was never rebuilt and neither was the Freeman fortune.

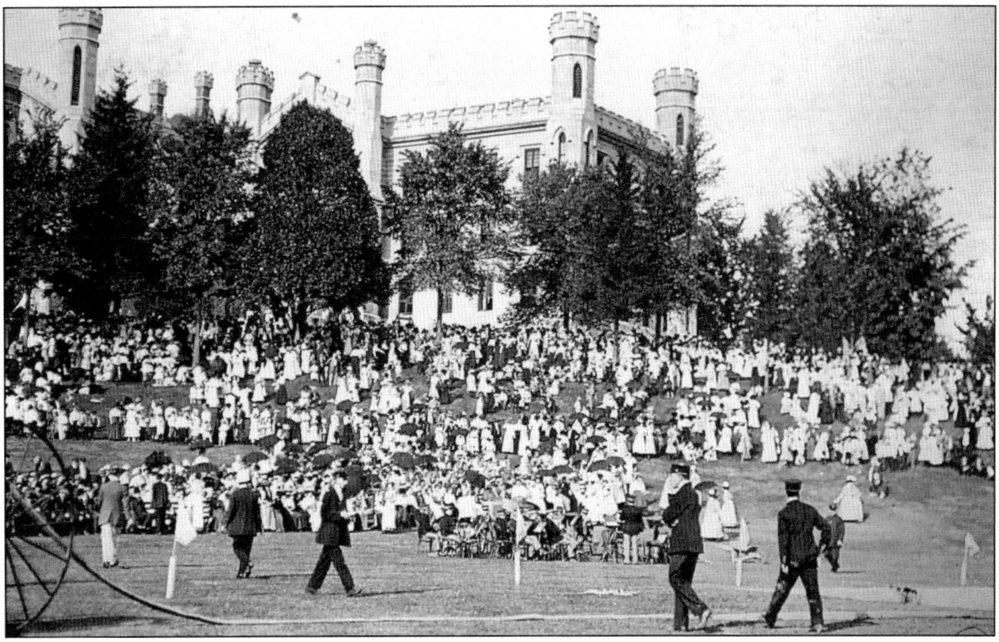

Local streetcar companies ran excursions to extensive grounds at the New York State Inebriate Asylum, the first institution of its kind in the nation. The public was encouraged to visit the impressive Gothic buildings and parklike gardens. In 1905, Binghamton fire companies put on the pictured demonstration for a large crowd of tourists.

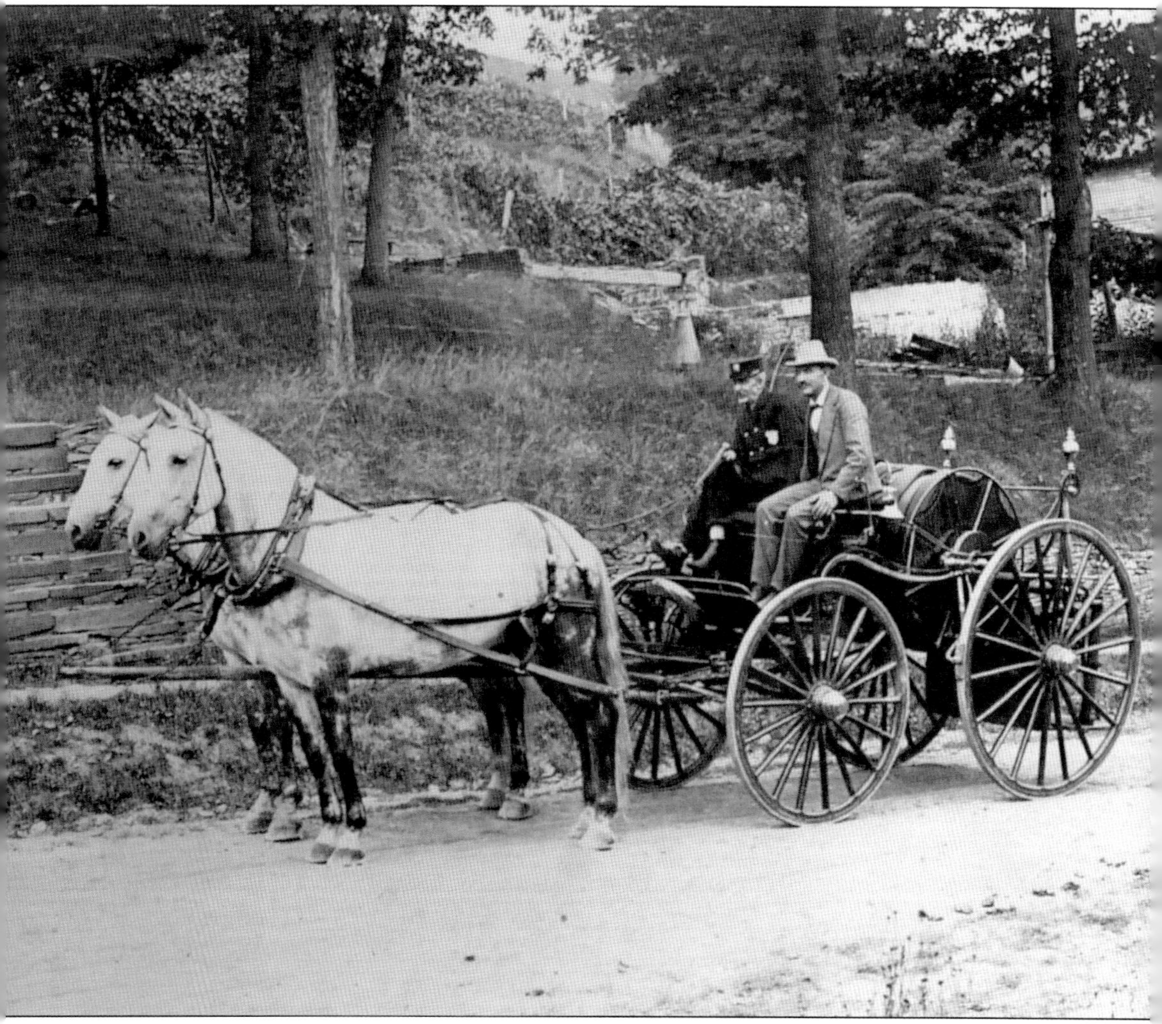

In the early 1800s, the first machine used to fight fires locally was a long, narrow wagon with poles and hooks for ladders and buckets. Late in 1838, Binghamton trustees were petitioned by the Crystal Hose Company to authorize funds for a new fire hose of not more than 30 feet. It was sanctioned and ordered to be crafted by "Uncle Tommy Allen." Allen made it to fit the capacity of the engine, sewing all seams by hand and using no rivets. The hose lasted longer than the wagon. The Binghamton Crystal Hose Company earned acclaim in 1858 for exhibiting a costly fire carriage mounted in heavy gold. It included several silver and bronze statuettes and elaborate lamps. By 1886, the parade carriage had been disposed of by lottery so that a horse-drawn carriage could be purchased. This photograph shows the Alert Company's fire wagon. Colonel and Major, who pulled the old reel cart, were a championship team who could run a mile in 2 minutes 42 seconds while drawing 2,800 pounds. The pair was killed by a train at the Liberty Street Station.

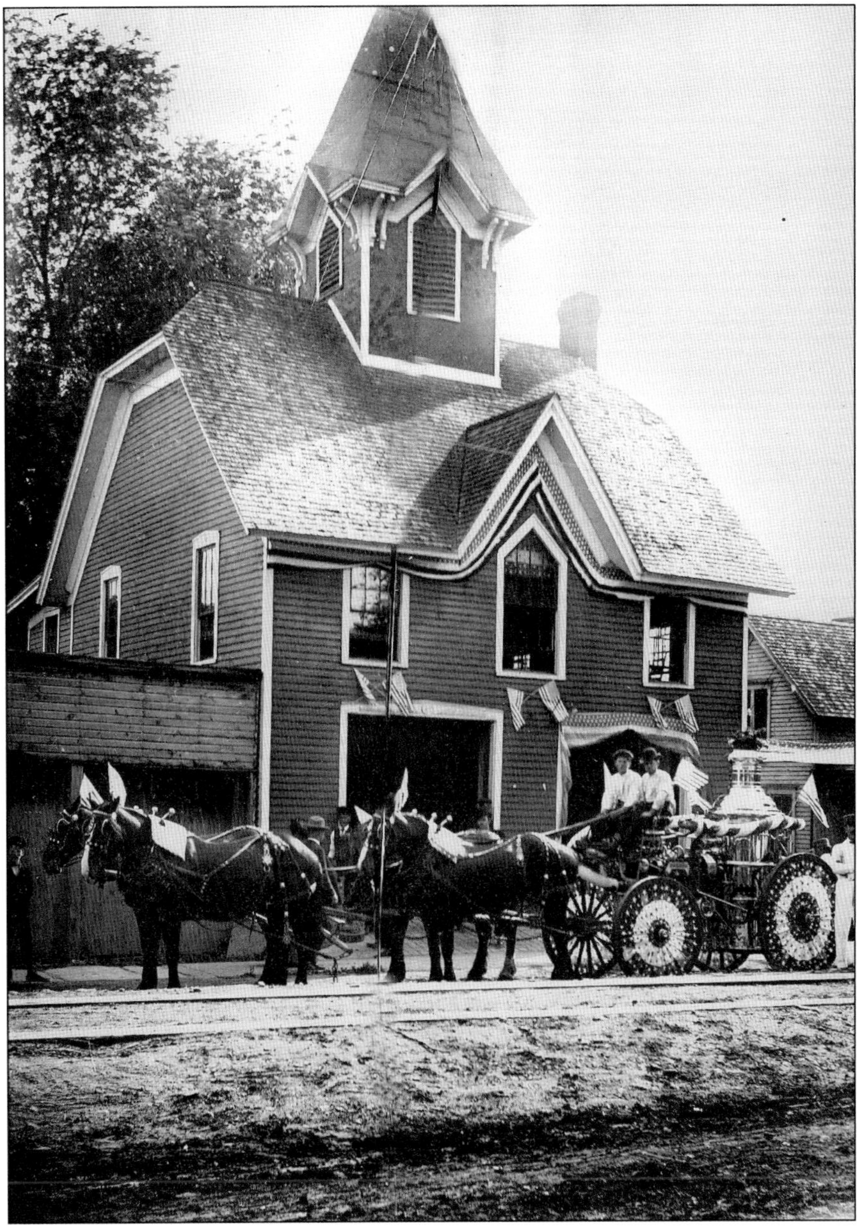

The first horse to pull fire duty in Binghamton was Colonel, one of the Alert Company's team of grays. He braved storms and answered alarms for 22 years, weighed 1,150 pounds, and was thoroughly game in spirit, not odor. Prince, of the Fountain Chemical Company, was a large bay stallion sold into retirement to a Syracuse woman. One day while out for a drive, he ran to the call of an alarm despite protests from the lady. He demolished property and his popularity in the process of responding to duty. Dick, a four-legged member of the Mechanics Hose Company, knew every word spoken to him and always wanted to be first at a fire. His only known fault was that he never refused a cooling draught of beer and, at celebrations, drank plenty of the amber fluid. The habit never interfered with his work, and he continued to serve until 1899, when he collapsed and died on the corner of Main and Beethoven Streets while responding to an alarm.

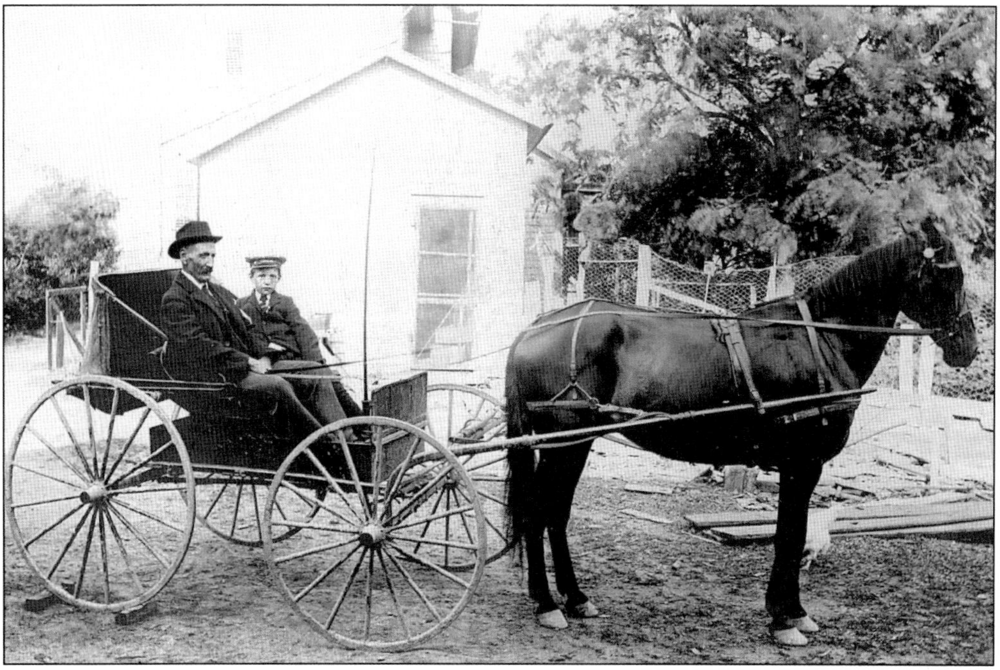

A horse and buggy could kick up a lot of dust. Government advisories such as the following were issued during the dry season: "Every resident should secure several barrels of road dust for use: Mix dust with your poultry guano or coal ashes in an old barrel it is the perfect fertilizer with no disagreeable odor. Road dust is an excellent deodorizer of vaults; throw down a pint of dust each time vault is used."

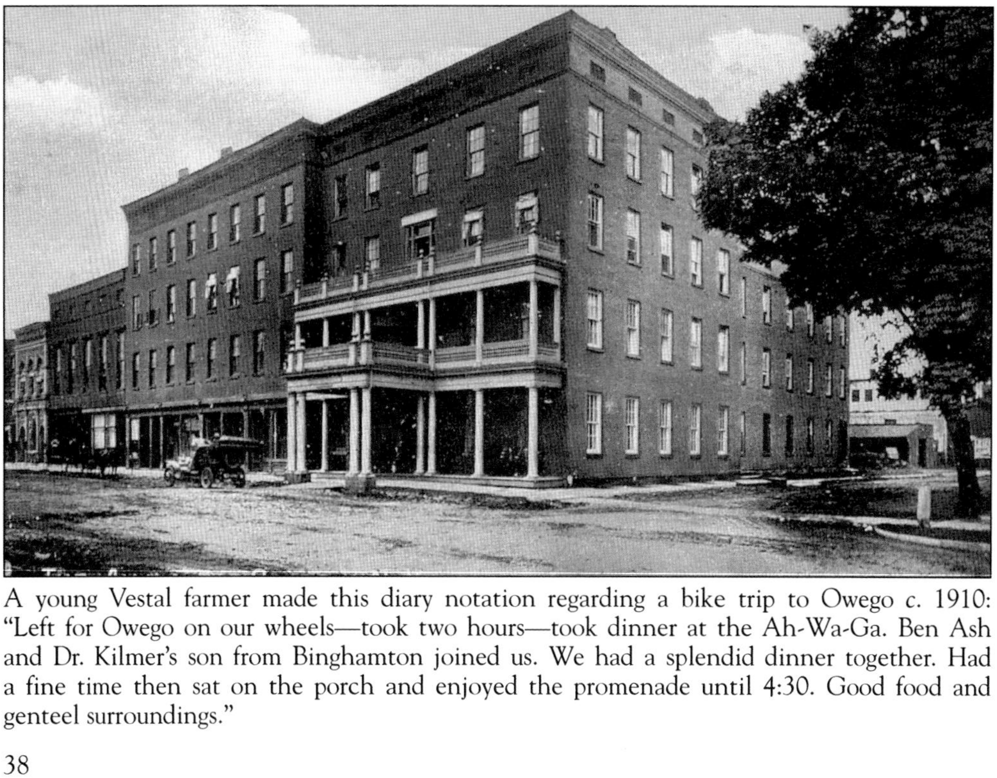

A young Vestal farmer made this diary notation regarding a bike trip to Owego c. 1910: "Left for Owego on our wheels—took two hours—took dinner at the Ah-Wa-Ga. Ben Ash and Dr. Kilmer's son from Binghamton joined us. We had a splendid dinner together. Had a fine time then sat on the porch and enjoyed the promenade until 4:30. Good food and genteel surroundings."

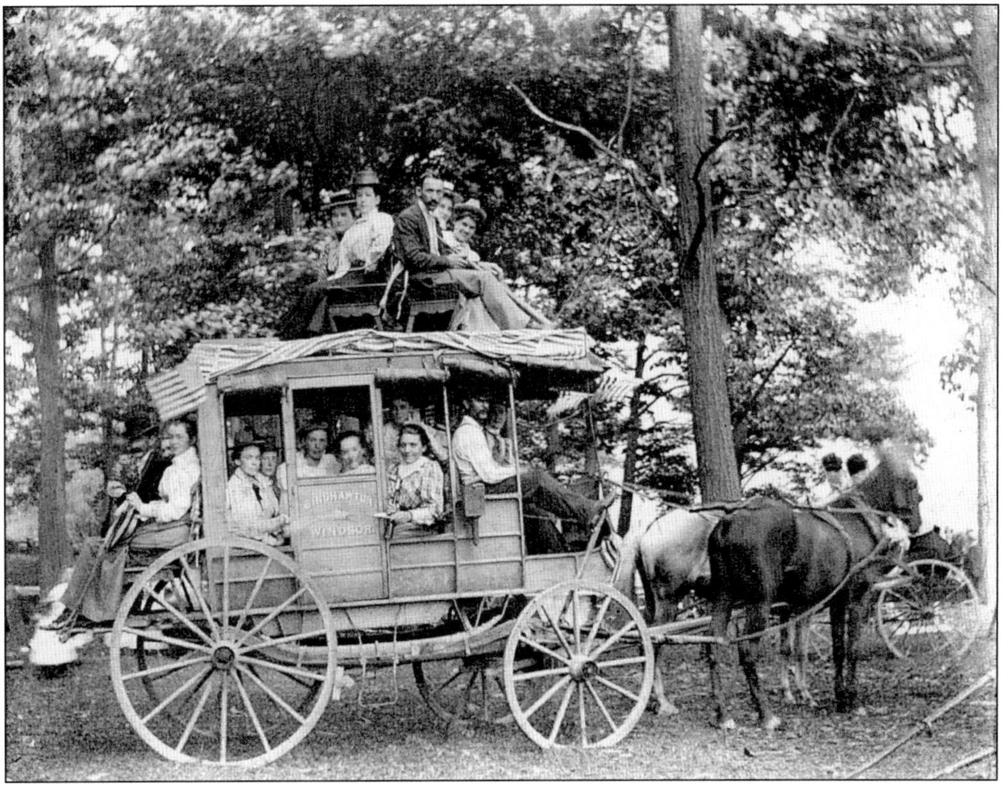

Travel changed from stage coach to motor coach in a few short decades, modernizing from horse to motor power, although it took the road system much longer to improve and provide a smooth journey. The stage pictured above was on a picnic outing near the Susquehanna River. The motorized coach was on its way from Vestal to a wedding in Binghamton.

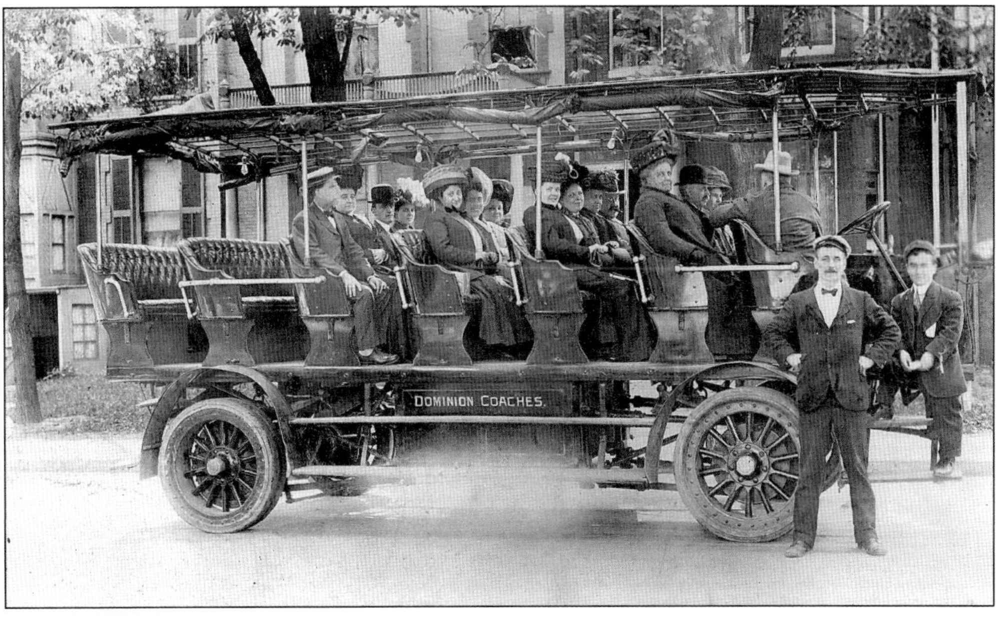

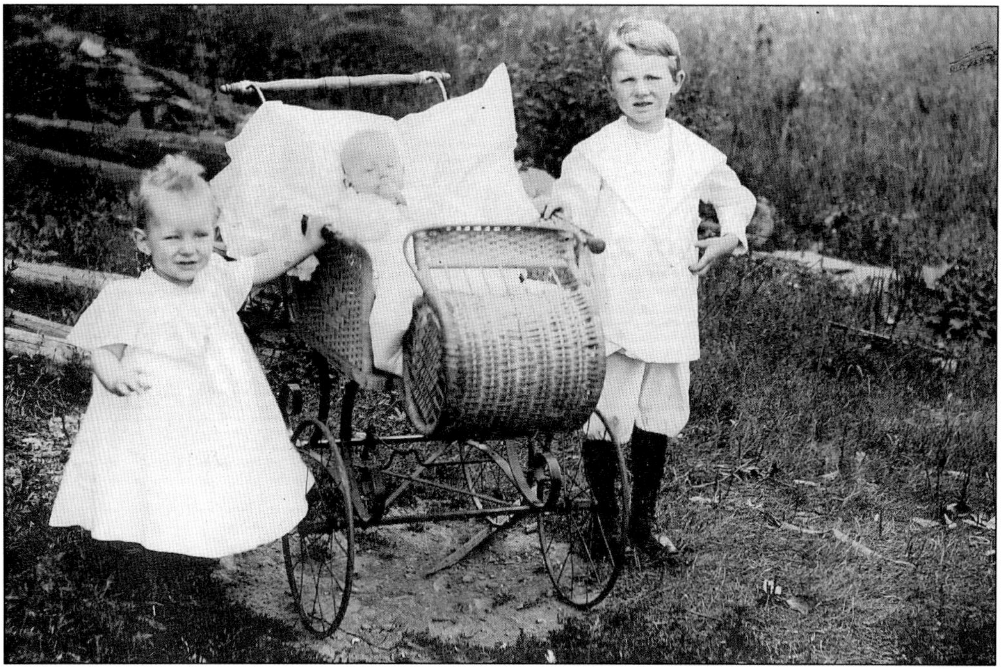

Maybe life was lived at a slower pace in previous centuries, but people and their children were always trying to get somewhere quicker and easier. Above, a wicker baby buggy is being used, and below, a dog-powered cart provides motion. There were several businesses in Broome County that made baby carriages, children's wagons, and toys.

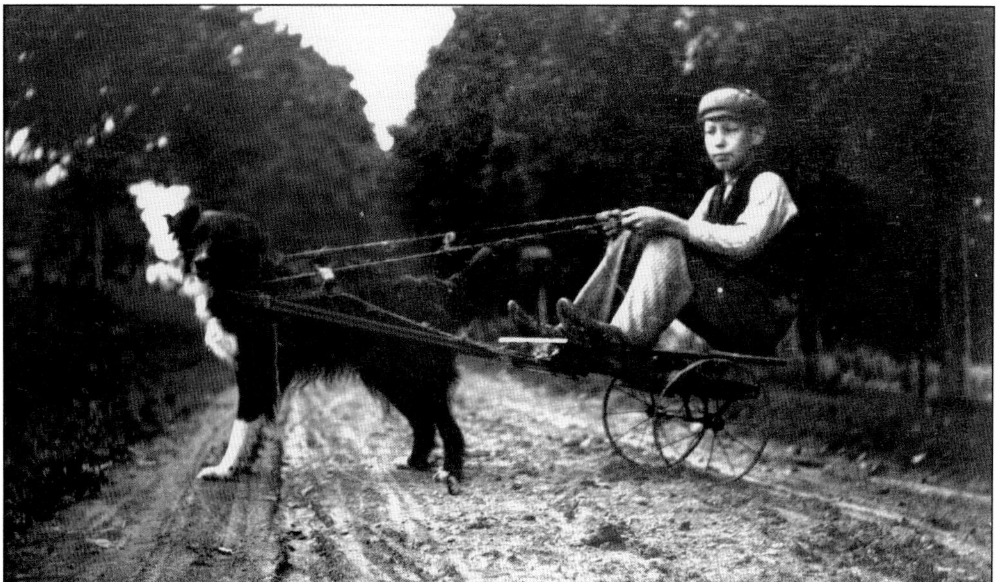

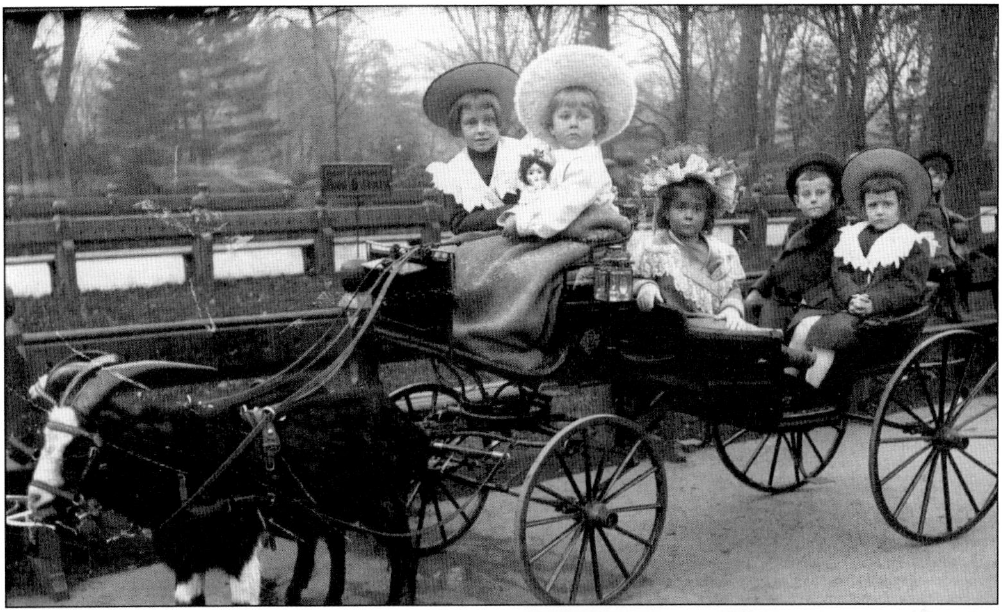

Itinerant photographers brought along their own props to make photographs more enjoyable for the children and more appealing to the paying parent. A goat-pulled wagon in 1900 was photographed in Vestal. A pony and cowboy gear came with the itinerant photographer as he traveled through Binghamton in 1939. The boy in the cowboy outfit is Ed Aswad.

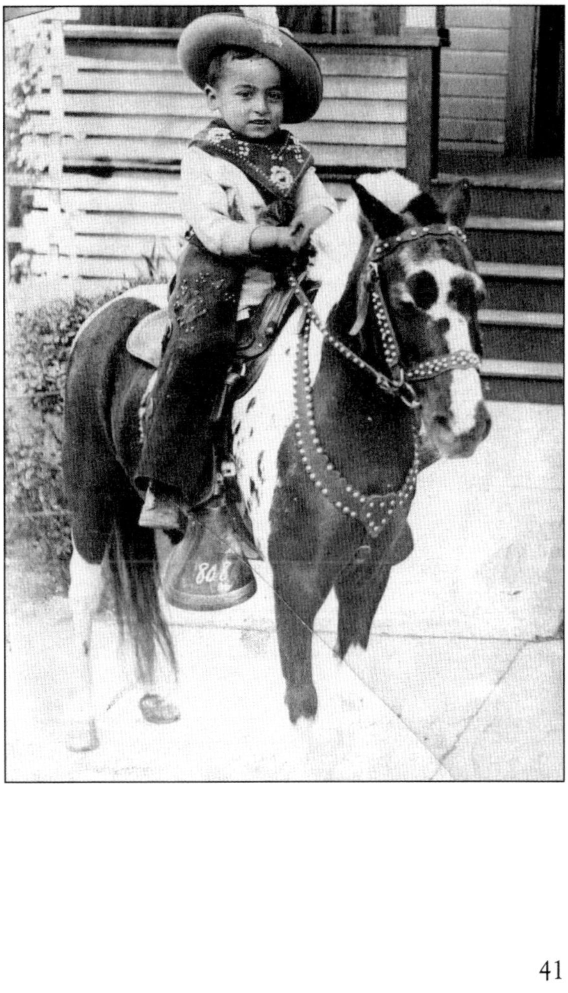

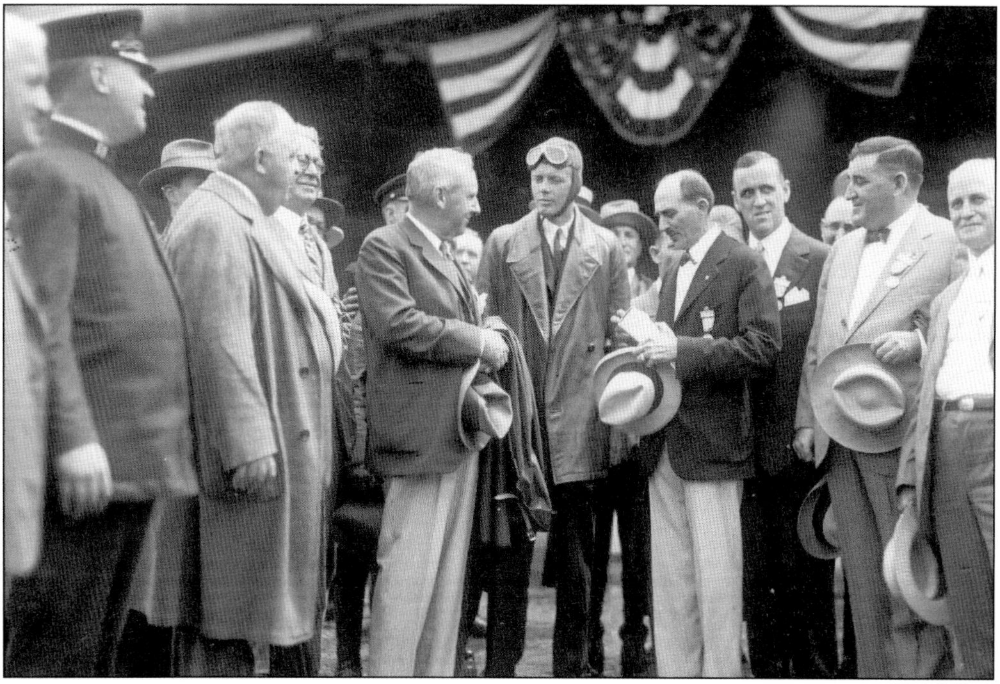

Charles A. Lindbergh flew solo across the Atlantic in May 1927. In November of that same year, the Binghamton newspaper headlines read, "Lindy Lands Here!" Just 16 miles south in a field near St. Joseph's, Pennsylvania, he had made an emergency landing because of snow and sleet. Broome residents came to see the history-making event all day Saturday and Sunday while waiting for Lindy's plane to be repaired. Captain Lindbergh and Major Lamphier, who was piloting a second plane, put on a show as they flew from the Twin Tier skies, astounding spectators. These photographs are originals of Lindbergh and the *Spirit of St. Louis*, taken in July 1927 by the author's uncle Walter Lewis at a Buffalo airfield.

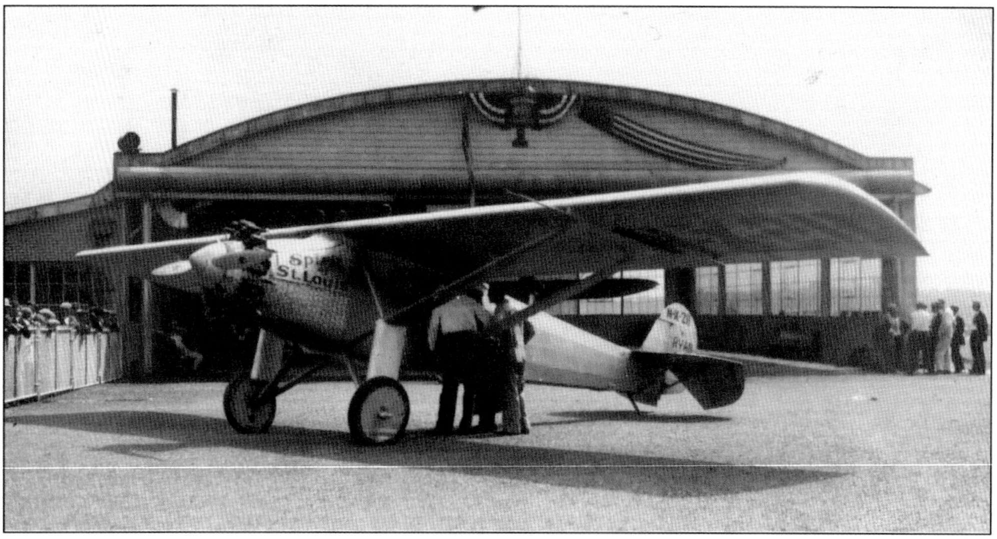

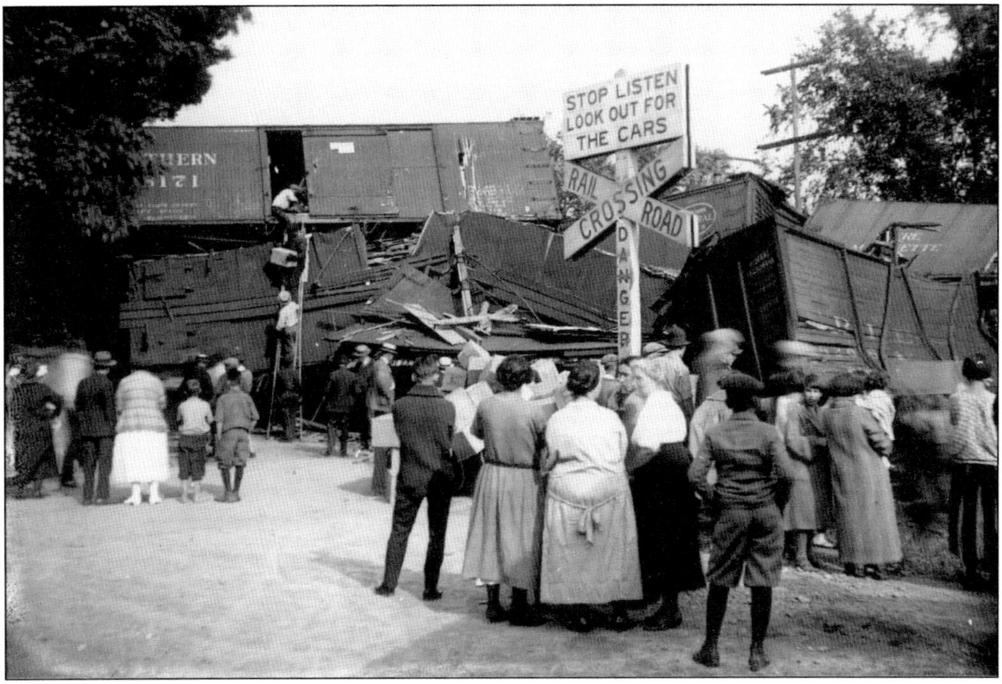

This photograph, made from a glass negative, captures the aftermath of a major train wreck in the town of Union c. 1910. Other hazards of early rail travel were flying cinders and soot from the engine. Frequent travelers carried a few flaxseeds in their pockets and would pop a seed into an eye that had caught debris. This procedure supposedly "cleansed the vexation from the orb."

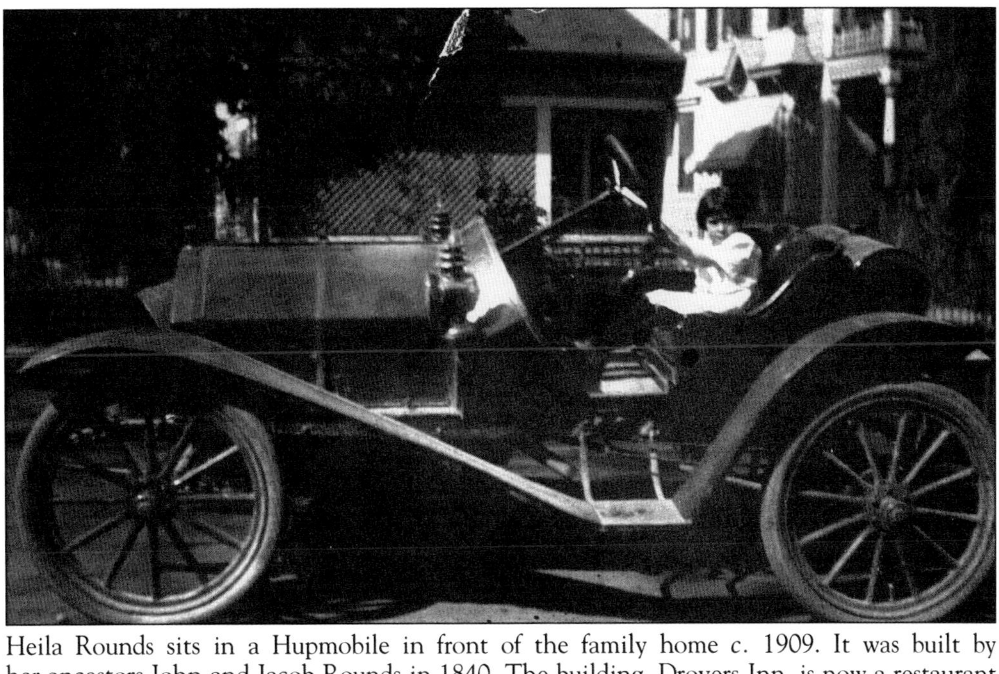

Heila Rounds sits in a Hupmobile in front of the family home c. 1909. It was built by her ancestors John and Jacob Rounds in 1840. The building, Drovers Inn, is now a restaurant in Vestal.

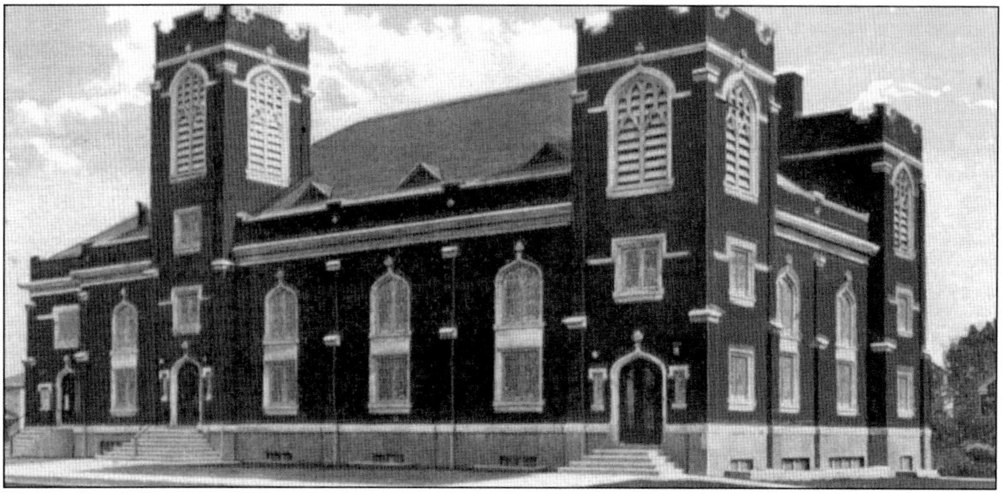

There has been a First Methodist Church of Endicott since 1902. The current impressive structure on McKinley Avenue has architectural details and woodwork with old-world charm. It also houses a very unusual stained glass window. At first glance the subject of this massive work of art could be Jesus in the garden. However, surrounded with children is George F. Johnson. The 10-foot-high by 20-foot-wide scene is depicted in brilliant cathedral glass colors. It was based on a 1935 photograph of Johnson at Ideal Park. The window was installed in 1945 in a prominent position in the church. Perhaps it was too prominent, as many parishioners believed Johnson's image didn't belong on the altar adjacent to God. It took nearly a decade to convince Johnson disciples a change was necessary, but the window was eventually moved to a space over the McKinley Avenue entrance.

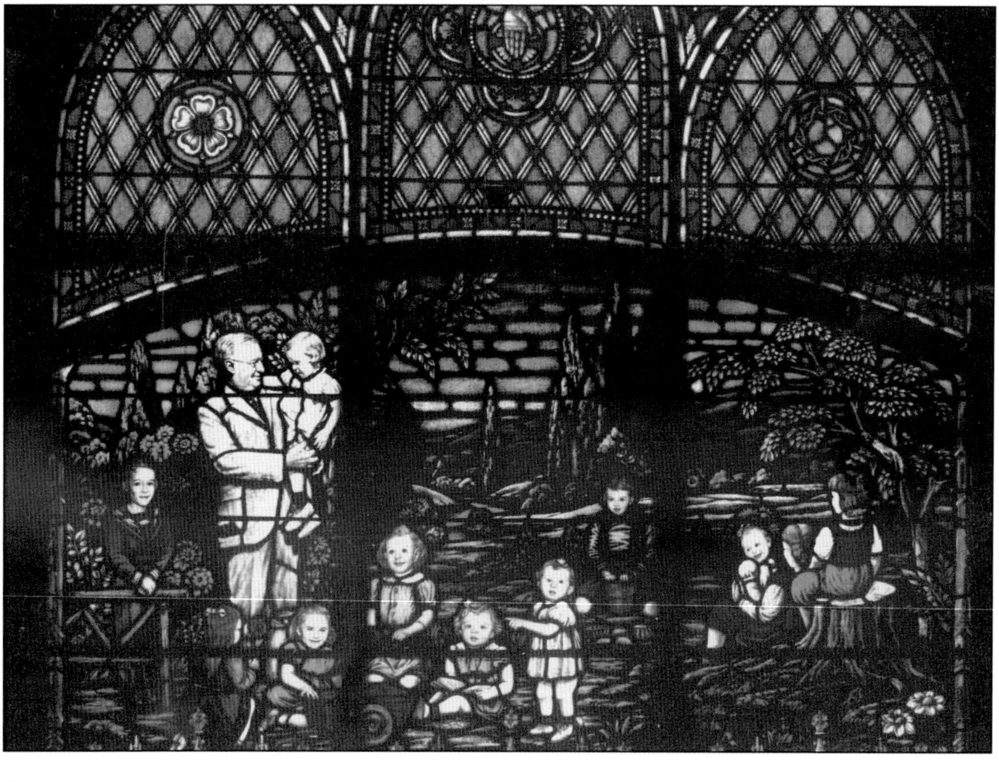

This flyer was distributed at the Binghamton Fair in 1912, advocating "Purity, Anti-White Slave and Colportage Work." Few could argue with the sentiments—if they could figure out where the problem existed. Chastity, temperance, and religion were hawked at every fair, carnival, and street gathering.

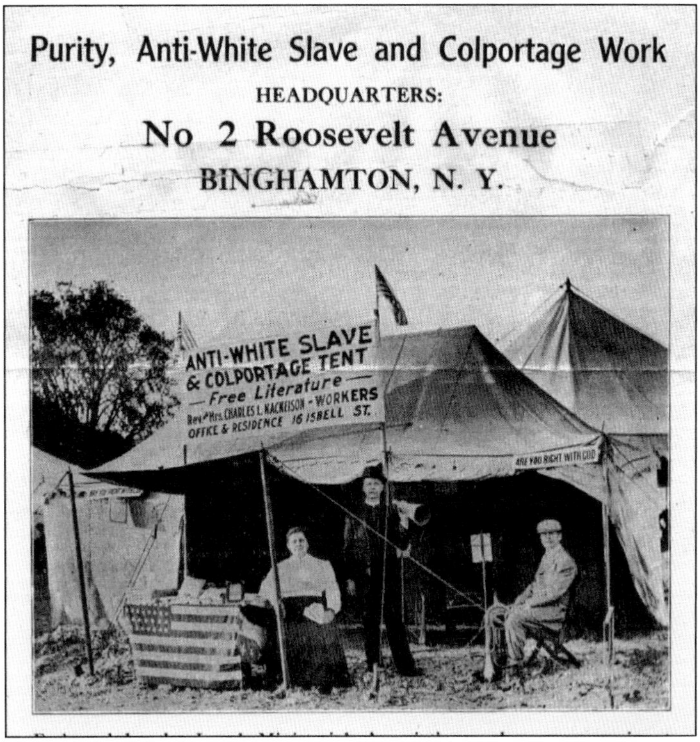

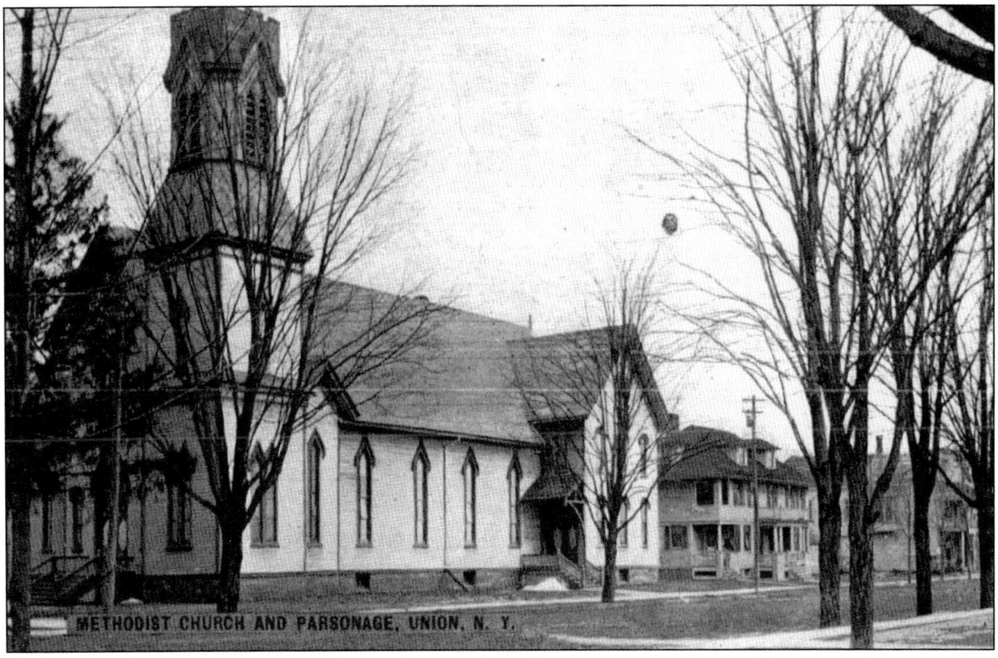

In 1892, a newspaper article informed the public that arrangements had been made to give an "oxy-hydrogen Stereopticon Entertainment" at the Methodist Episcopal Church in Union. Also advertised was one of the largest and most expensive dissolving-view stereopticons ever made, along with an exhibit of the Edison phonograph. "Hear it sing without the use of ear tubes!" Admission was 25¢.

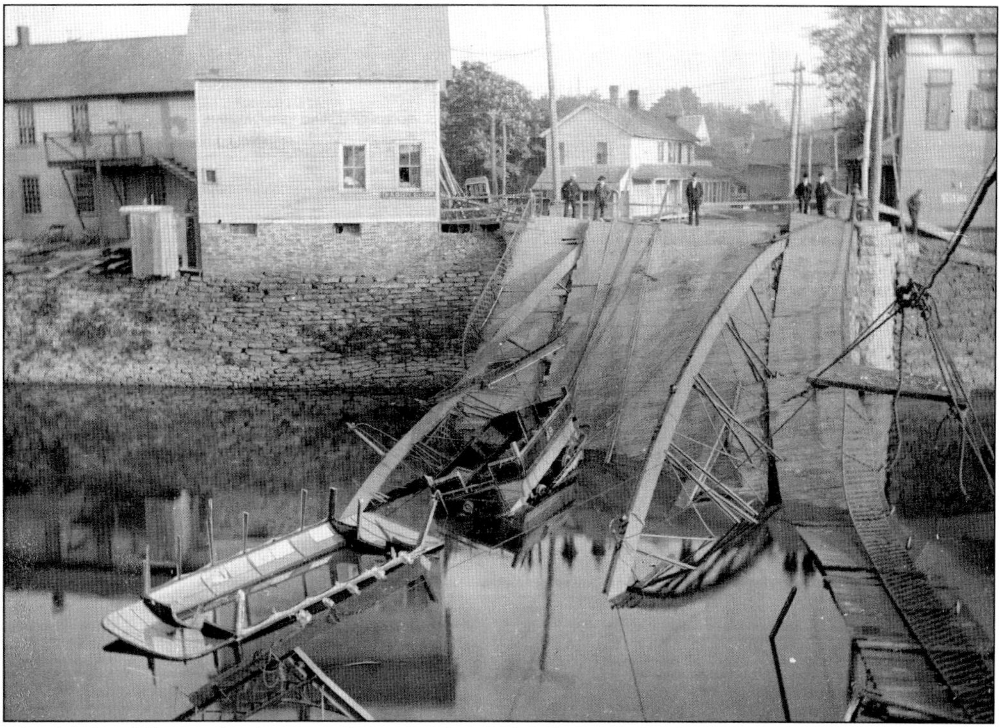

This bridge fell once by disaster, the second time by design. The first Rock Bottom Bridge, built in 1874, collapsed in 1903 while a trolley was crossing, as shown in the photograph above. A new bridge was constructed in 1904, remaining in service until 1970, when it was closed as unsafe. In 2001, charges were set, and the bridge exploded into the past. Ed Aswad took the second photograph as the bridge was being demolished.

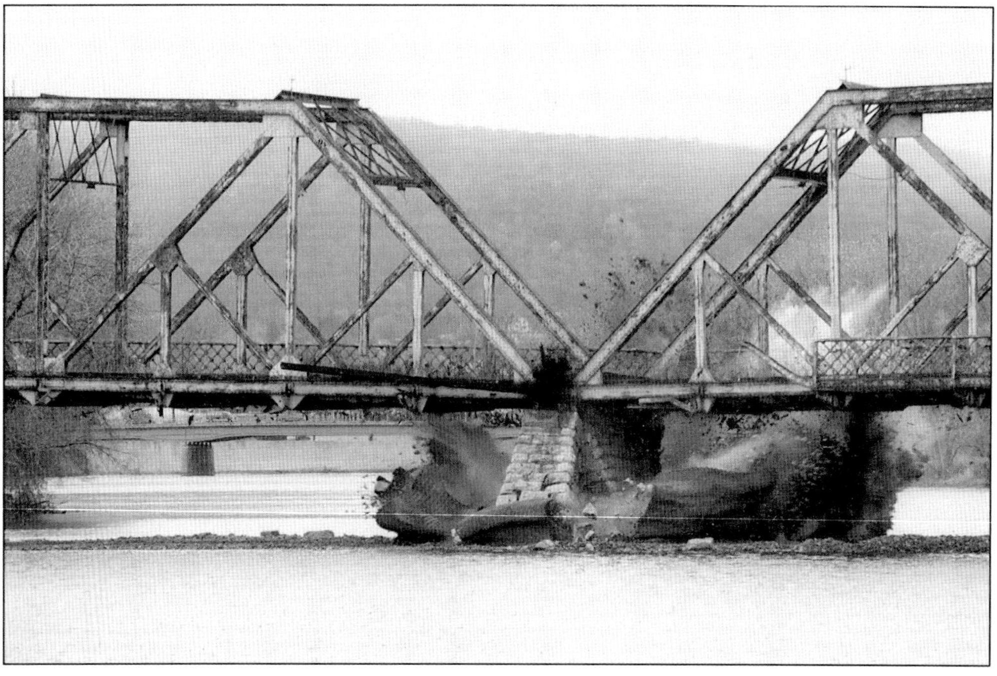

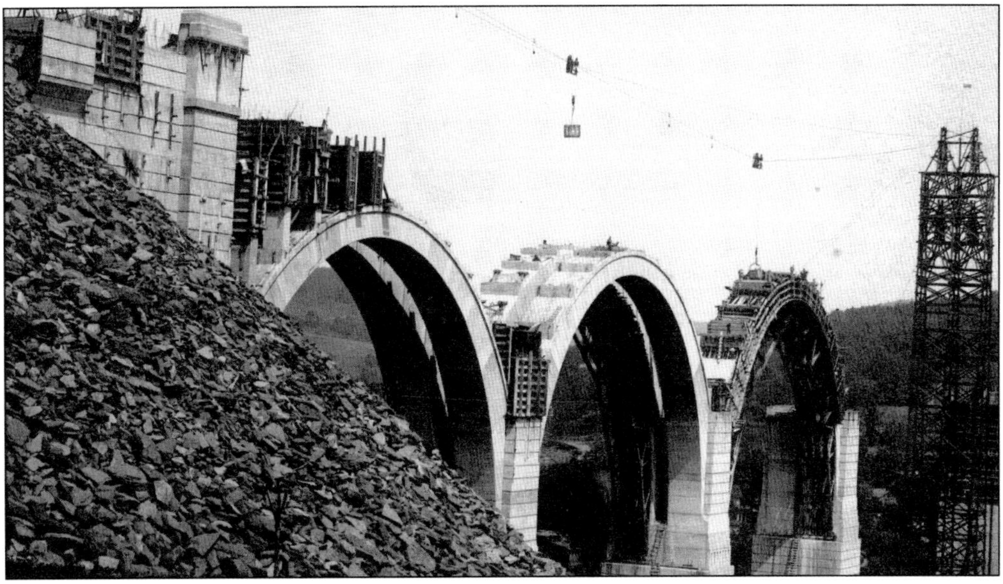

Still hailed as an engineering marvel, the Martins Creek Viaduct, also known as the D L & W Railroad Bridge at Kingsley, Pennsylvania, is one of the largest concrete bridges in the world. As it was being constructed, it attracted many skilled workers from Broome County. Completed in 1915, it "changed the face of nature, to accommodate the 'Road of Anthracite.' " For the duration of bridge construction, the town of Kingsley experienced unparalleled prosperity, providing room and board for the out-of-town crews. In an attempt to save hours of travel time, the railroad cutoff made history and impressed the world with the greatness of the work. The structure is a National Historic Civil Engineering Landmark.

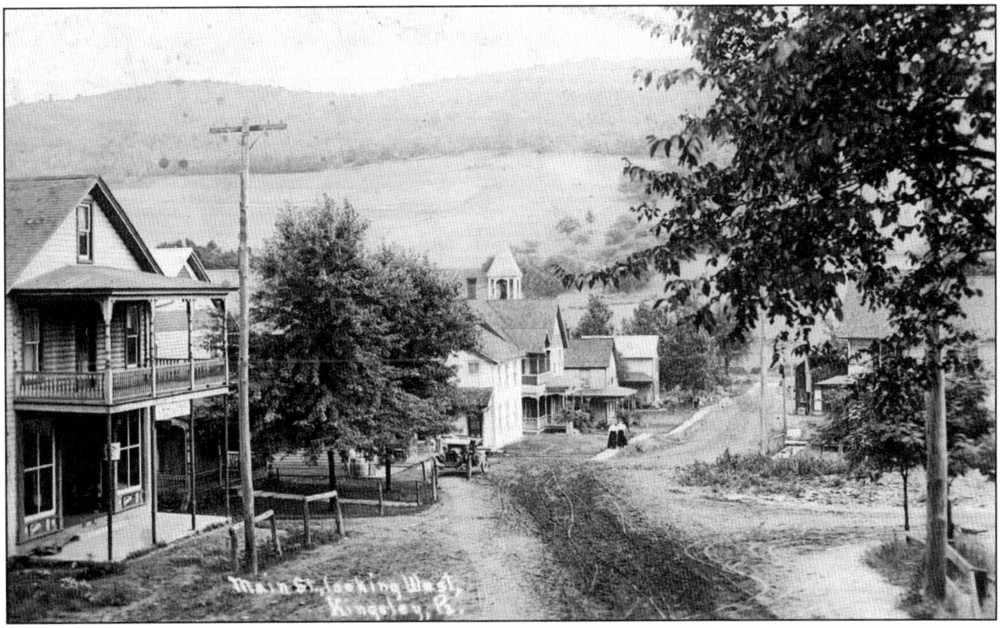

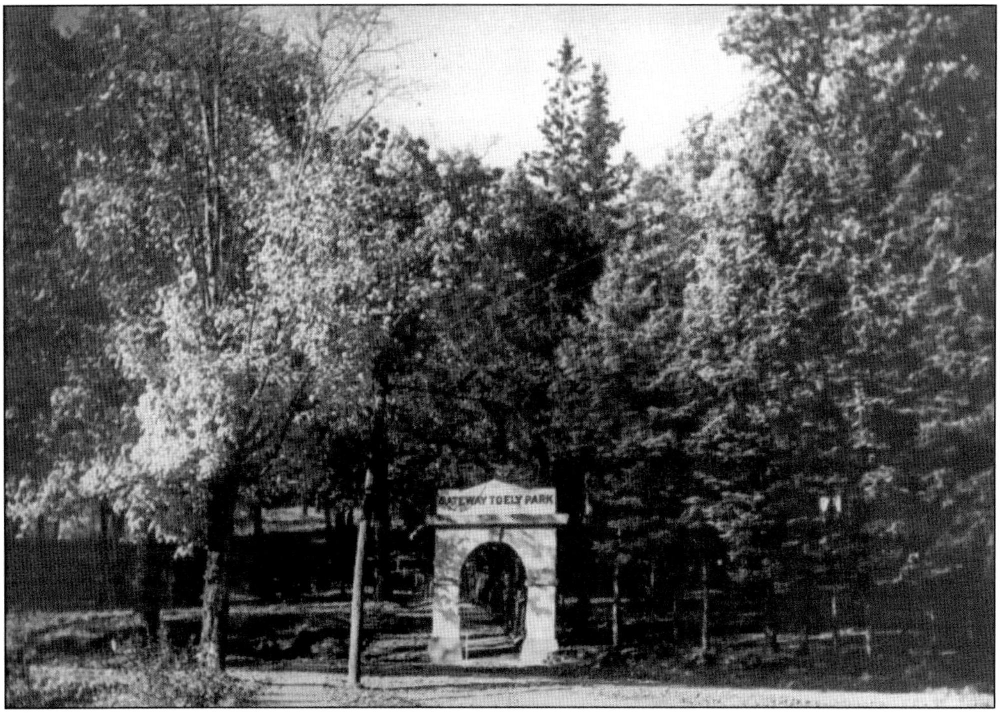

The gateway to Ely Park was an impressive arch, which led to hundreds of steps and paths to Ely Park at the top of Prospect Hill. A nearby cave in the mountain—closed off with wrought-iron gates—resembled the fabled cave of Aladdin, but in reality was a remnant of the West Kress Brewery cooling vaults. The arch and the cave were sacrificed to progress when the Kamikaze Curve section of Route 17 was constructed.

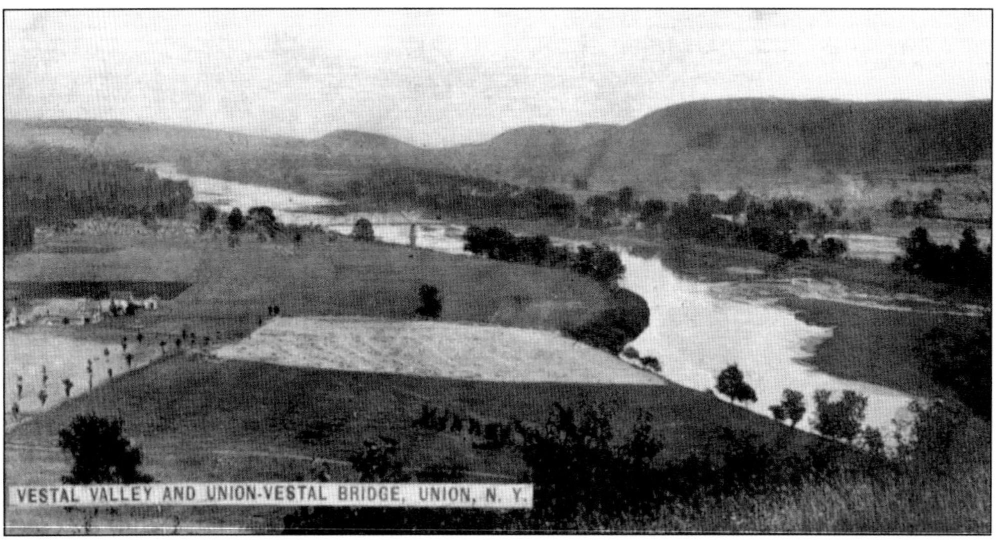

The *Union News* reported this shocking accident in 1867: "A terrible crash was heard as the bridge over the Susquehanna gave way with 127 head of cattle on it. It was the worst sight we ever witnessed. A great loss to the drover in killing and injuring his cattle, to the Union & Vestal Bridge Company, and to citizens whose communication between towns has been cut off. Rebuild the bridge! Action! Action!"

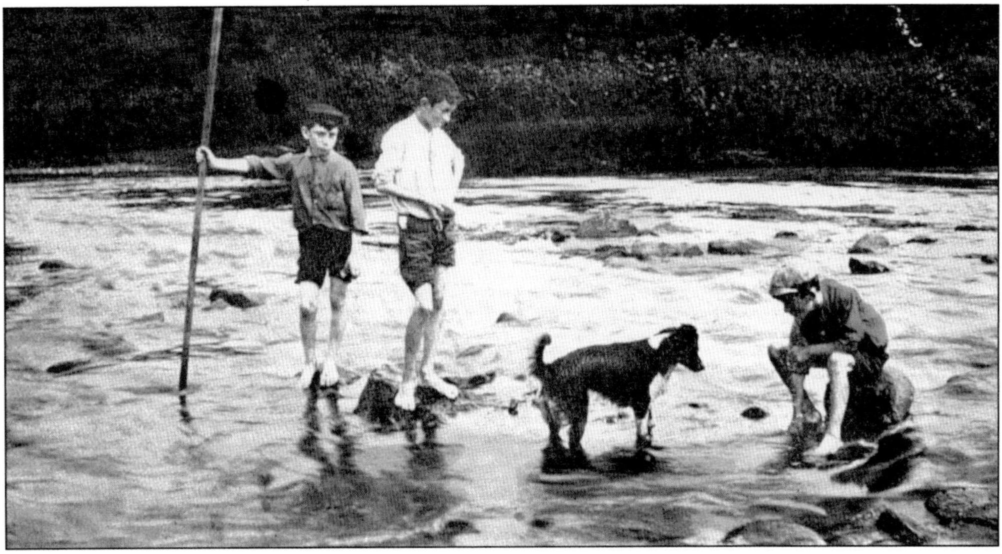

Some Susquehanna River lore and laws are as follows:

1798—River water is hailed as a remedy for tortures of overindulgence in strong drink.
1808—Settler Robbins describes the river valley as "60 acres of deep swampland," with mud "deep as a horse's belly."
1868—A small boy hooks a bullhead weighing 155 pounds. Many men helped to land the monster!
1897—Effort will be made by authorities to prevent fishing on Sundays. Officers will arrest violators.

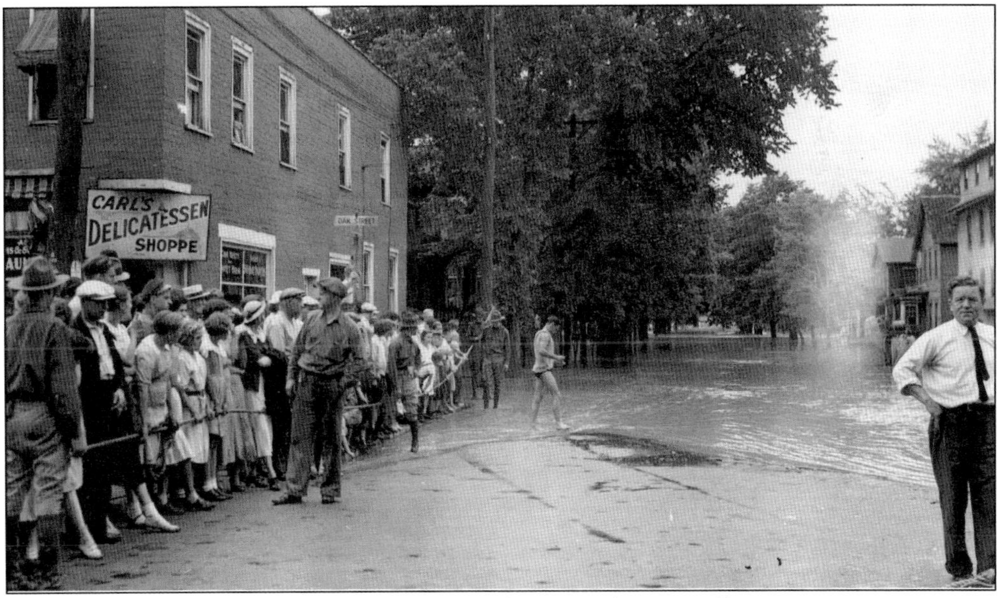

The great floods of 1935 and 1936 devastated the Susquehanna Valley region, inspiring many dam and engineering projects to prevent future disasters. We assume this postcard message of 1935 was an indication of humor: "Jonas, Just a note to let you know we have been held up here in Binghamton on account of very high waters. Noah."

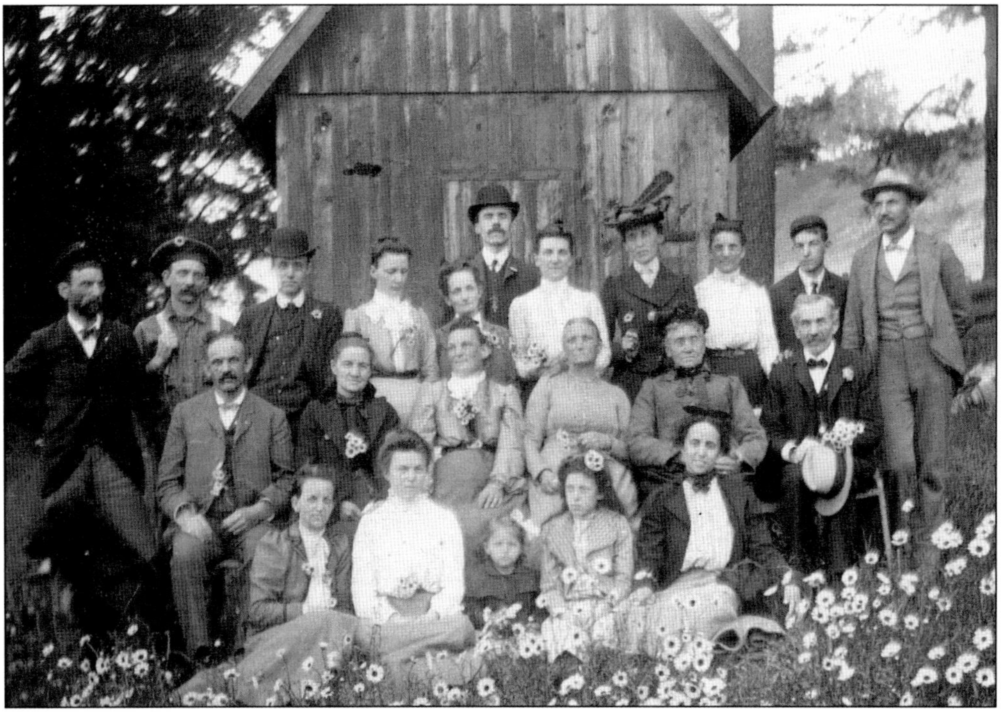

A traveler in the 1880s described the natural beauty of Broome as "magnificent hillsides, sheltering meadows, carpeted with daisies as large as trade dollars, the sweet pure air festooned with the perfume of nature, beguiling the senses with wonder." Shown is a picnic party in a field of daisies of the same era.

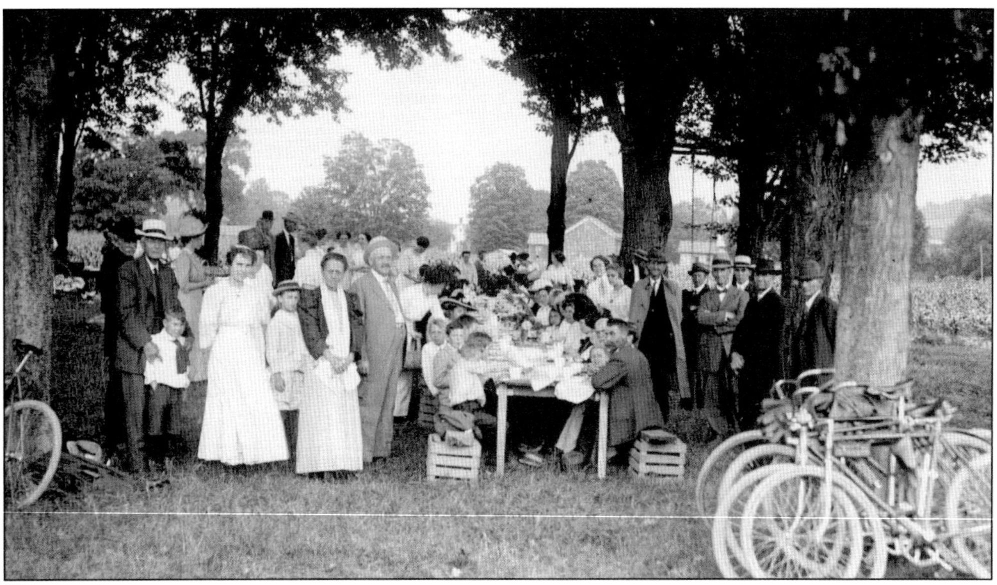

The Bradley Creek School in the town of Union hosted this picnic *c.* 1910. Travel was by horse or balloon tire bicycle. Seating was comprised of crates and boards, but the lawn of Howard Early's home between cornfields was welcoming, and the food was homemade.

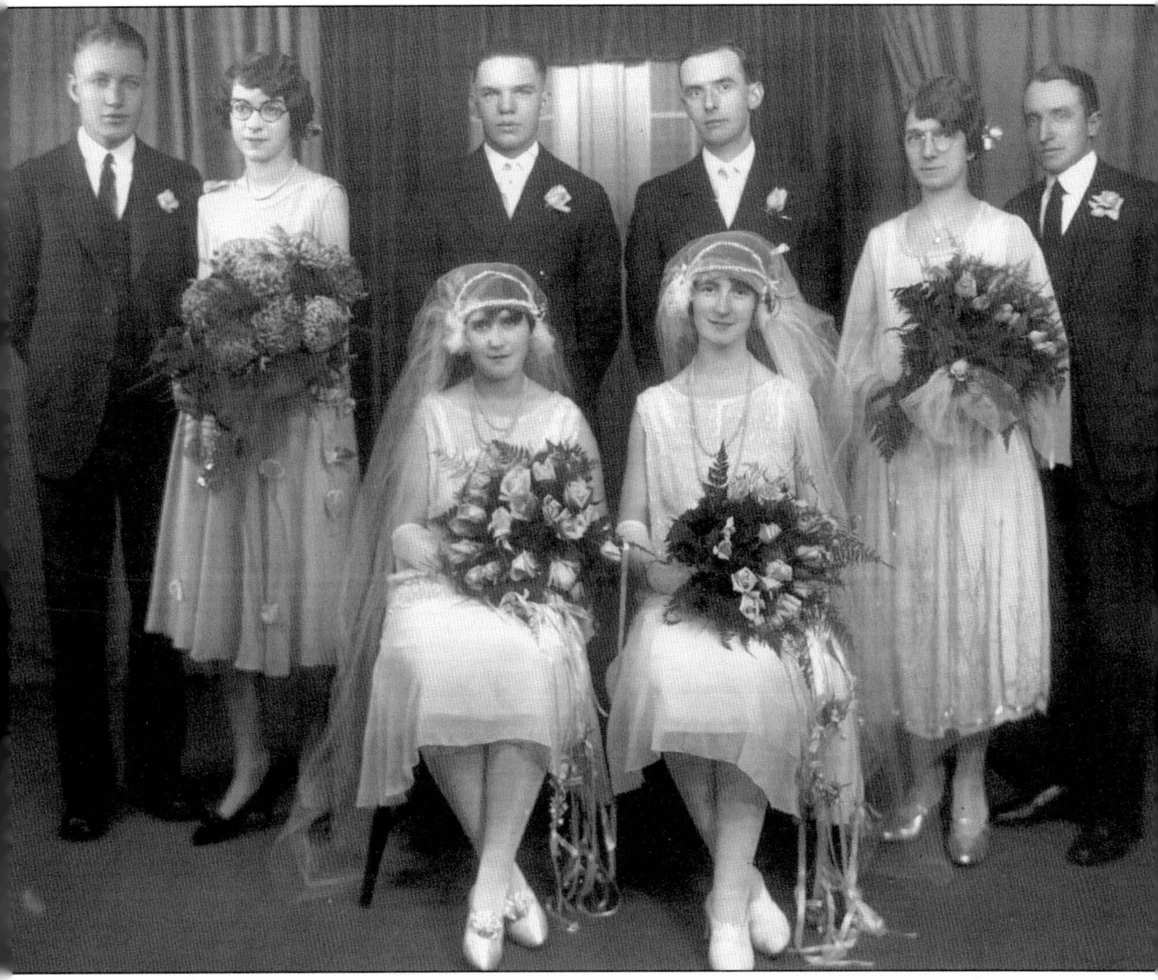

Love and marriage always inspires advice such as this:

> 1910—I hardly think you need any advice on the management of a man. Kindness and plenty to eat are said to be the best way to keep them happy. Love, Mother.
> 1913—Here is my advice on marriage pal, I don't need any exercise, but if I did I would argue with a woman.
> 1916—Have been celebrating for the past three weeks and visiting after the ceremony. It is a nice city but don't equal Union Center. I am the only old maid left here now. I think the only way you and I will ever get married is to marry each other. I am on my "honeymoon" now, all I lack is the man.

The photograph is a double wedding for sisters in the 1930s.

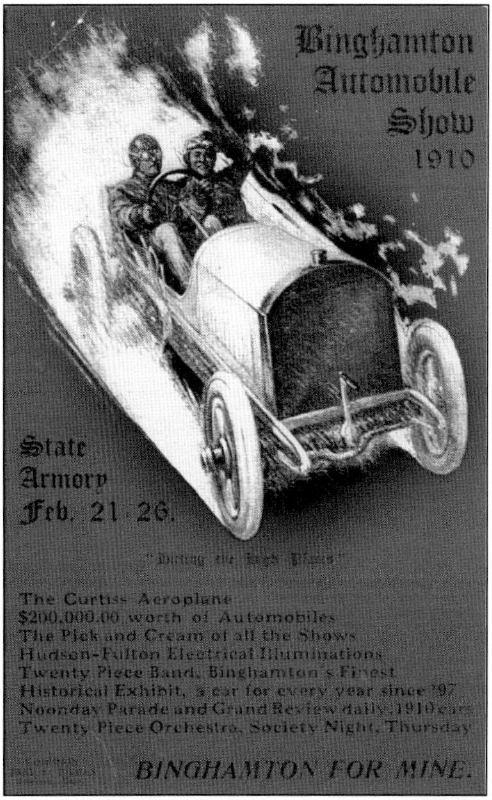

Broome County has always had active organizations to promote the agreeable way of life in a community with a congenial atmosphere. Among the plans to attract attention were numerous extravagant fairs and spectacular exhibits. The 1910 Binghamton Auto Show offered a 20-piece orchestra and $2 million worth of automobiles on display. The Binghamton Fair of 1930 charged an admission of only 35¢ for three days of attractions.

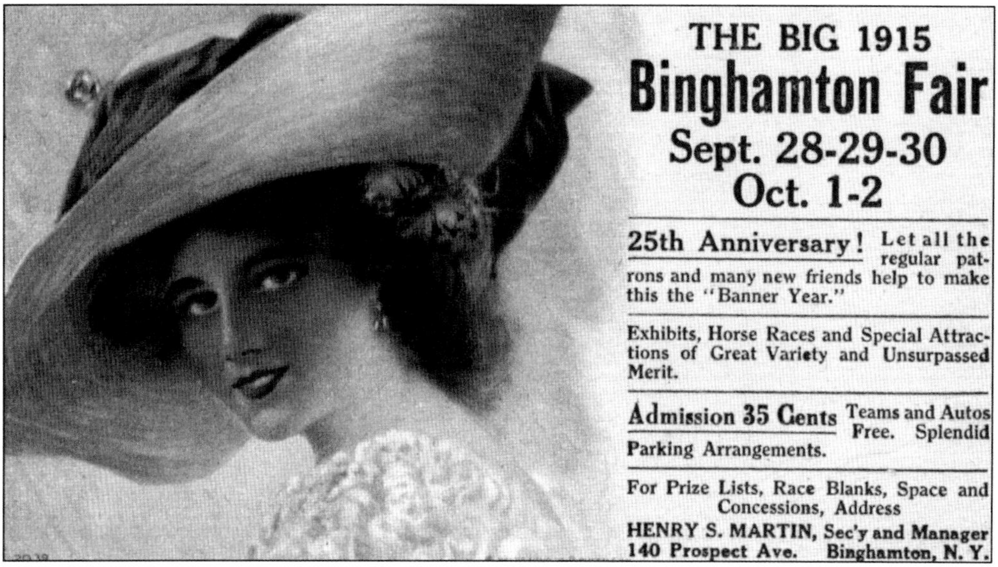

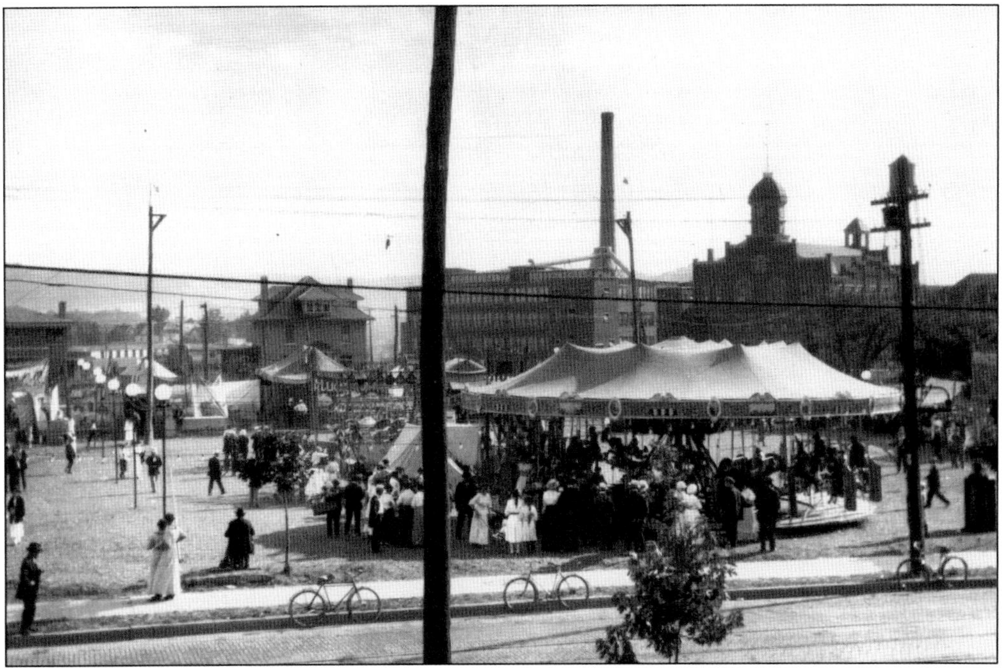

The village of Johnson City, *c.* 1912, encouraged traveling carnivals and circuses to set up attractions in the heart of the village. A carousel was a novelty before the Endicott Johnson Corporation donated six Hershell machines to the community.

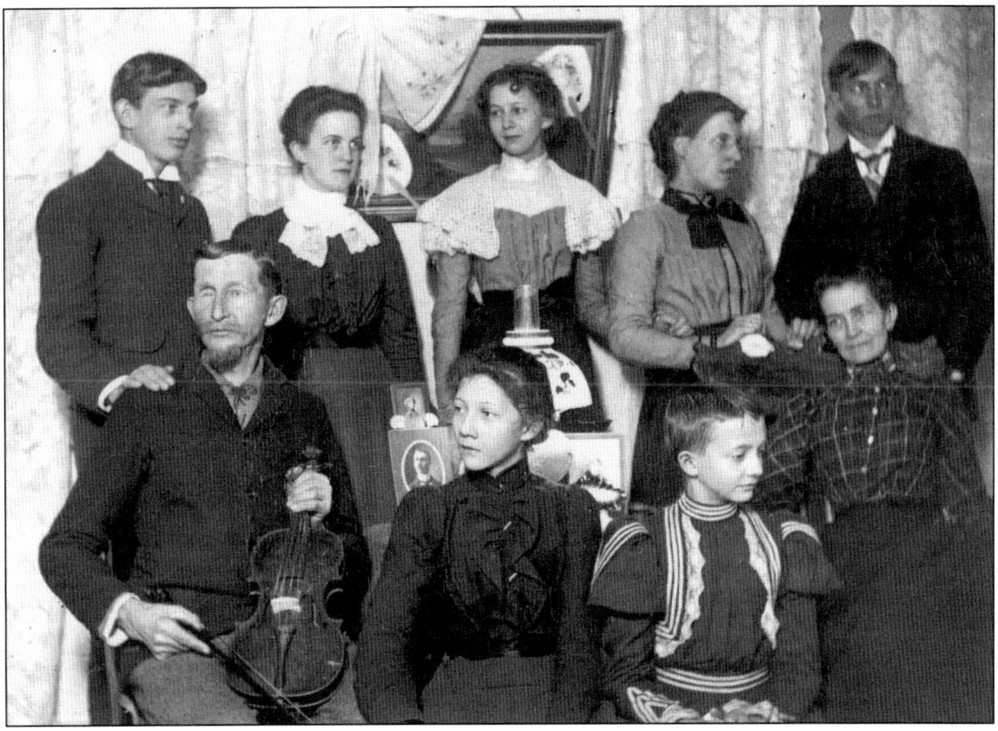

Entertainment in 1898 consisted of a group of any size and a talented person with a fiddle.

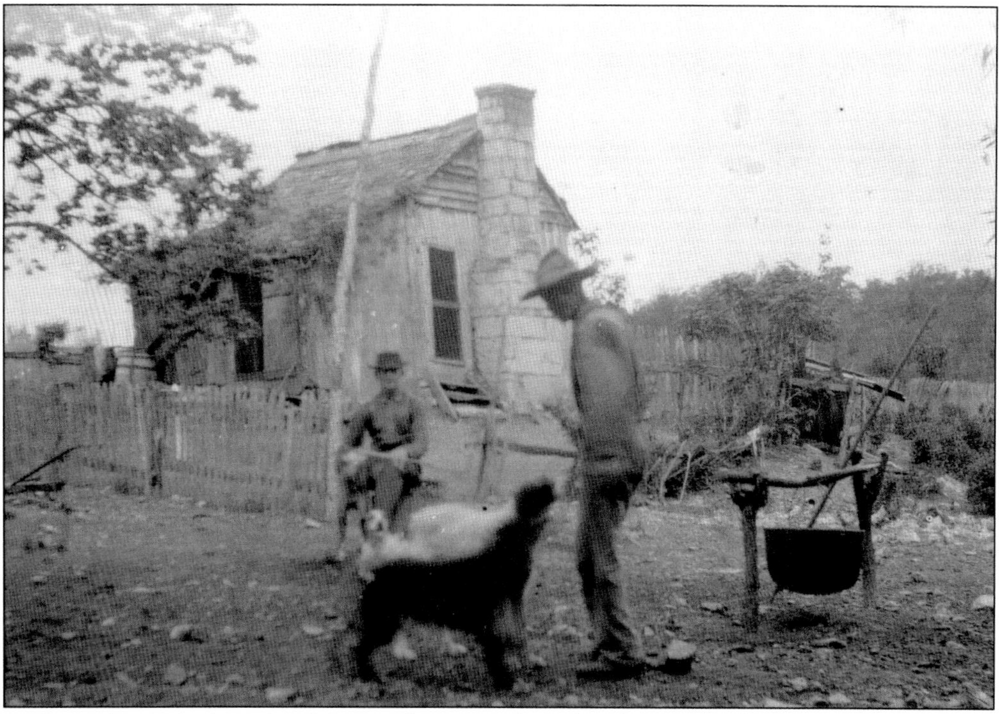

In the early 1900s, large local farms often were dotted with tiny shacks for itinerant workers. Although transient farm laborers were not as common in northern fields, many families found it necessary to travel to maintain a meager income. Low wages, hardship, poor housing, and lack of health care and sanitation facilities were common problems. These images were recorded on glass-plate negatives *c.* 1900.

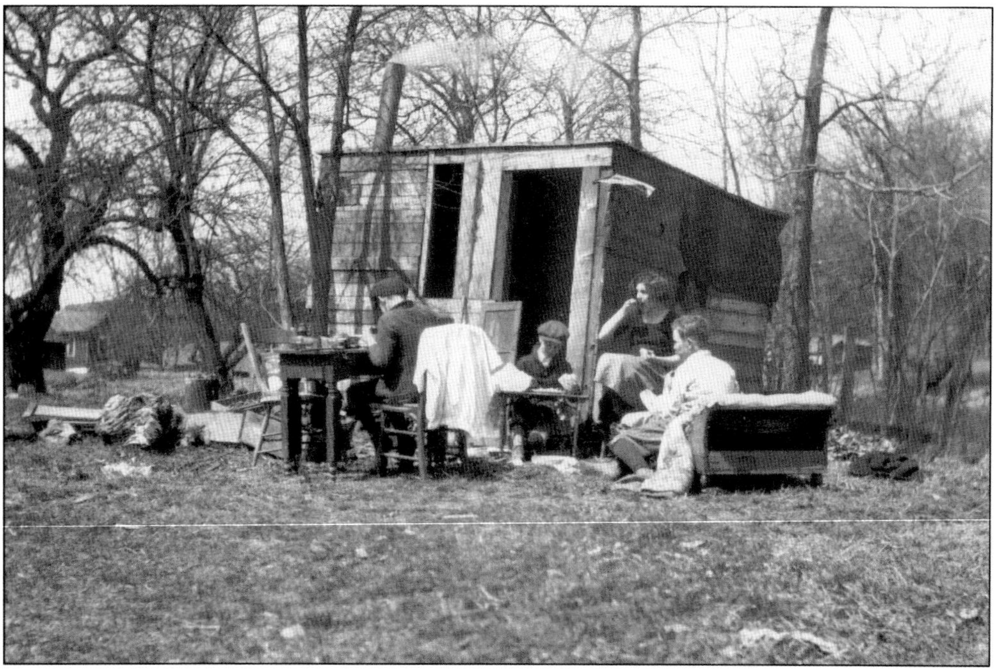

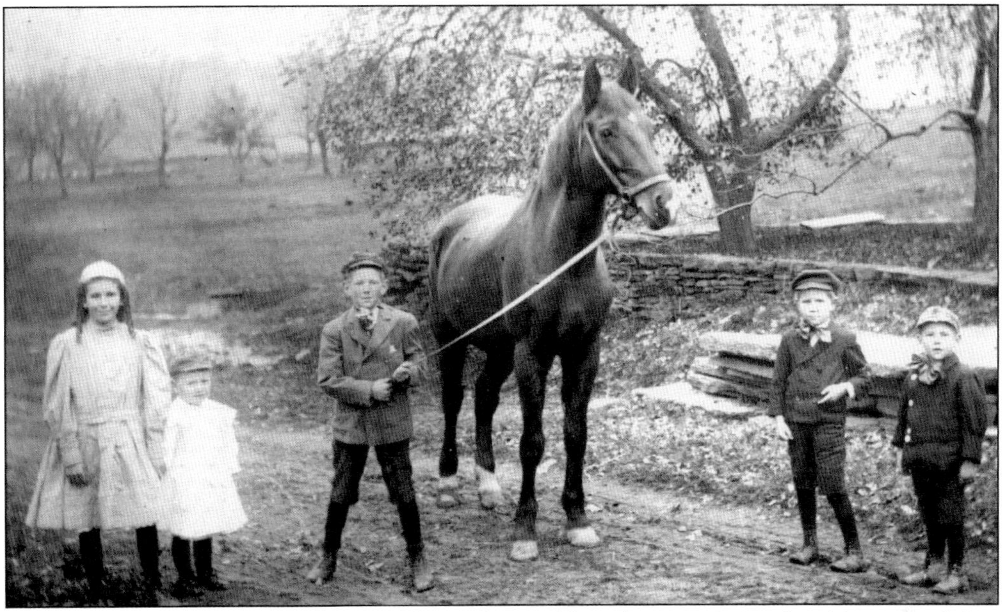

Larry the horse would probably never have this problem, but in 1811, a local law stated that "no horse shall be allowed to run on the common and any horse found at large will be liable to be taken to plow." The photograph of Larry and his friends was imprinted on a glass negative in 1909.

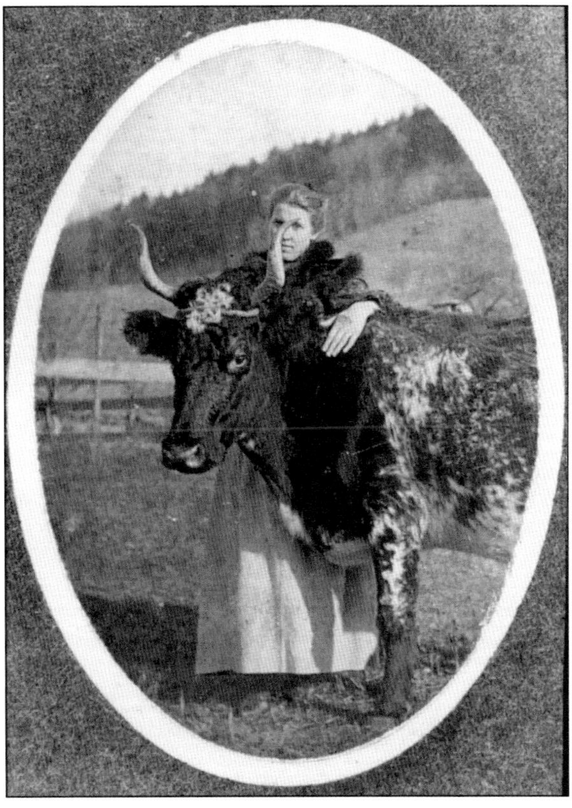

Each year, many rural churches have a special Blessing of the Animals ceremony. Usually held outdoors, the ceremony's purpose is to share God with all of his creatures. The tradition is still followed in many churches. This bovine is bedecked for presentation to the deity *c.* 1897.

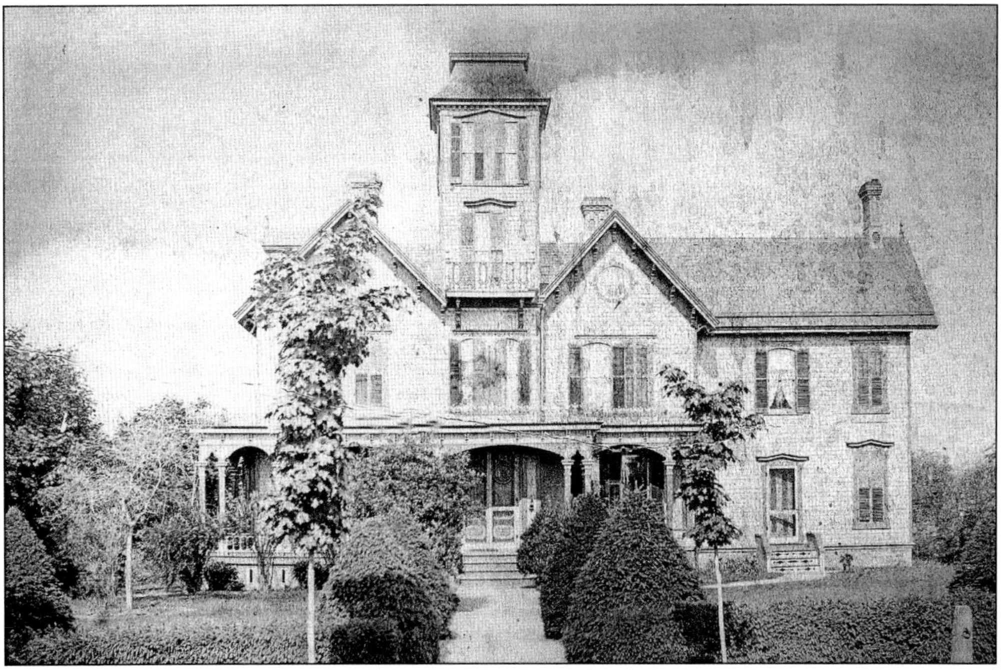

The Charles Pumpelly Home was located on Nanticoke Avenue in the town of Union and was built pre-1876. Charles Pumpelly was an active community member who served as road commissioner and member of the assembly. He was also successful at growing superior crops of tobacco.

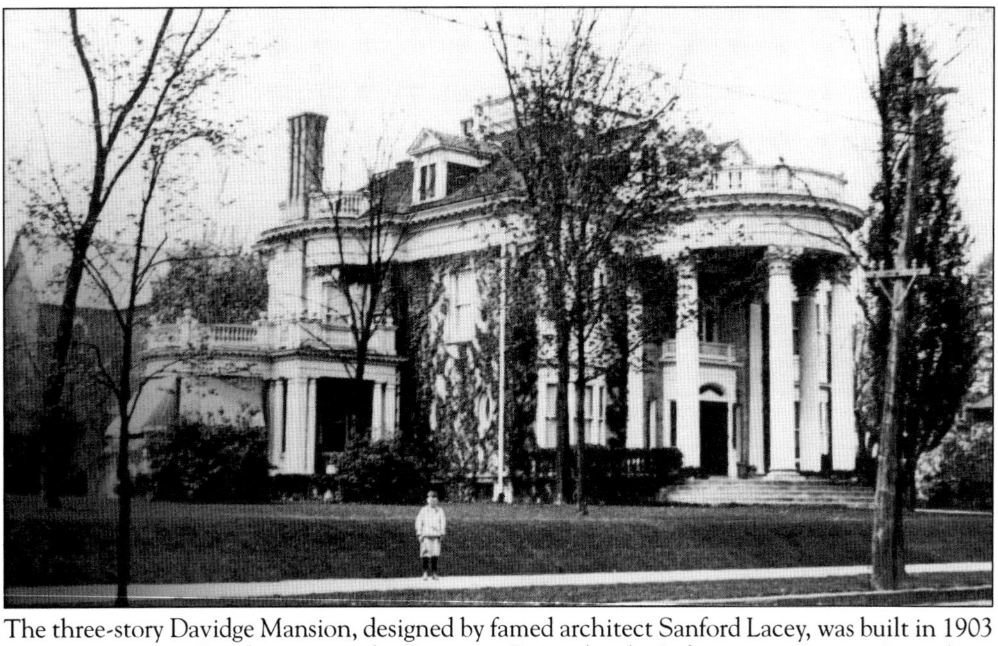

The three-story Davidge Mansion, designed by famed architect Sanford Lacey, was built in 1903 on Front Street in Binghamton in the Georgian Revival style. It features two-story Corinthian columns that support a portico. In 1920, it was purchased by St. Patrick's Church for use as a convent. The mansion still stands, now housing various commercial and charitable offices and the headquarters for the local Junior League.

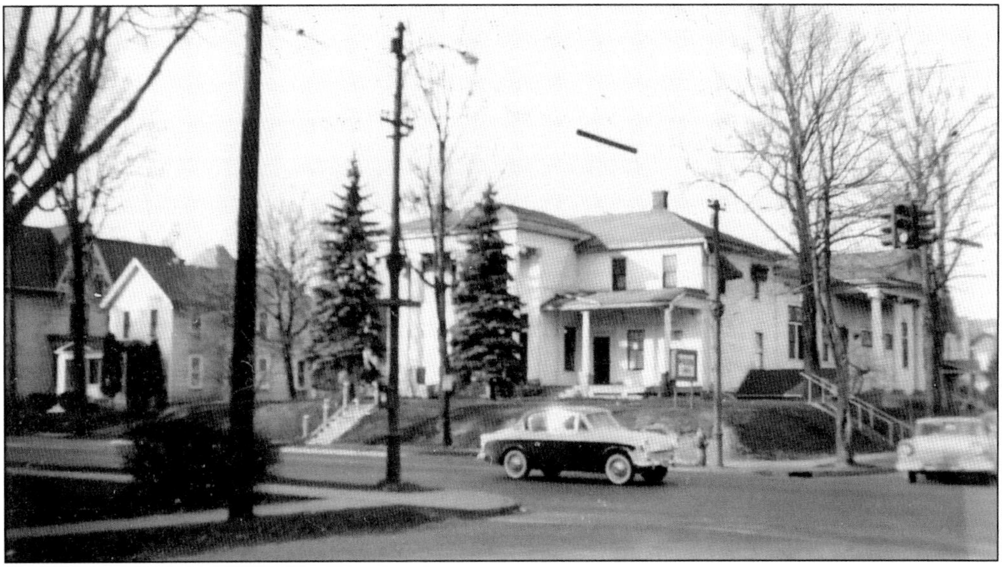

Lawrence Mercereau built this distinctive home on Main Street in Union *c.* 1837. It eventually became the Moose Lodge and, in 1975, was torn down for the very necessary construction of another fast-food restaurant.

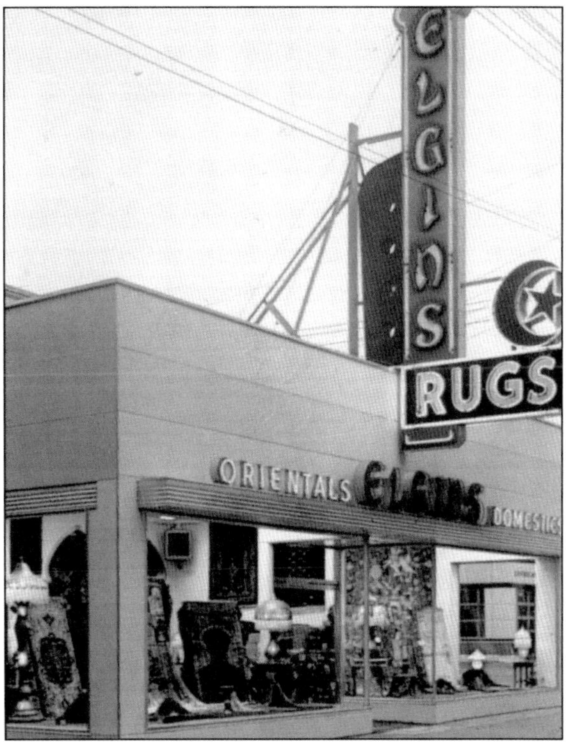

An exotic-looking store in Binghamton sold quality home furnishings from the Middle East. George T. Elgin began the business in 1924 and moved to this Main Street location in 1950. The retail shop was built on the front of a mansion once owned by Fred Weed, manager of a tannery founded by his father in the mid-1800s. The house contained locally crafted Victorian-style oak woodwork.

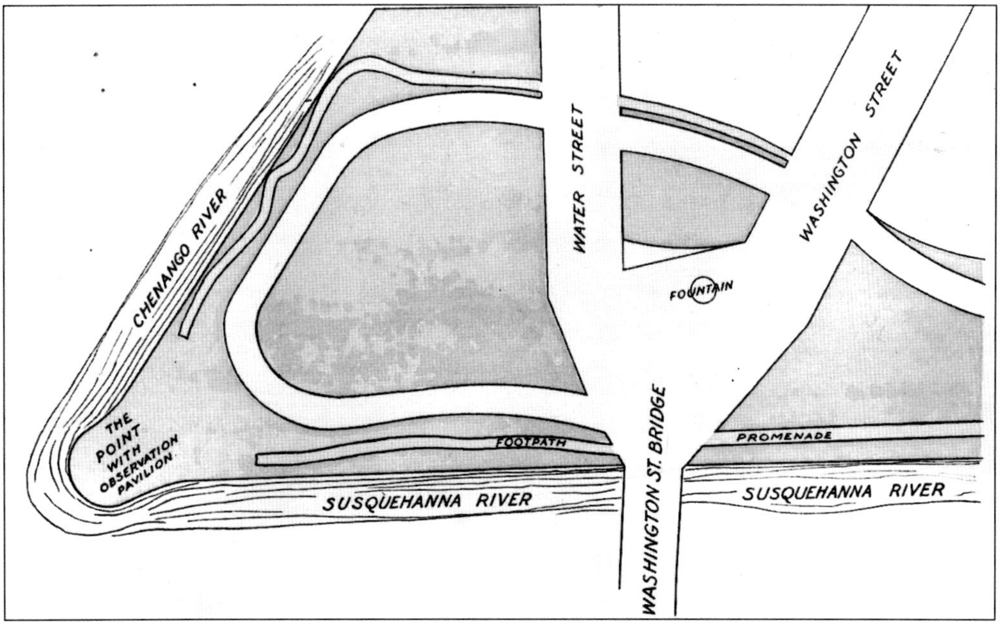

A detailed study was made of Binghamton that gave practical suggestions for physical changes and thus prepared the city for growth to hasten a "Better Binghamton." The expensive plan recommended riverbank improvement, including lights, a promenade, and an outlook at the apex of the point near the confluence of rivers. The proposal was completed in 1911. Some 90 years later, political powers—in their usual swift response—are following some of the recommendations. Confluence Park, under construction in 2002, is shown in the photograph below. The drawing above is from the original book of advice commissioned nearly a century earlier by the Mercantile-Press Club of Binghamton.

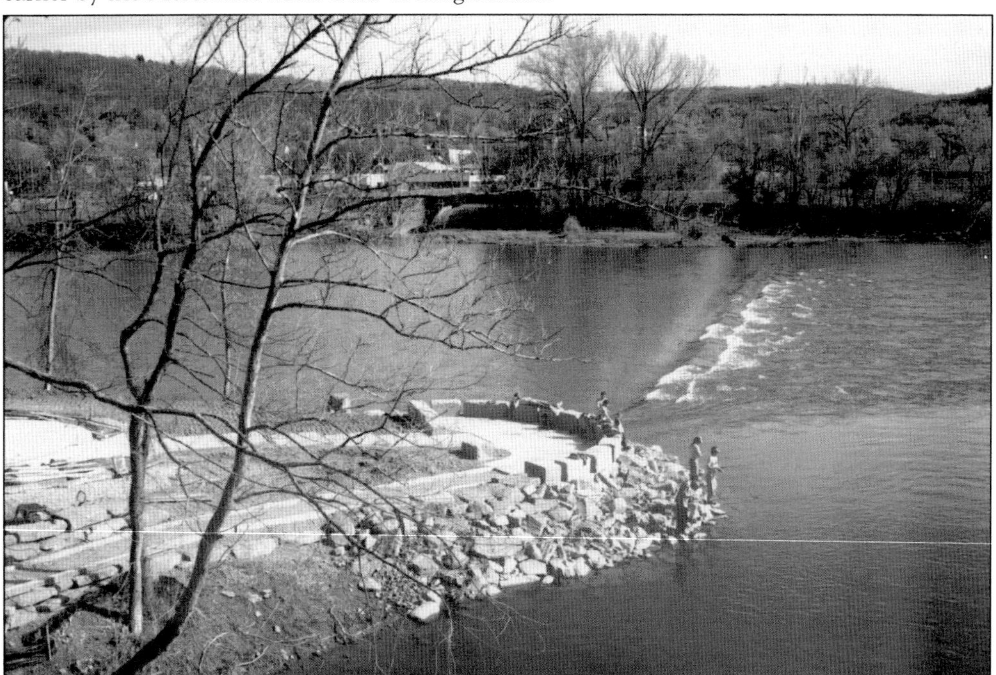

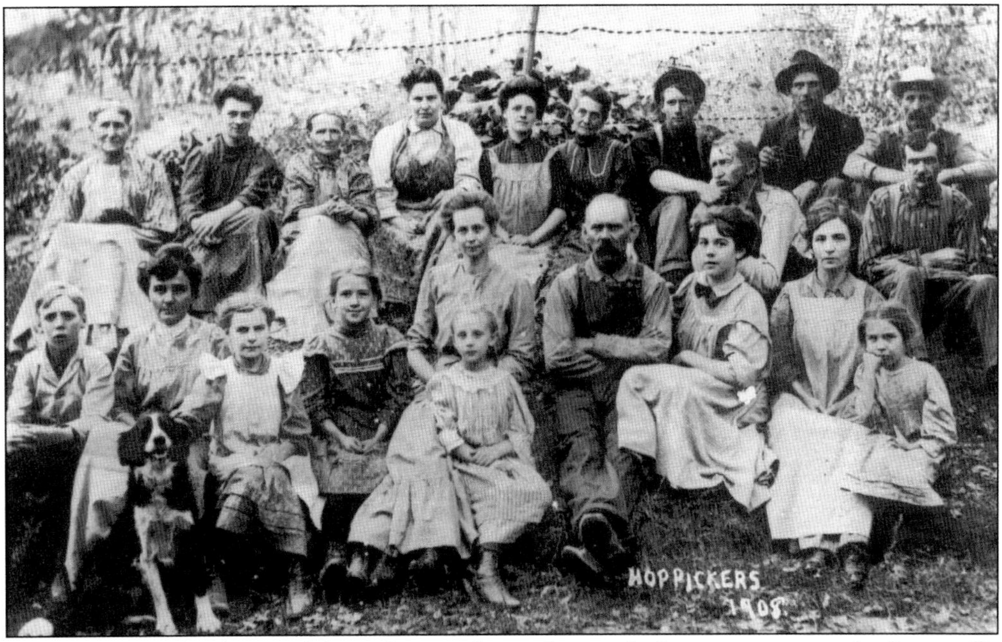

Hops are a hardy plant and have been cultivated since before written records. Regionally grown hops, picked in large baskets such as those shown, earned the pickers from 4¢ to 7¢ per bushel. Pickers had to know which hops to harvest, as the riper the hop the stronger the lupulin content and, thus, the more it was worth. This photograph was taken in 1908.

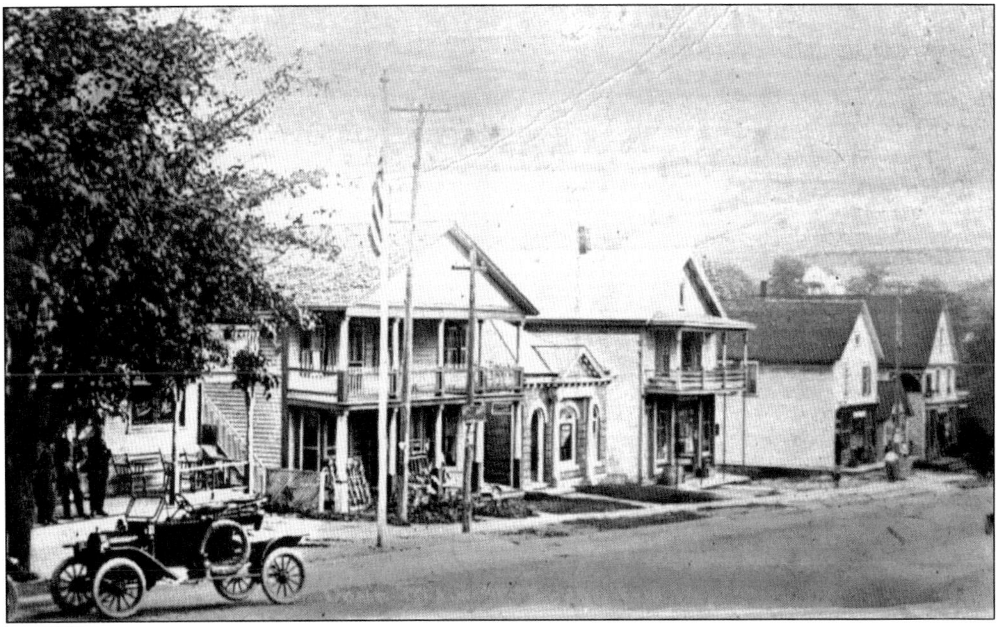

The small village of Hop Bottom, a few miles from Binghamton, was named for the wild hops that grew in abundance along a ravine through town. However, around 1812, outsiders jokingly referred to the settlement as "Hopping Bottom" to poke fun at the Methodists, who were "wont to exhibiting spiritual joy by leaping and shouting." The picture shows Main Street *c.* 1924.

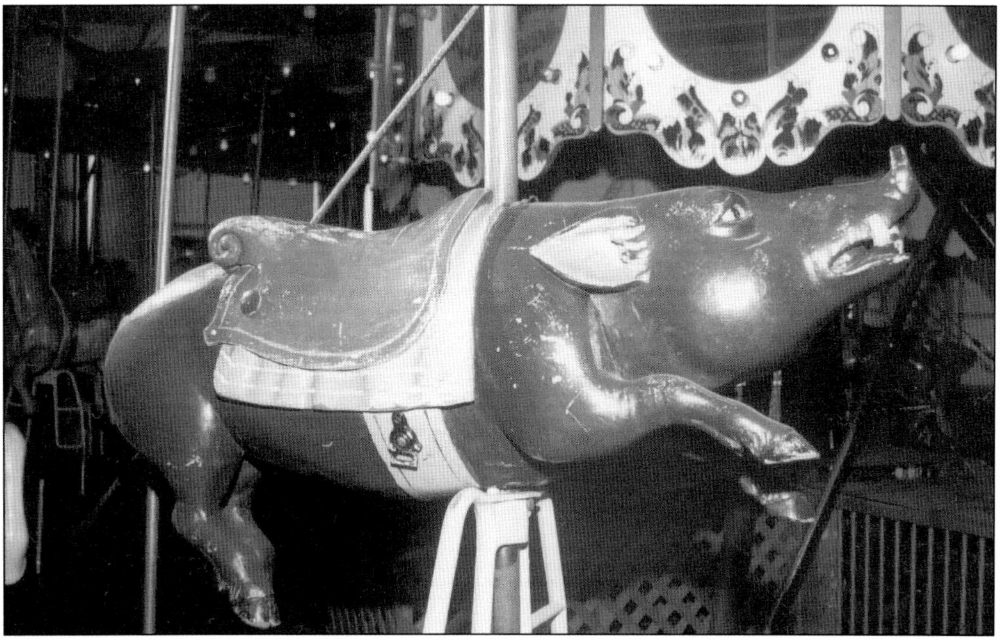

Corralling livestock was a continuing problem in early America. A local town enacted a law in 1791, stating, "Hogs may run on the common, boars excepted. All boars found on the common over two months old shall be liable to immediate castration by any person." The only porker running around today is this one on the historic carousel in West Endicott Park.

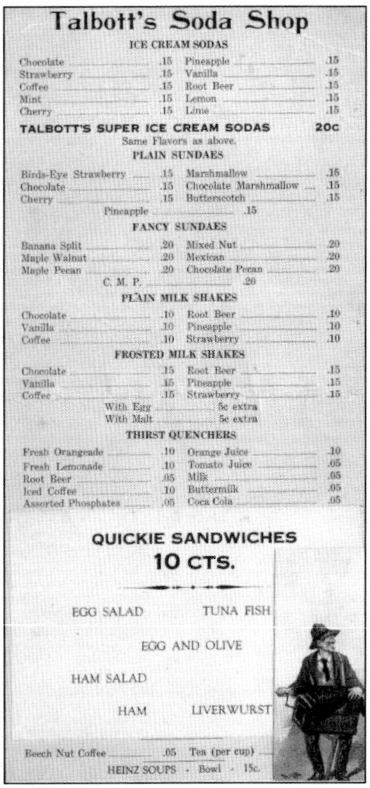

Talbott's Soda Shop

ICE CREAM SODAS

Chocolate	.15	Pineapple	.15
Strawberry	.15	Vanilla	.15
Coffee	.15	Root Beer	.15
Mint	.15	Lemon	.15
Cherry	.15	Lime	.15

TALBOTT'S SUPER ICE CREAM SODAS 20c

Same Flavors as above.

PLAIN SUNDAES

Birds-Eye Strawberry	.15	Marshmallow	.15
Chocolate	.15	Chocolate Marshmallow	.15
Cherry	.15	Butterscotch	.15

Pineapple .15

FANCY SUNDAES

Banana Split	.20	Mixed Nut	.20
Maple Walnut	.20	Mexican	.20
Maple Pecan	.20	Chocolate Pecan	.20

C. M. P. .20

PLAIN MILK SHAKES

Chocolate	.10	Root Beer	.10
Vanilla	.10	Pineapple	.10
Coffee	.10	Strawberry	.10

FROSTED MILK SHAKES

Chocolate	.15	Root Beer	.15
Vanilla	.15	Pineapple	.15
Coffee	.15	Strawberry	.15

With Egg 5c extra
With Malt 5c extra

THIRST QUENCHERS

Fresh Orangeade	.10	Orange Juice	.10
Fresh Lemonade	.10	Tomato Juice	.05
Root Beer	.05	Milk	.05
Iced Coffee	.10	Buttermilk	.05
Assorted Phosphates	.05	Coca Cola	.05

QUICKIE SANDWICHES
10 CTS.

EGG SALAD TUNA FISH
EGG AND OLIVE
HAM SALAD
HAM LIVERWURST

Beech Nut Coffee .05 Tea (per cup)
HEINZ SOUPS - Bowl - 15c.

An 1897 newspaper announced, "Street hawkers abound! . . . A sweet cider man [is] charging a nickel for a small cupful of the stuff, and coming soon is the roast chestnut man." In 1940, there were fewer traveling merchants, but each summer the hurdy-gurdy man and a smelly little monkey would stand near Beethoven and Main Streets by Talbot's Soda Shop collecting coins. The organ grinder and his tunes now live only in memories.

Two

The Business of Commerce and Community

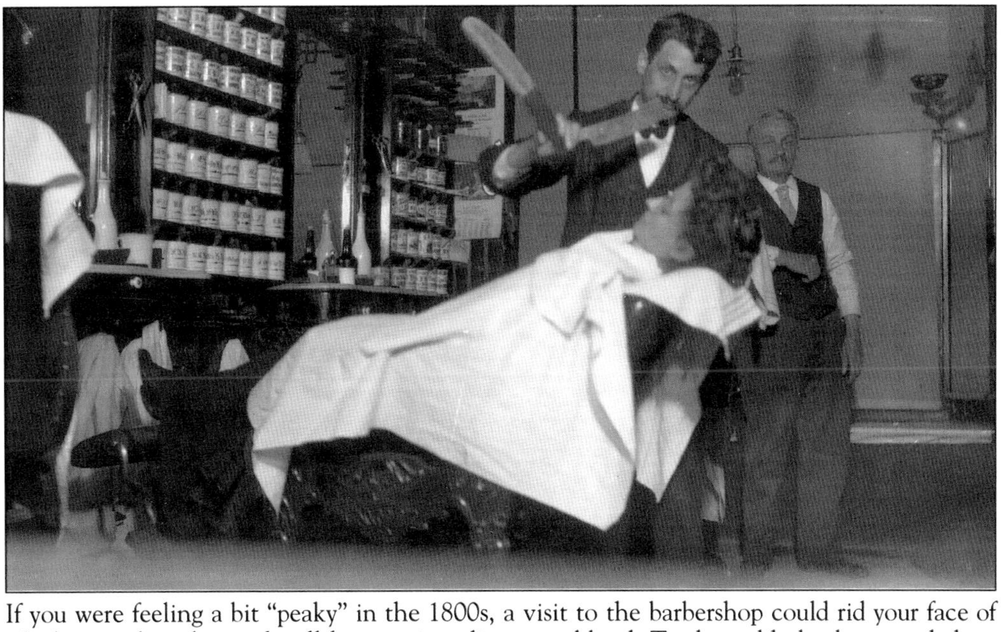

If you were feeling a bit "peaky" in the 1800s, a visit to the barbershop could rid your face of whiskers and eradicate the ill humors invading your blood. Teeth could also be attended to, but only by being pulled. The familiar red-and-white barber pole indicated bloodletting and bandages were available at the tonsorial artist establishment. A shave and a cut had a more inclusive meaning in previous centuries.

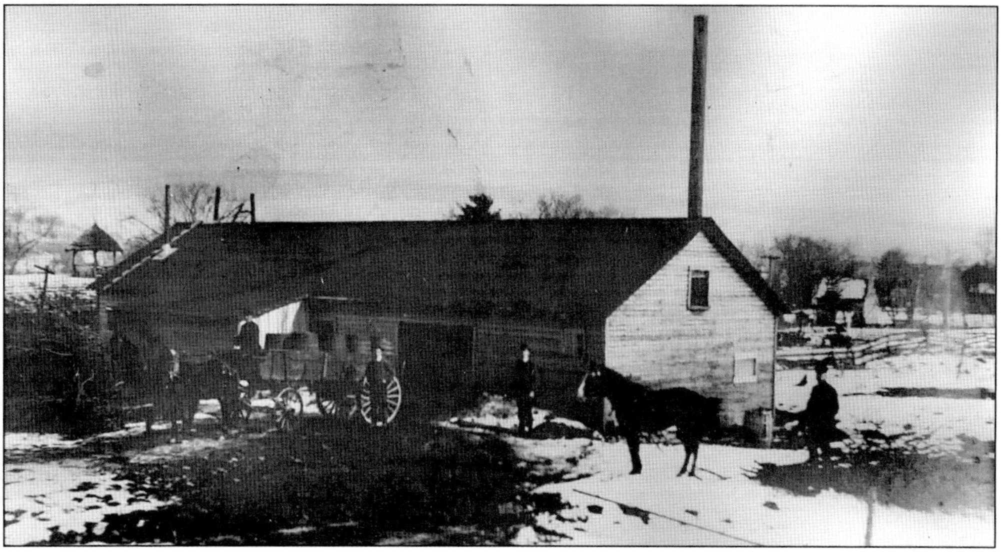

The town of Triangle had a witch hazel plant *c.* 1910. American witch hazel is a fall-blooming shrub or small tree. The ripe fruits discharge seeds by an unusual explosive action, often shooting seeds many feet. An astringent is made from the leaves and bark for use on cuts, bruises, and bites. The branches of the hazel tree were the choice for use as divining rods and bows.

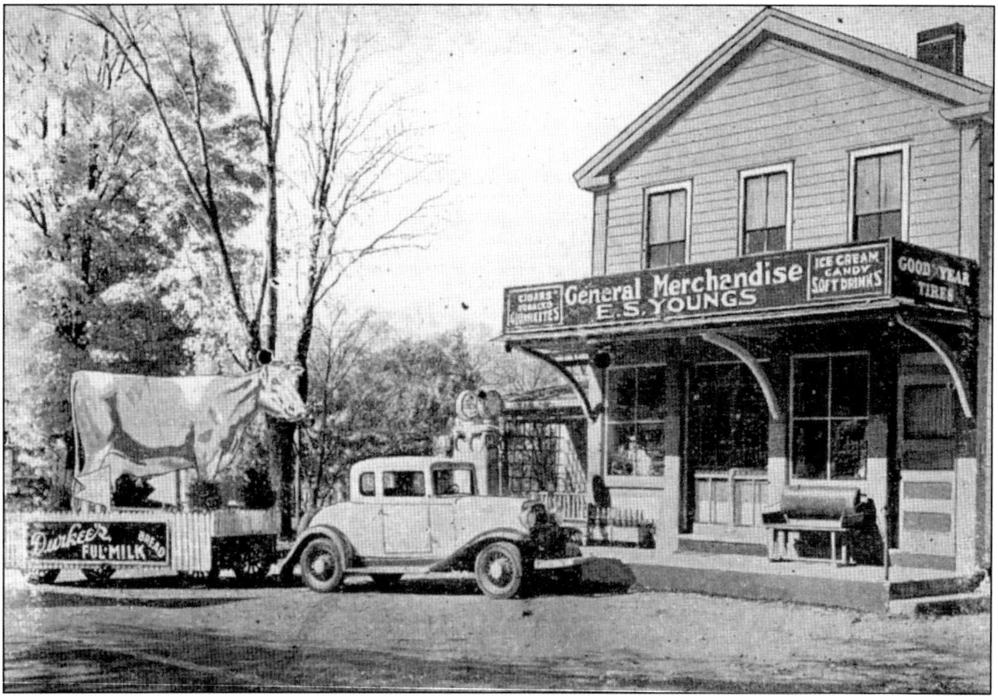

Youngs Store operated for many generations in Port Crane. From 1836 to 1878, the Chenango Canal operated practically at its front door, creating prosperous days for the merchant. Canal people were of "rough character with little respected for laws." At one point, there was a hanging on the store's front porch. A few months later, an attempted murder occurred in the barn.

The Lyric Theater offered entertainment on Washington Avenue in Endicott. In 1919, community members wished to end an ordinance that banned movies on Sundays. The village board voted with the clergy, who protested this step to perdition. Prevailing thoughts contended that young women would be snared into lives of shame by attending movies. George F. Johnson intervened on the side of change. Another ballot was taken, and Sunday afternoon shows were allowed.

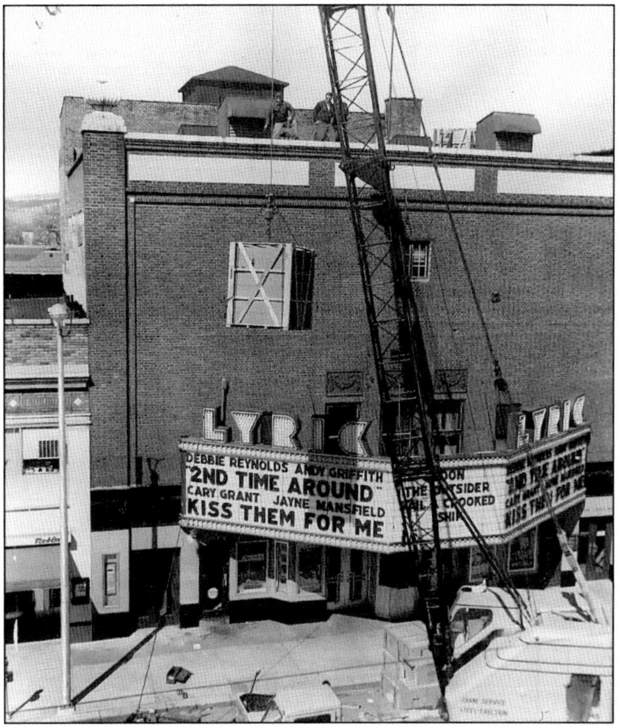

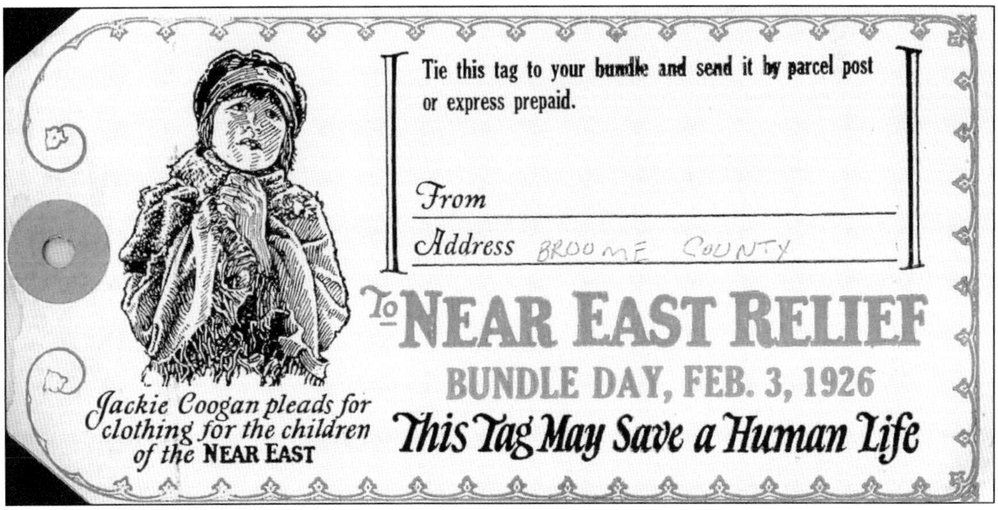

A Near East Relief Bundle Day occurred in 1926. The business of charity in Broome County is exemplified by a fan of child actor Jackie Coogan, who put this tag in her scrapbook with a note saying, "We did send clothes to the children even if we don't have much but wanted to keep the Jackie tag. Jenny gave her shoes without holes."

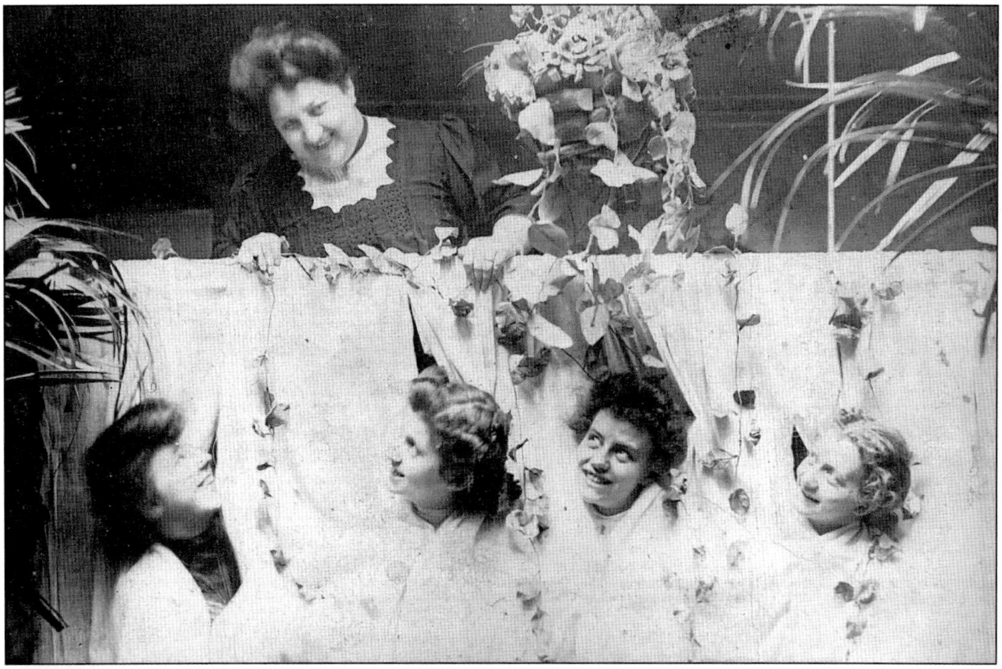

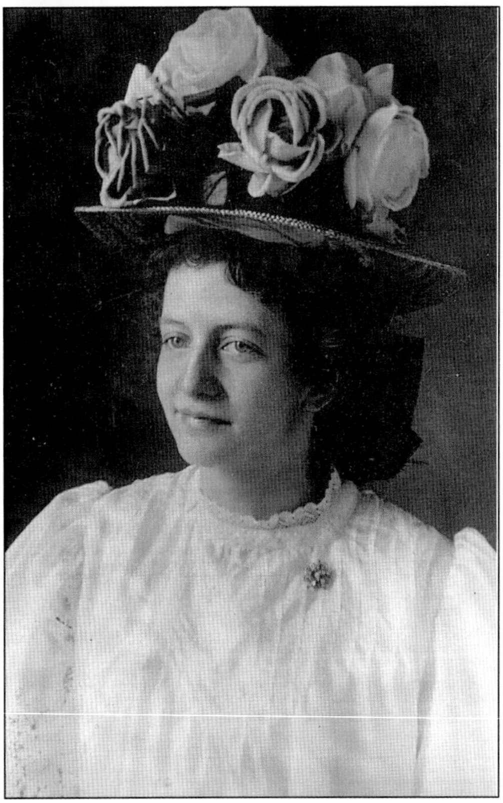

The excitement on the faces of these women is for the beginning of their new venture at a millinery shop. The lady in the photograph at the left looks like a very satisfied patron. The term "mad as a hatter" originated due to the brain damage that often resulted when a hatter breathed in chemicals used to preserve straw and the fragile material needed to create hats. The worst of the chemicals was a creosote derivative—all part of the price of fashion. The business next-door to the hat establishment was a "Tailor and Draper, specialists in the Toggery trade."

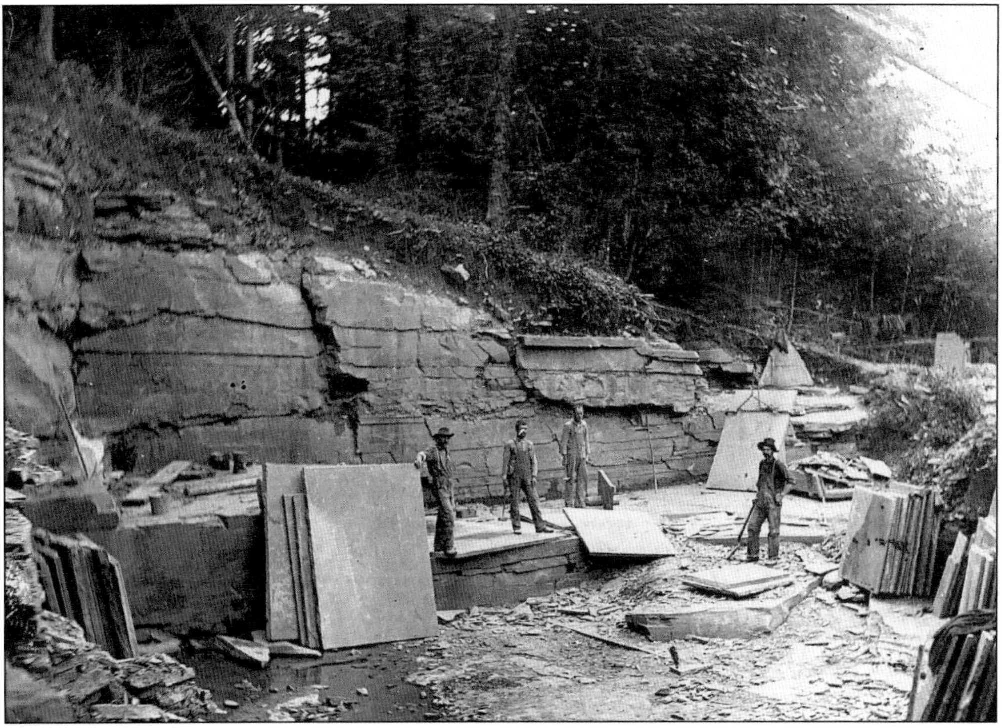

Hewing bluestone from the local mountains was a profitable business for those with a strong back and a feel for stone. It was also a very dangerous profession that required the use of dynamite and heavy primitive tools. Many quarries in Broome County thrived in the early 1900s until concrete, a cheaper building material, came into common use.

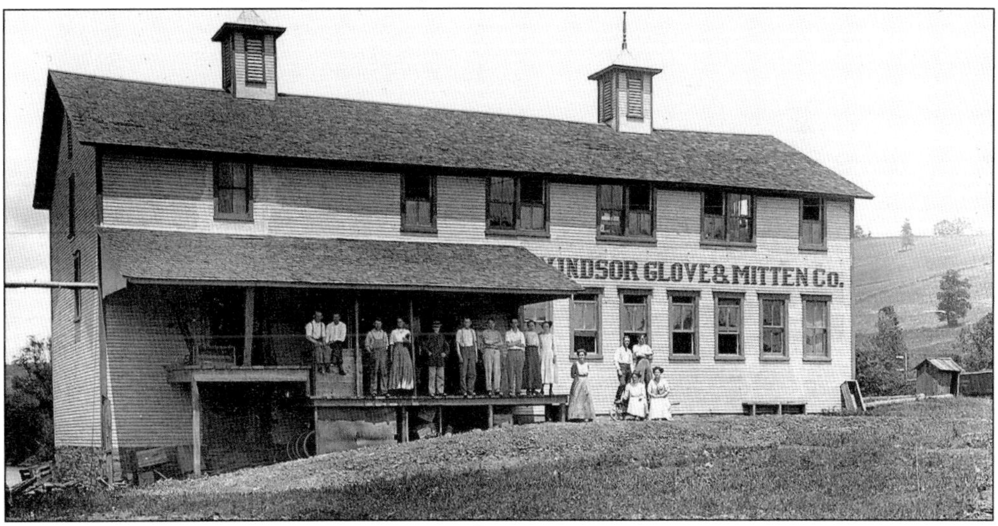

The emotions of women working in a glove factory are reflected in these letters:

> 1911—It is impossible for me to come home, the company is not to close except for x-mas day so I will be alone, am so disappointed.
>
> 1914—There has been a glove strike here for months and it does not add to holiday festivities. I have work only part time on a frog farm.

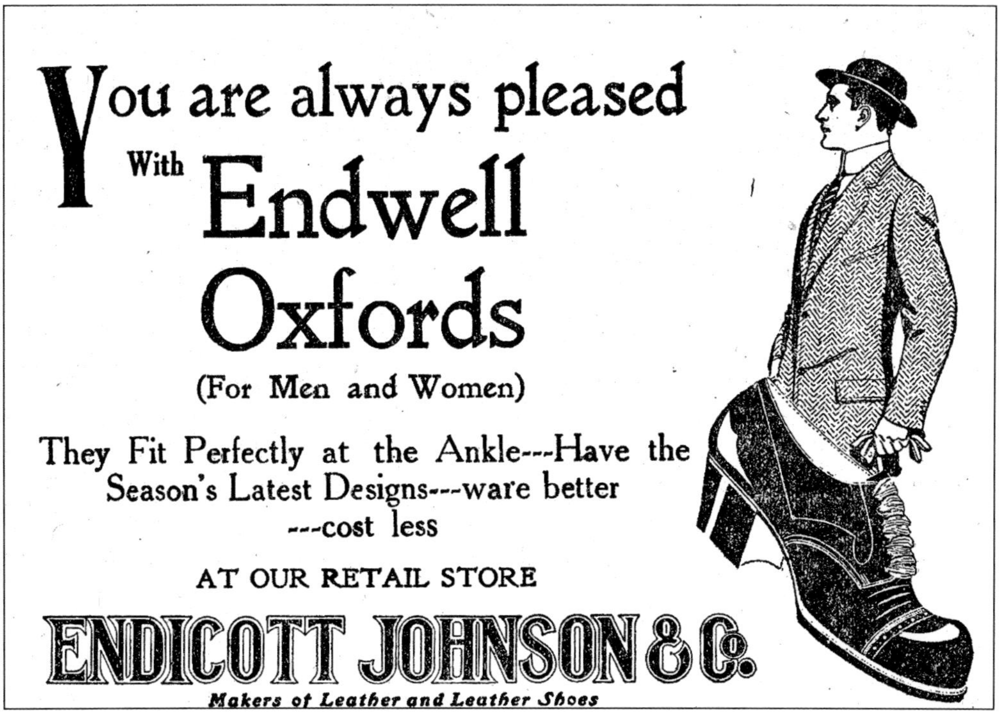

In 1921, residents of Hooper were required to change the hamlet name so that a post office could be established. Mystery has surrounded the choice of the name Endwell. However, this advertisement of 1912 indicates the Endicott Johnson Company produced a popular brand of shoe, "the Endwell where your feet would always end well." Perhaps the puzzle is solved.

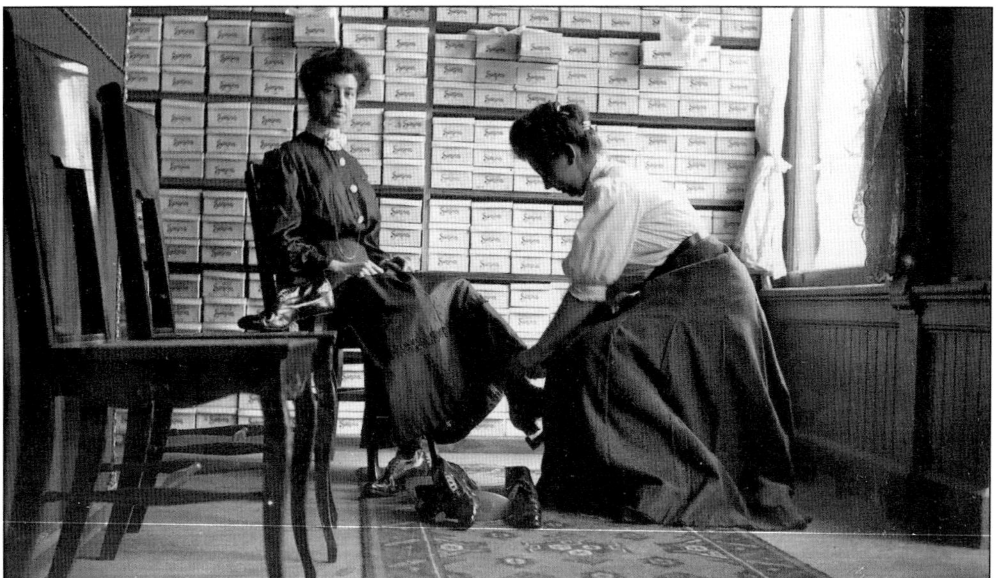

As shoe production proliferated, so did sales shops. Personal attention and advice from the store clerk made choosing footwear an enjoyable experience in 1909. For decades there were dozens of EJ retail shoe stores in the southern tier of New York—now there are none.

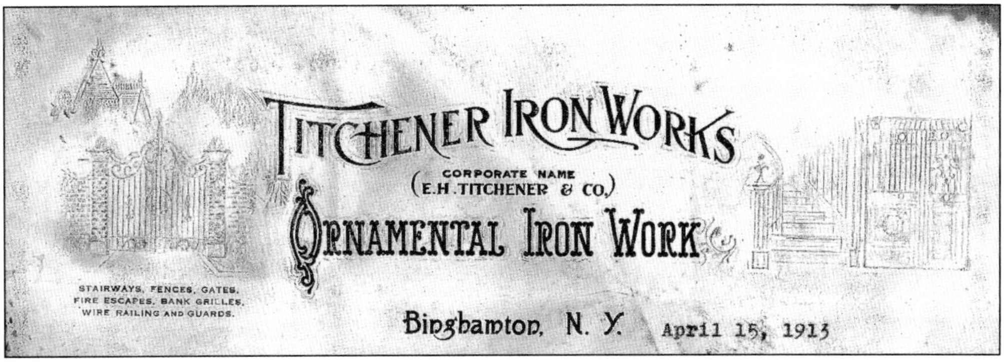
TITCHENER IRON WORKS
(CORPORATE NAME E.H. TITCHENER & CO.)
ORNAMENTAL IRON WORK
STAIRWAYS, FENCES, GATES, FIRE ESCAPES, BANK GRILLES, WIRE RAILING AND GUARDS.
Binghamton, N. Y. April 15, 1913

The Titchener Iron Works was in business from the mid-1800s, producing impressive ornamental iron. The company fashioned architectural embellishments for some of Broome County's most elaborate homes. All the ironwork on the Phelps Mansion, now the Monday Afternoon Club, was created by this concern. Built in 1870, the elegant mansion is lovingly preserved by a dedicated membership. The building has undergone extensive exterior restoration of the third floor and closely resembles this picture taken in the 1920s. The letterhead is from the Titchener Iron Works in 1913.

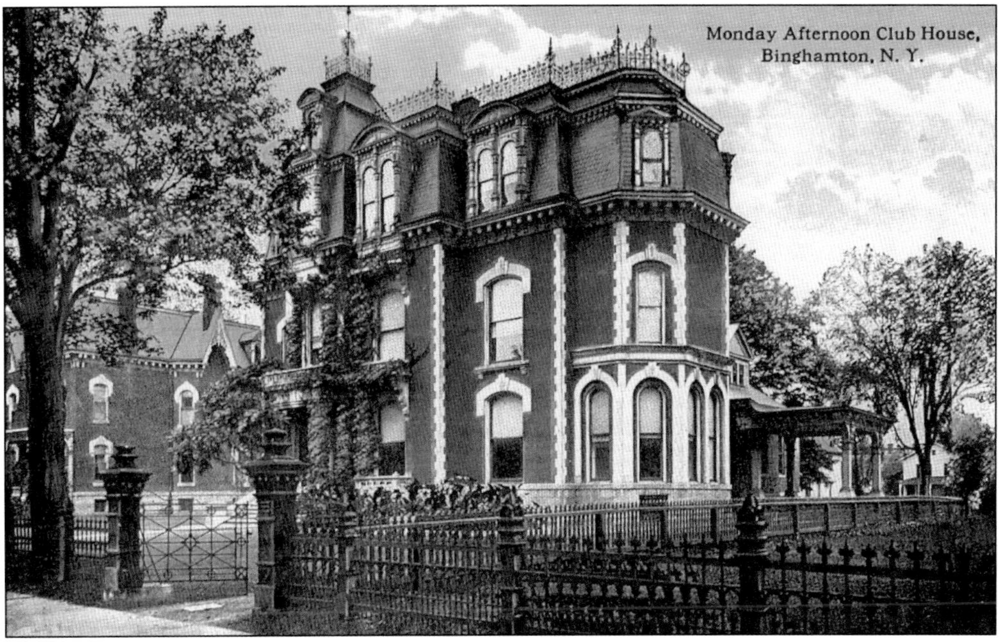

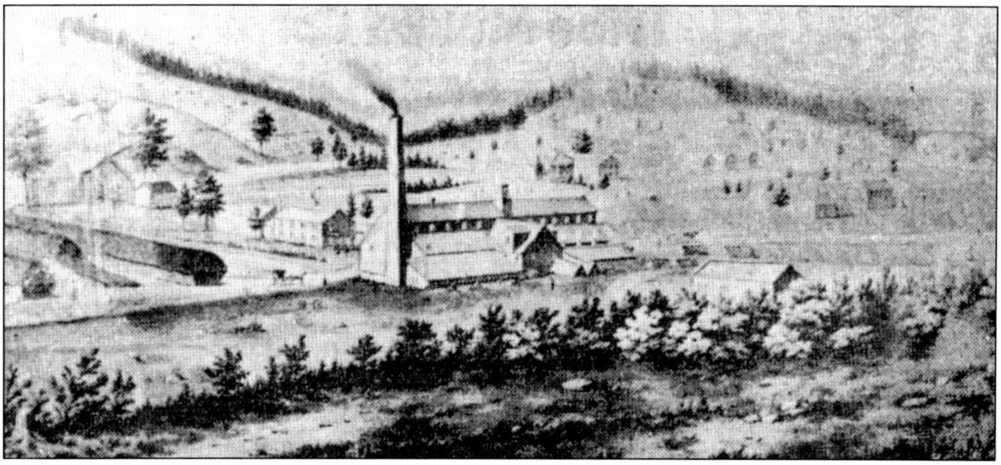

The vast forests were valuable natural resources to early entrepreneurs. In 1848, Lewis C. England operated a tannery near the current site of the IBM Glendale laboratory. Mountainous piles of oak, hemlock, and chestnut bark were ground, then soaked in vats of warm water until the tannic acid leached out. Houses were built, the creek was dammed, and the fledgling village was called Englandville. All evidence of the business has now disappeared.

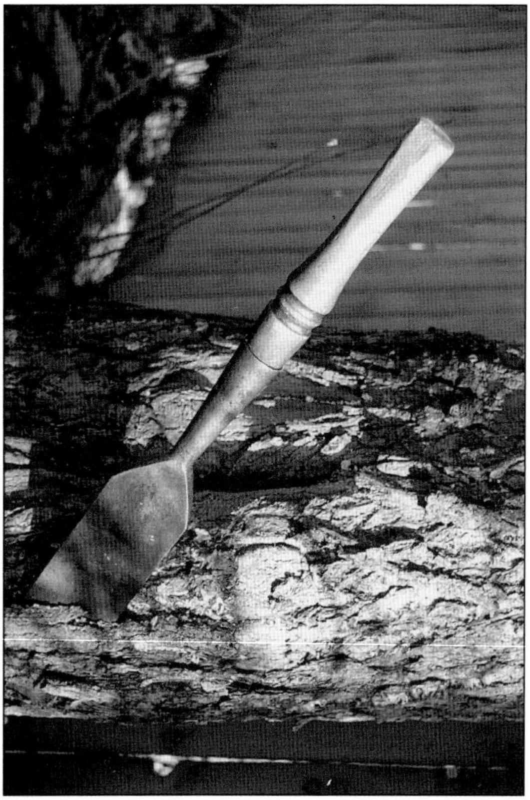

The first local person in the leather trade may have been Col. Joseph Abbott, who settled in Binghamton in 1811. He made leather in the summer and tanned it in the winter. At the opening of spring rafting season, Abbott set up shop on a raft and made shoes along the river wherever he could find a customer. The photograph shows a bark spud, or bill, used for peeling bark from logs.

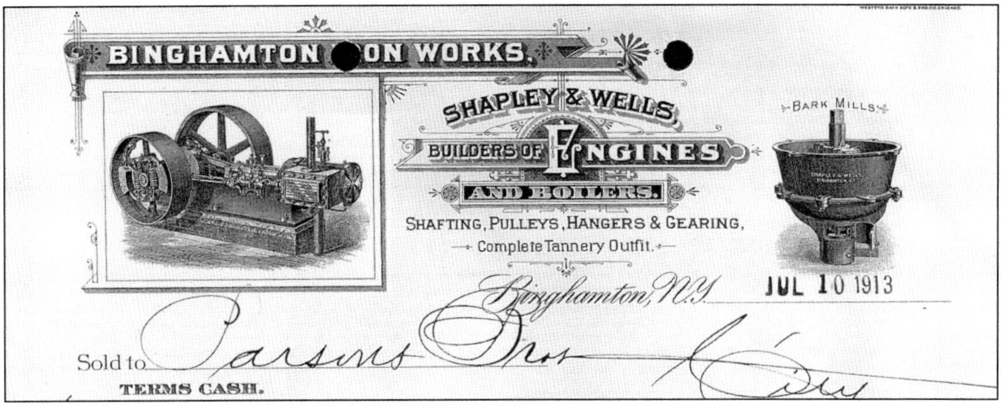

BINGHAMTON IRON WORKS.

SHAPLEY & WELLS,

BUILDERS OF ENGINES

AND BOILERS.

SHAFTING, PULLEYS, HANGERS & GEARING,

Complete Tannery Outfit.

BARK MILLS.

Binghamton, N.Y. JUL 10 1913

Sold to Parsons Bros

TERMS CASH.

The Binghamton Iron Works was founded in 1850 by Martin Shapley and Alfred Dunk. The firm manufactured bark mills and complete tannery outfits for the numerous area tanneries. The Iron Works also engaged in extensive engine building and machinery production and was still operating a successful business in 1913, when this letterhead was used. A drawing of a bark mill is on the company letterhead.

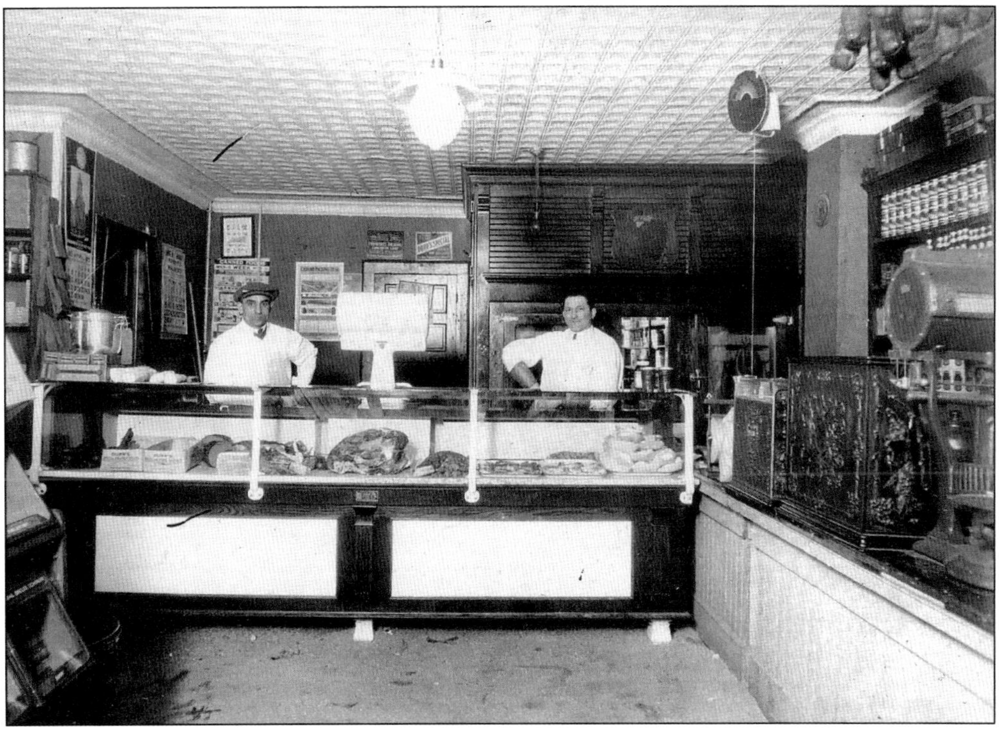

The neighborhood grocery store of the early 1900s provided personal service, custom-cut meats, and delivery to your home. The meat locker at the back of this store is disguised by quality woodwork. A tin ceiling, sawdust-covered floors, and a string ball hanging from above complete the nostalgic photograph.

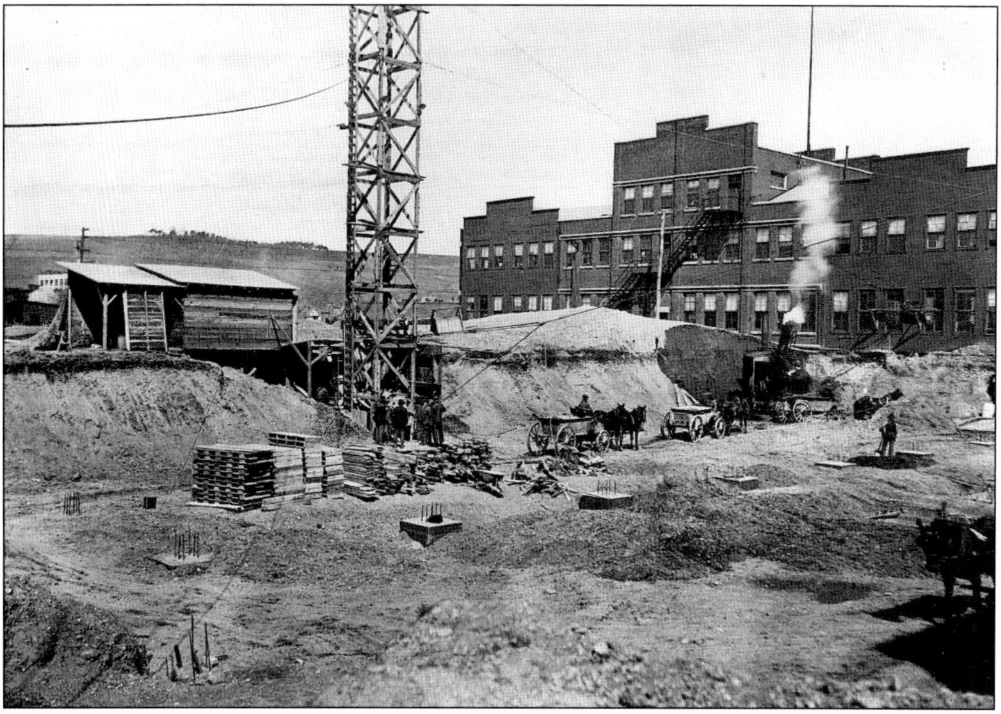

IBM began its role as a major influence in Broome County when the Bundy Company moved from Binghamton in 1905 and began building factories in Endicott. This photograph shows one of the early buildings under construction in 1920.

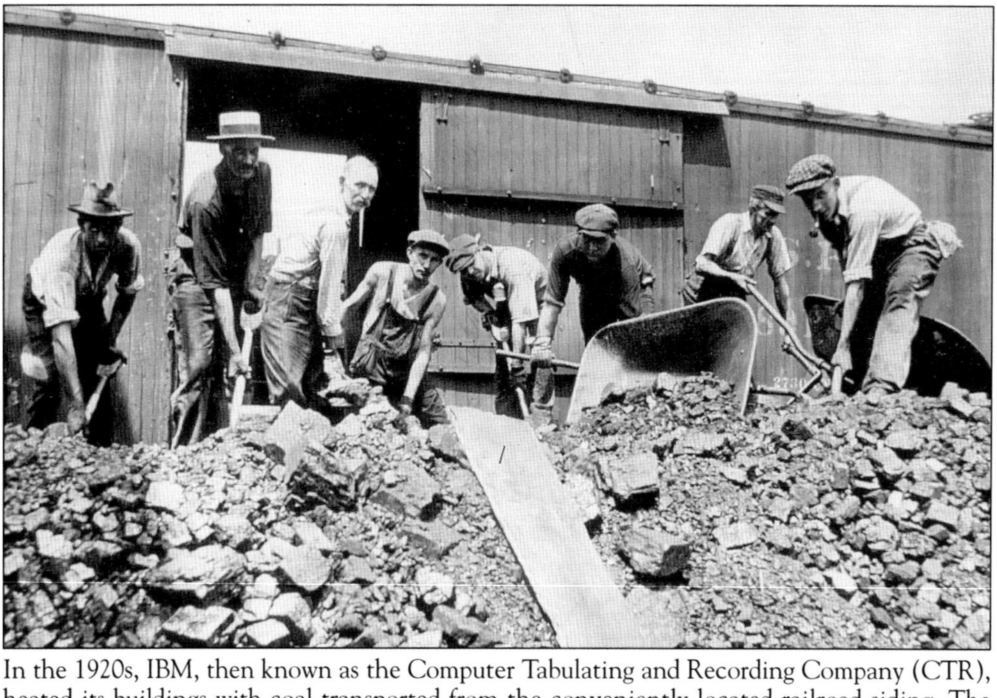

In the 1920s, IBM, then known as the Computer Tabulating and Recording Company (CTR), heated its buildings with coal transported from the conveniently located railroad siding. The fuel was transferred by wheelbarrow and fed to boilers through manpower.

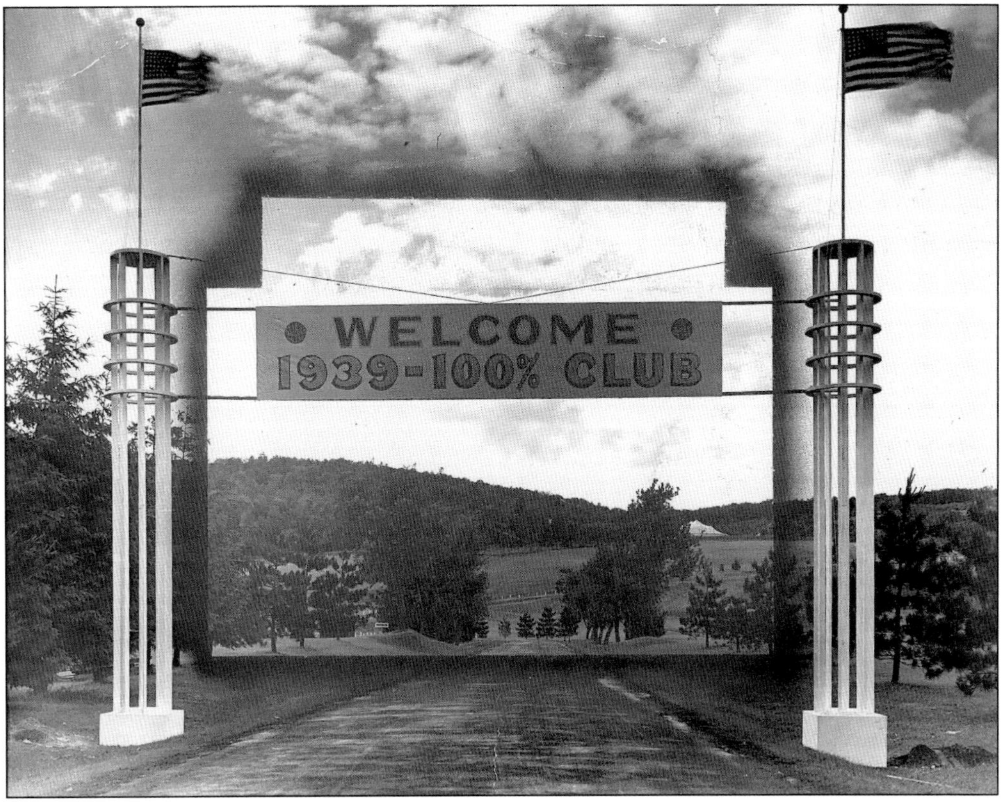

Early in its history, IBM realized success would depend on several factors: development, service, and sales. To recognize outstanding effort in the sales division, the 100 Percent Club was organized. Corporate "pep rallies" were held at Tent City in Endwell, near the IBM Country Club. A three-day stay in one of the 400 two-man tents covering the homestead hillside was considered a reward for meeting sales goals. The central convention center was a massive circus tent 38 feet high and 98 feet wide. A thousand people at a time could attend sessions, sing "Hail to Watson" and "Ever Onward IBM," and review the newest product line.

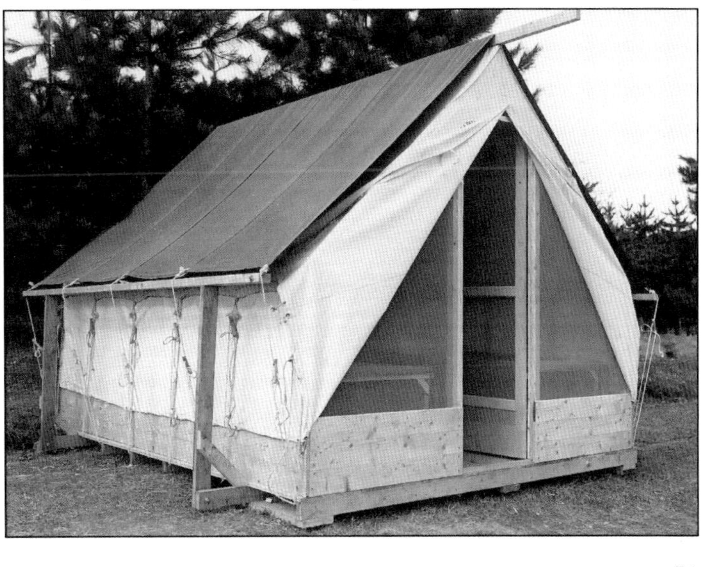

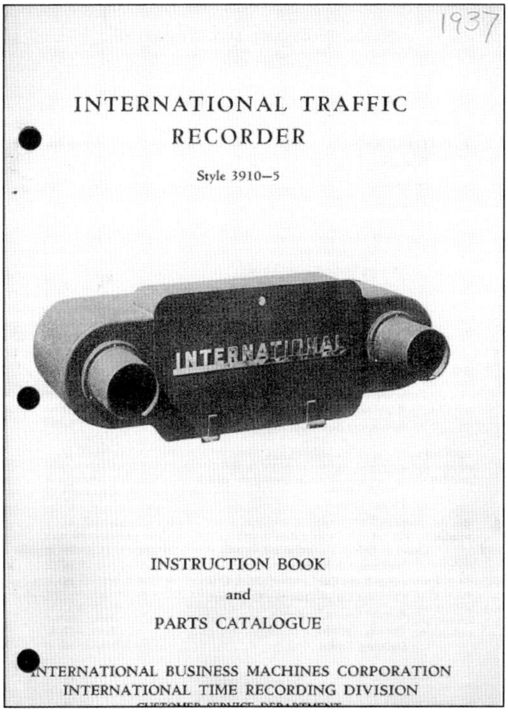
1937

INTERNATIONAL TRAFFIC RECORDER

Style 3910–5

INSTRUCTION BOOK

and

PARTS CATALOGUE

INTERNATIONAL BUSINESS MACHINES CORPORATION
INTERNATIONAL TIME RECORDING DIVISION

A little-known item produced by the IBM Corporation was the International traffic recorder, manufactured in 1937. Using the modern technology of photoelectric cells, it was guaranteed to count only vehicles, not humans or animals.

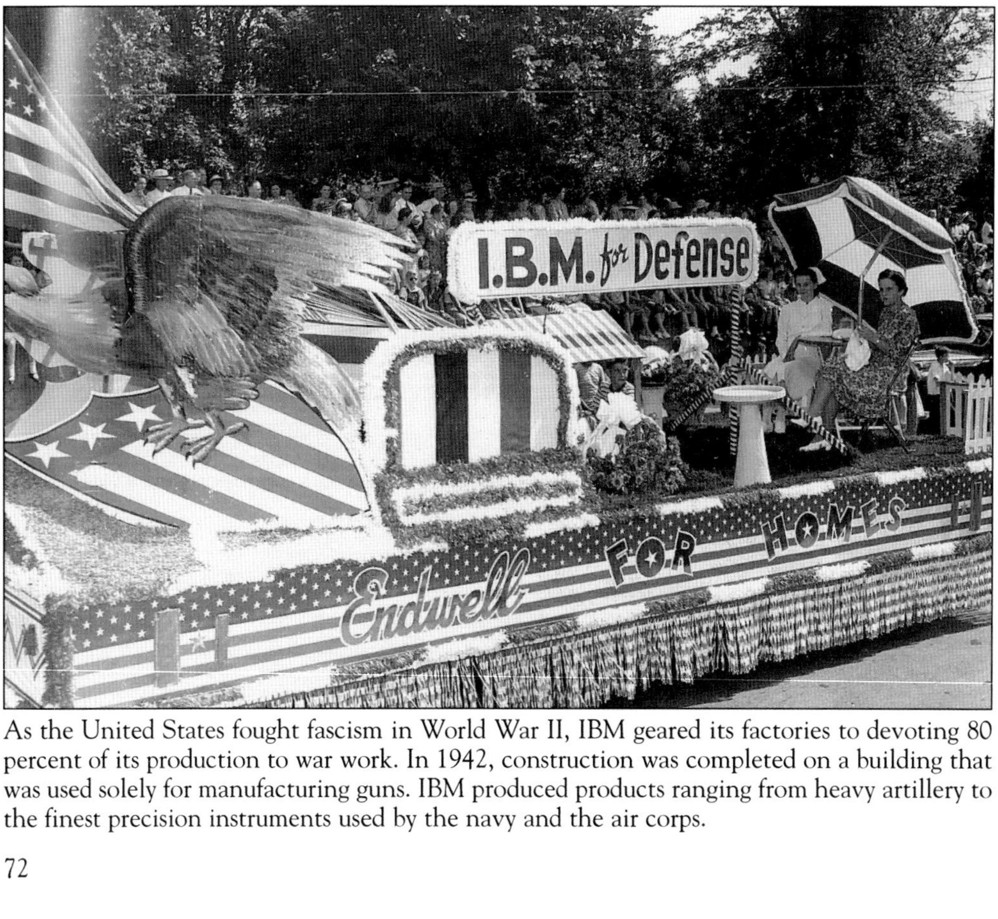

As the United States fought fascism in World War II, IBM geared its factories to devoting 80 percent of its production to war work. In 1942, construction was completed on a building that was used solely for manufacturing guns. IBM produced products ranging from heavy artillery to the finest precision instruments used by the navy and the air corps.

A small pet cemetery in Binghamton is the final resting place for one of the greatest racehorses of the 20th century. Exterminator, nicknamed "Old Bones," was not thought to be championship material and was gelded. Proving everyone wrong, the horse eventually won 50 races, including the 1918 Kentucky Derby. His great heart and gentle nature made him an American folk legend. Exterminator lived out his life at the Kilmer stables on Riverside Drive in Binghamton.

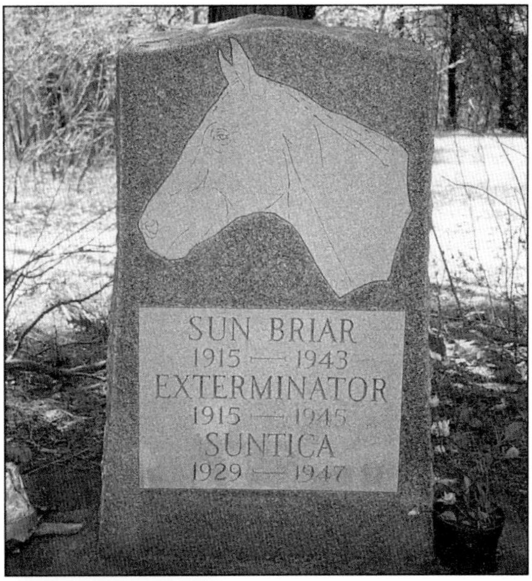

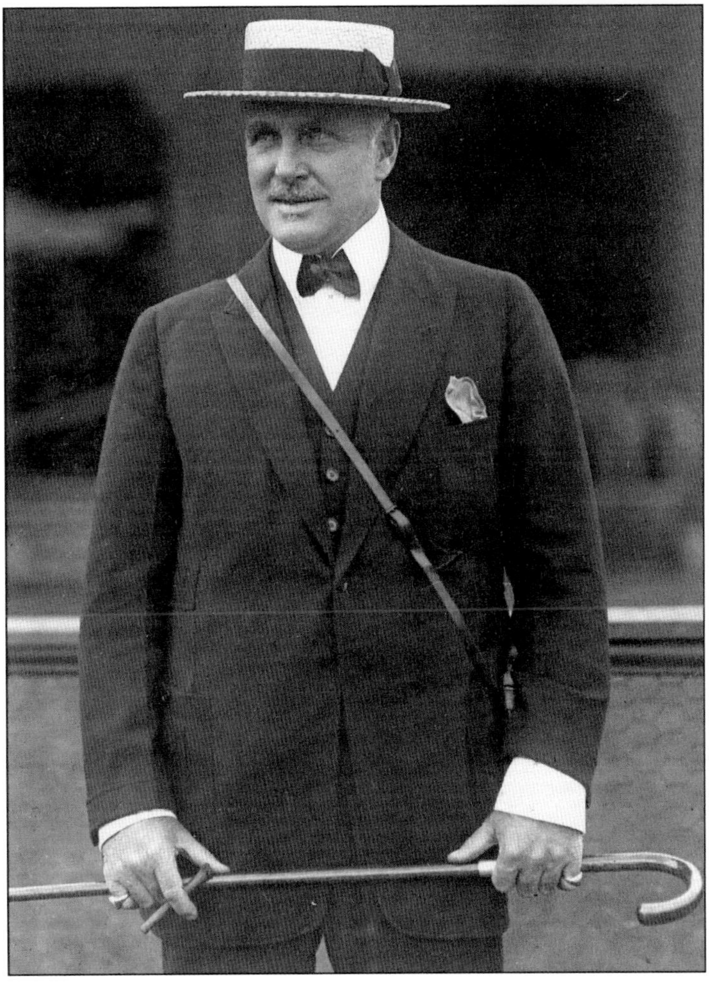

The *Binghamton Press* was established by patent medicine mogul Willis Sharp Kilmer in a fit of anger against existing newspapers. Kilmer resented the publishing of details about his divorce, such as the story that he had clobbered his wife with a beer bottle. In 1904, he installed a quadruple printing press capable of producing 48,000 completed papers in one hour. Fifteen feet high, it could be observed through the windows at sidewalk level of the Binghamton Press building on Chenango Street. He did indeed eliminate the competition.

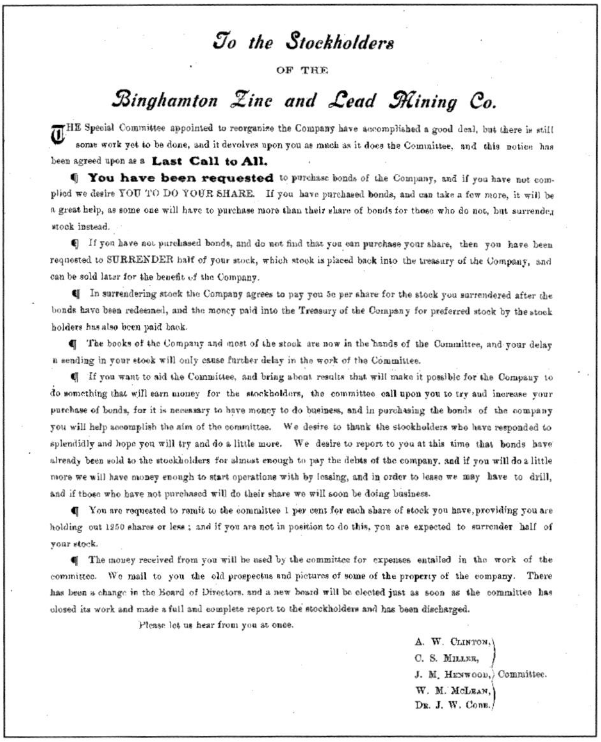

To the Stockholders

OF THE

Binghamton Zinc and Lead Mining Co.

THE Special Committee appointed to reorganize the Company have accomplished a good deal, but there is still some work yet to be done, and it devolves upon you as much as it does the Committee, and this notice has been agreed upon as a **Last Call to All.**

¶ **You have been requested** to purchase bonds of the Company, and if you have not complied we desire YOU TO DO YOUR SHARE. If you have purchased bonds, and can take a few more, it will be a great help, as some one will have to purchase more than their share of bonds for those who do not, but surrender stock instead.

¶ If you have not purchased bonds, and do not find that you can purchase your share, then you have been requested to SURRENDER half of your stock, which stock is placed back into the treasury of the Company, and can be sold later for the benefit of the Company.

¶ In surrendering stock the Company agrees to pay you 5c per share for the stock you surrendered after the bonds have been redeemed, and the money paid into the Treasury of the Company for preferred stock by the stock holders has also been paid back.

¶ The books of the Company and most of the stock are now in the hands of the Committee, and your delay n sending in your stock will only cause further delay in the work of the Committee.

¶ If you want to aid the Committee, and bring about results that will make it possible for the Company to do something that will earn money for the stockholders, the committee call upon you to try and increase your purchase of bonds, for it is necessary to have money to do business, and in purchasing the bonds of the company you will help accomplish the aim of the committee. We desire to thank the stockholders who have responded so splendidly and hope you will try and do a little more. We desire to report to you at this time that bonds have already been sold to the stockholders for almost enough to pay the debts of the company, and if you will do a little more we will have money enough to start operations with by leasing, and in order to lease we may have to drill, and if those who have not purchased will do their share we will soon be doing business.

¶ You are requested to remit to the committee 1 per cent for each share of stock you have, providing you are holding out 1250 shares or less; and if you are not in position to do this, you are expected to surrender half of your stock.

¶ The money received from you will be used by the committee for expenses entailed in the work of the committee. We mail to you the old prospectus and pictures of some of the property of the company. There has been a change in the Board of Directors, and a new board will be elected just as soon as the committee has closed its work and made a full and complete report to the stockholders and has been discharged.

Please let us hear from you at once.

A. W. CLINTON,
C. S. MILLER,
J. M. HENWOOD, Committee.
W. M. MCLEAN,
DR. J. W. COBB.

The Binghamton Zinc and Lead Mining Company was at work during the 1880s. Most of the members of the board of directors were prominent in Broome County businesses. Although there was a mine in Osborne Hollow, no mention is made of it ever earning a profit.

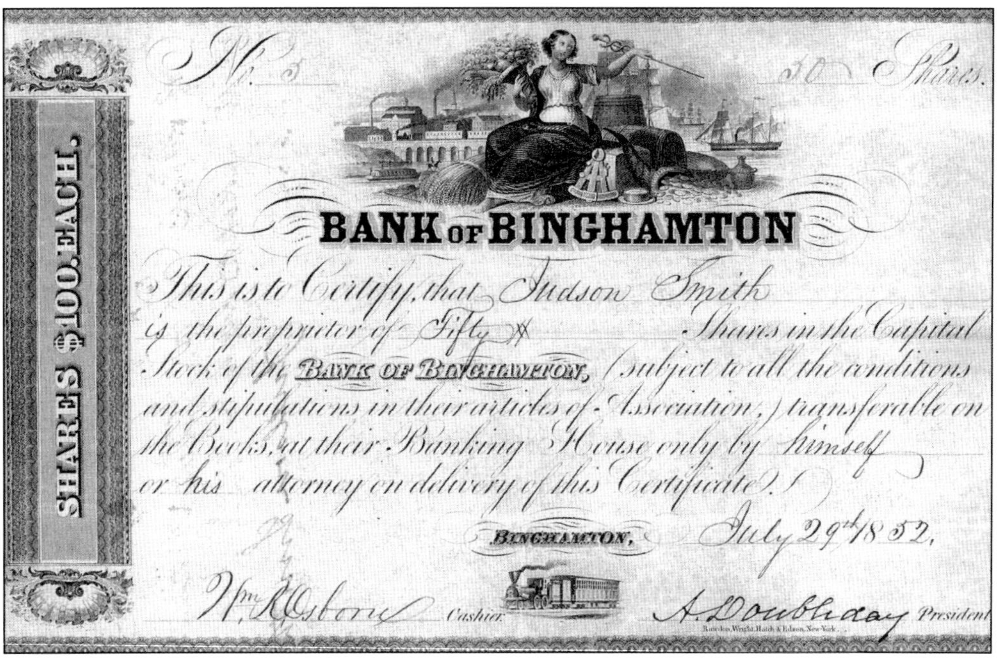

The Bank of Binghamton was chartered in 1852, and Dr. Ammi Doubleday was elected the first president. He had retired from the medical profession and the drugstore business because of the small income generated. His obituary stated, "He was a worthy citizen with an extraordinary memory and an authority on local history." He also owned the "gun house," located on Water Street, where the only village cannon was stored.

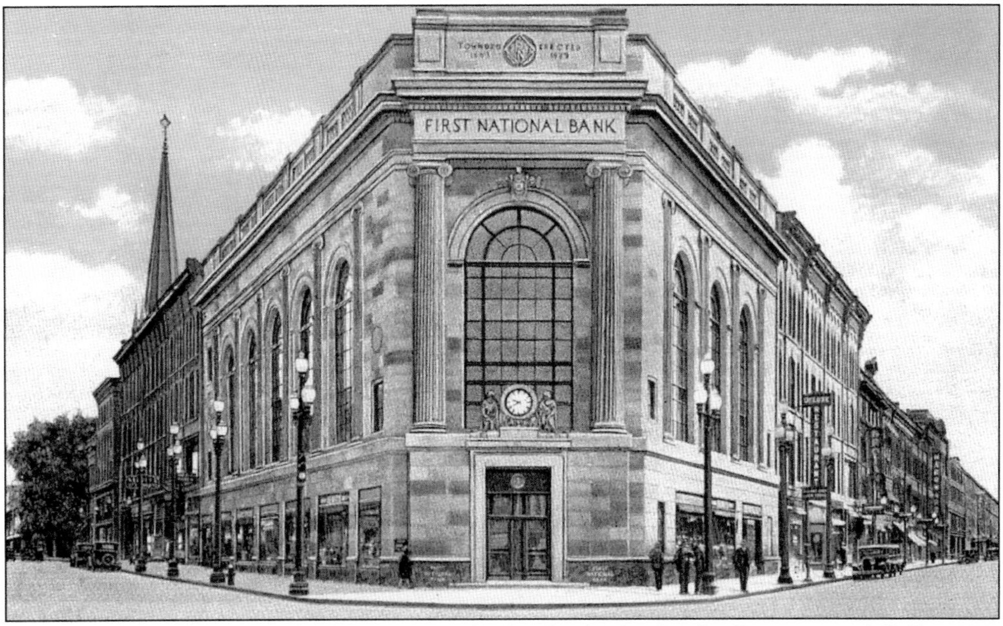

The First National Bank of Binghamton was the first bank of its kind in Broome in 1863. By 1929, it was located on the corner of Court and Chenango Streets in the Phelps Bank Building. This landmark was constructed in 1871 under the direction of architect Isaac Perry on a site that has always housed a bank. These photographs show the bank exterior and interior *c.* 1930.

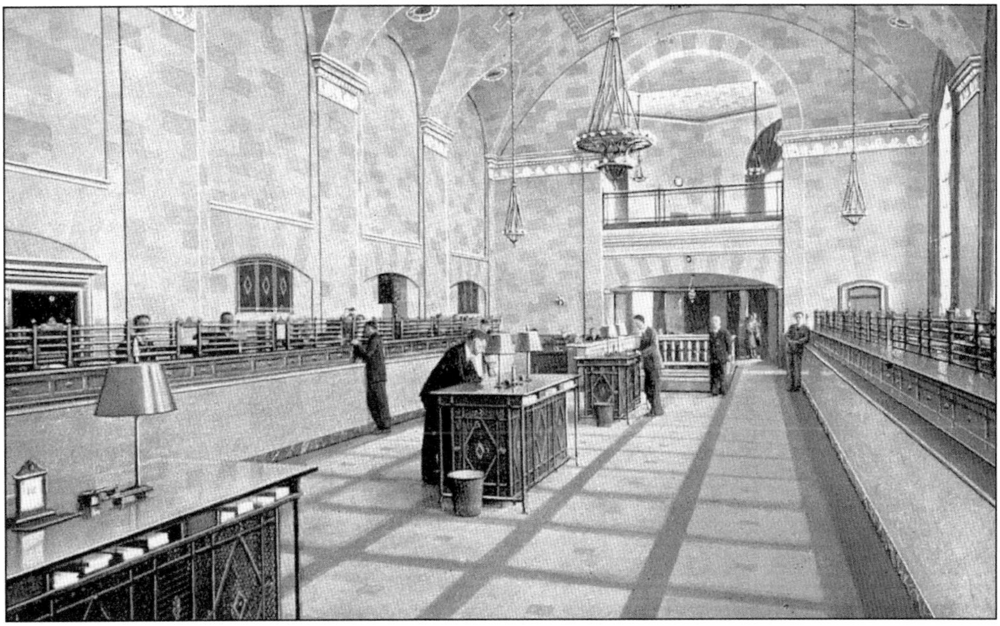

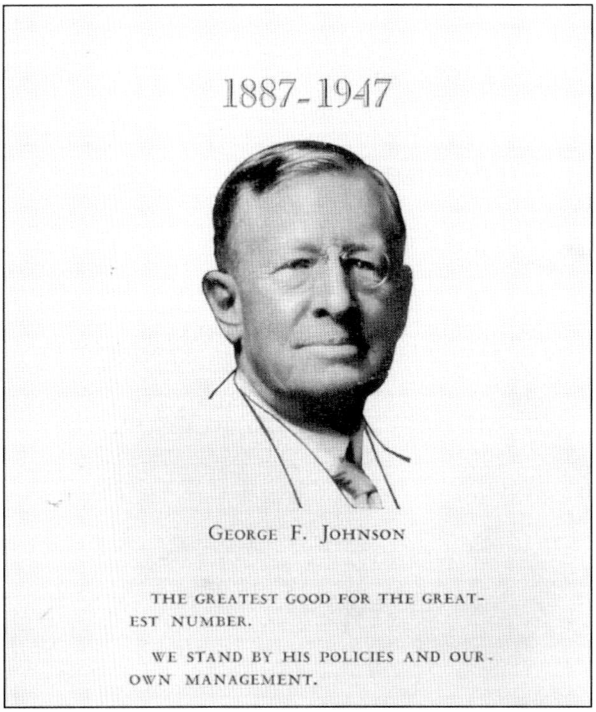

George F. Johnson is regarded as a great patriarch of Broome County. From humble beginnings he rose to be president of one of the largest shoe manufacturing concerns in the country. Innovative policies regarding labor relations and guidance of the employees in every facet of life kept his memory alive many years after the company ceased to exist. The program imprinted with the image of Johnson was used for a banquet in the 1950s. Each child born to an EJ worker was given a silver spoon and a $10 certificate to begin a savings account; the one below is dated 1926. This was all part of the Johnson policy of cradle-to-grave attention.

Ten Dollars has been deposited to the credit of

James William Biddle

An Endicott-Johnson Baby

In the Savings Department of

State Bank of Endicott

Compliments of Mr. George F. Johnson

Date Nov. 10, 1926 No. E-1291

Present this card at the above named Bank and obtain Pass Book

Pictured are Endicott Johnson Company tannery workers in the 1920s (not a delicate one is in the lot). Notes on the back of the photograph indicate some names and personalities:

#1 Tranaway now wed to third wife
#5 constantly jumping
#6 Runniberger, who knows everything
#2 Dietzer
#9 Digger
#4 Dickie Sticks
#12 Billie the Dutchman

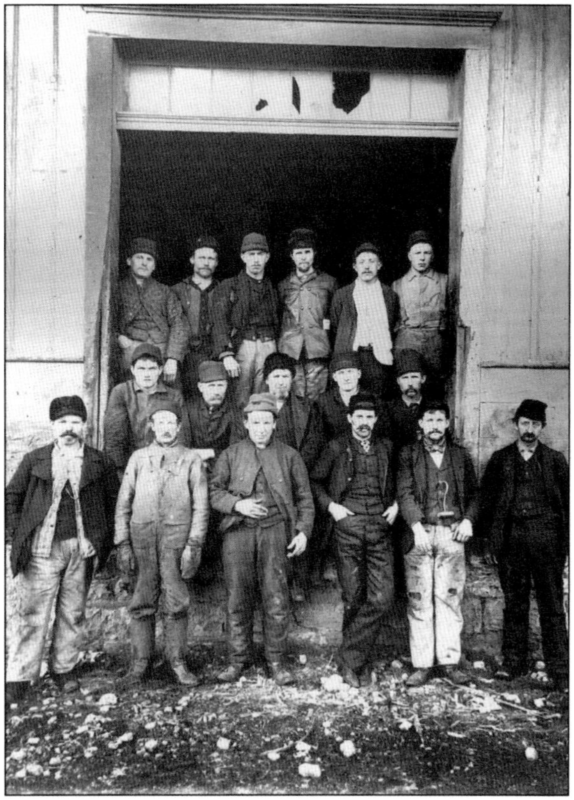

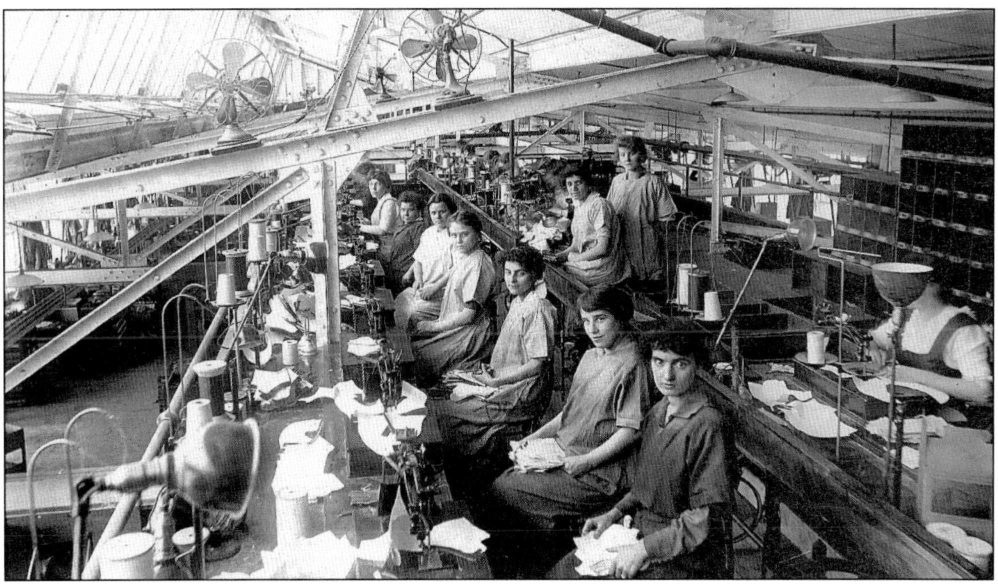

Endicott Johnson gained dominance in commerce on the strength of its immigrant labor force. The newcomers to America were grateful for the opportunity to earn a few cents by piecework. These women are operating sewing machines in the EJ Men's McKay plant in Johnson City in 1915, receiving, possibly, as much as $4 a week.

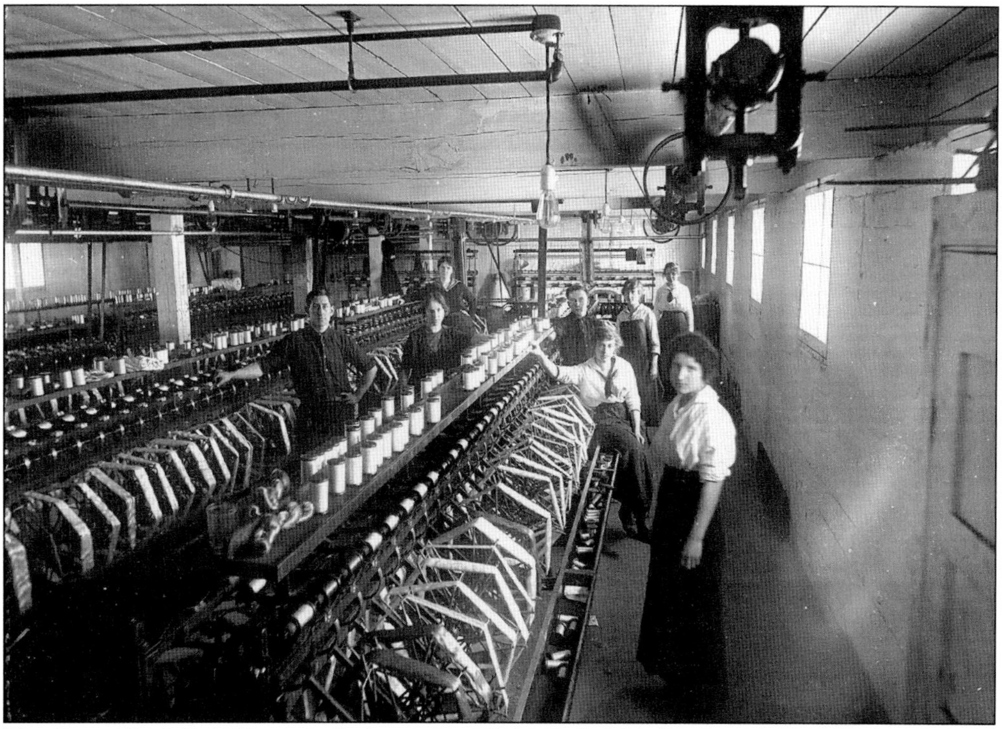

The Roseville Silk Mill, on Park Avenue, and the Ballard Silk Company, on Milford Street, operated in Binghamton in 1916 when these photographs were taken. Women were anxious to make the transition from long days of unpaid drudgery on farms. They moved to cities and worked long hours in unsafe conditions for meager wages, no benefits, and no childcare, but the possibility of new opportunities made factories preferable to rural life. Mothers would bring small children to the factory floor, sharing the danger of machinery and the hope for a better future. The life of a working woman in 1916 is reflected on every face in this portrait of mill workers. The photograph above is the interior of the Ballard Silk factory that specialized in "Crepe de Chine, Georgettes and Crepe Metoers." The picture below shows workers from the Roseville Silk Mill.

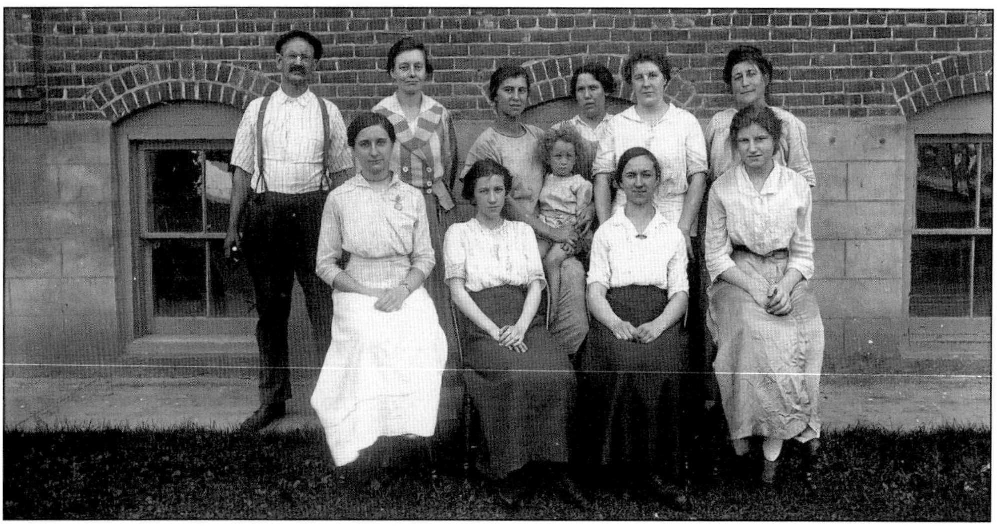

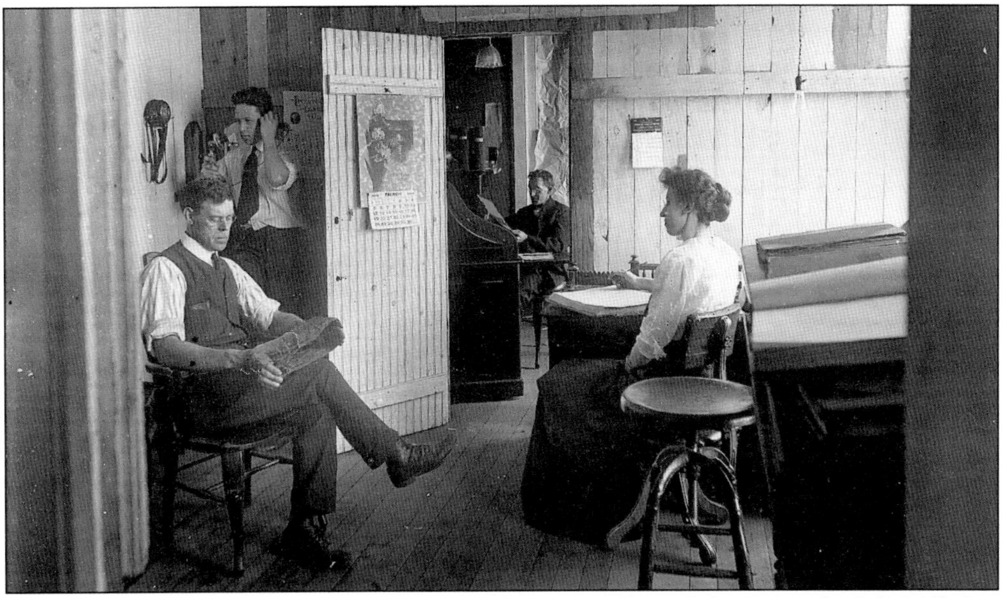

Working conditions were somewhat safer in the main office of the Roseville Silk Mill, but the hours were just as long. The company manager (seated) looks at a skein of silk thread in his hands, an assistant answers the modern telephone just behind him, and the faithful scribe awaits dictation at her desk.

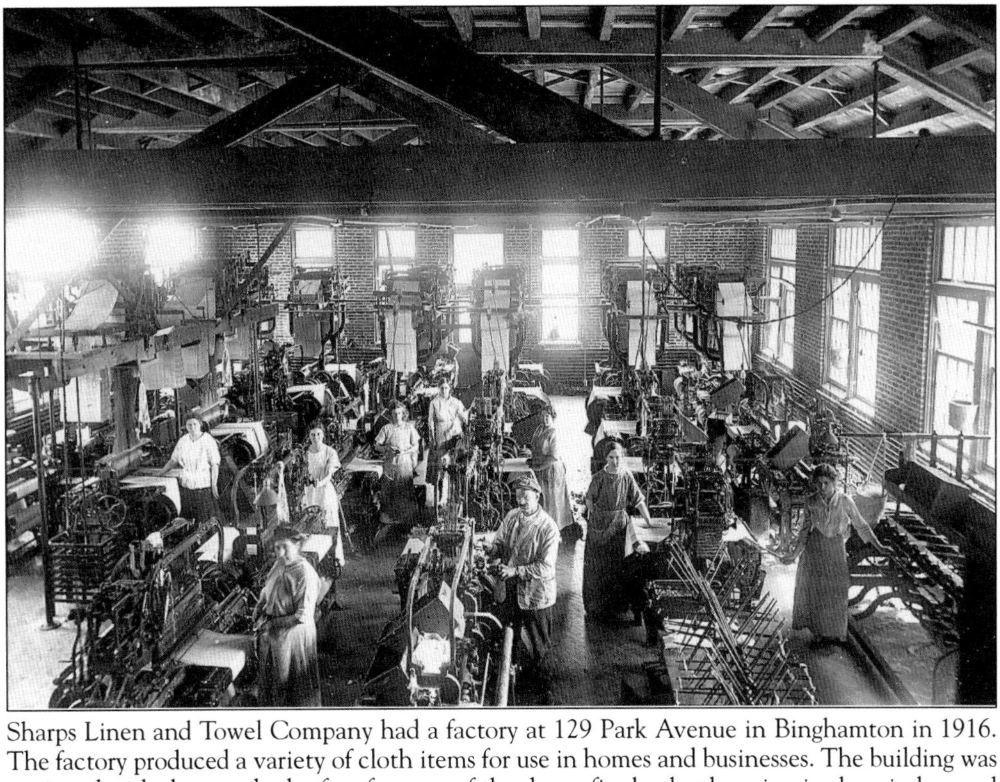

Sharps Linen and Towel Company had a factory at 129 Park Avenue in Binghamton in 1916. The factory produced a variety of cloth items for use in homes and businesses. The building was equipped with the standard safety features of the day: a fire bucket hanging in the window and electric wires hanging from the ceiling.

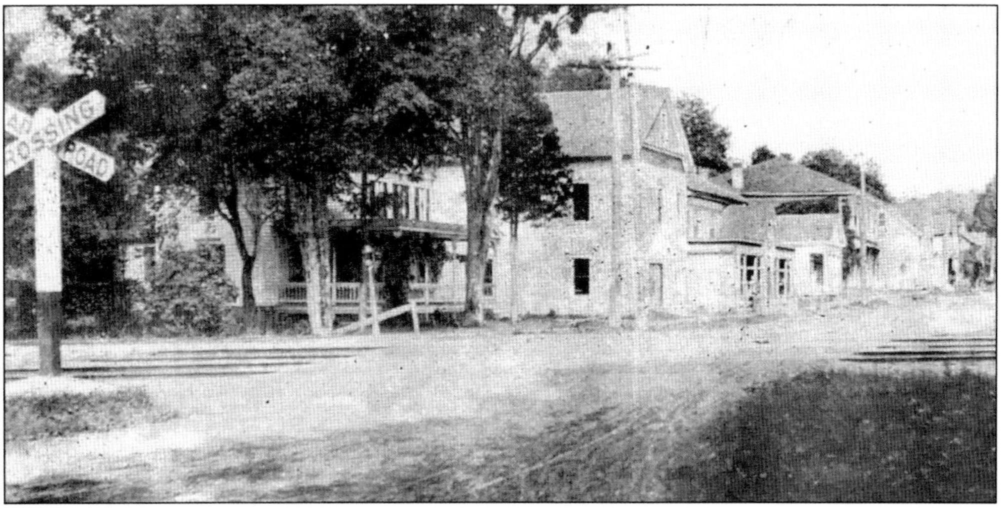

Shown is a thriving Main Street in Lisle *c.* 1910. Some milestones in Lisle's history follow:

1850—The Congregational church issues a list of Sunday sins including rafting, working, and do not pass a post office to mail or retrieve letters.
1860—A mastodon skeleton is found.
1900—A prosperous beer-shaving factory exists in town.
1917—Two years before the 19th Amendment passes, Lisle allows women to vote.

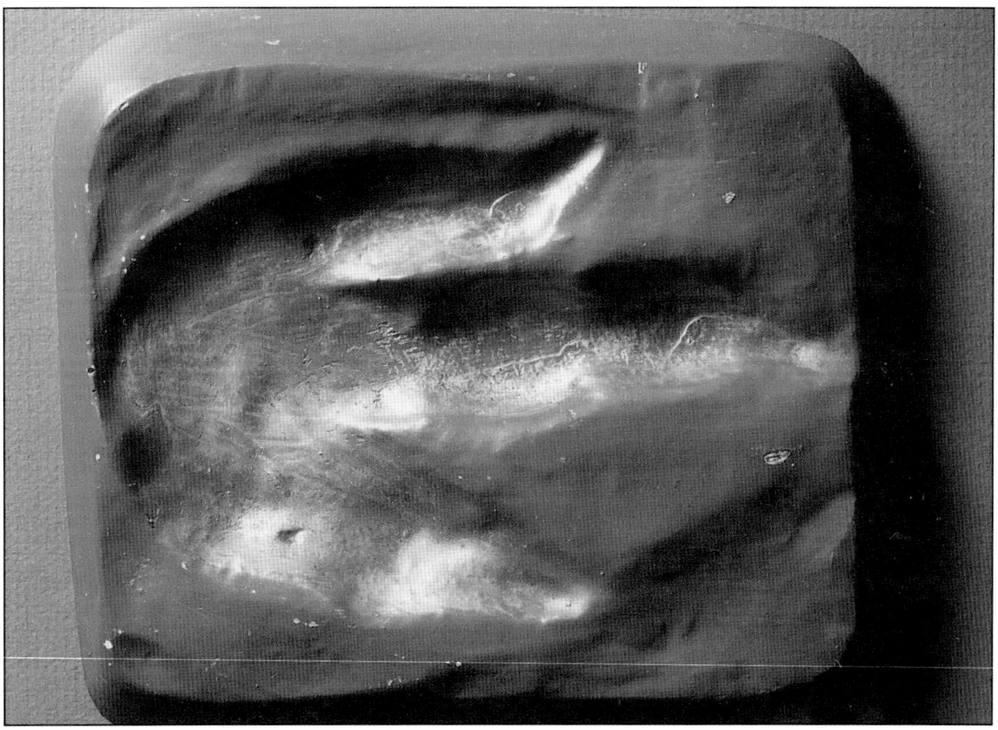

Kattelville, a hamlet in the town of Chenango, was founded *c.* 1796 but, in 1928, the remains of a much earlier inhabitant were found. The discovery of the fossilized footprints of a giant three-toed thunder lizard amazed the community.

The hamlet of Apalachin made world news in 1957 when dozens of the most prominent mobsters in the nation held a meeting at the hillside home of Joseph Barbara Sr. The police raid on the gangland convention reached into the lives of many Broome residents. Local "godfathers" were among those captured running from the rural crime party. Media and law enforcement attention in Broome County continued for years after the event.

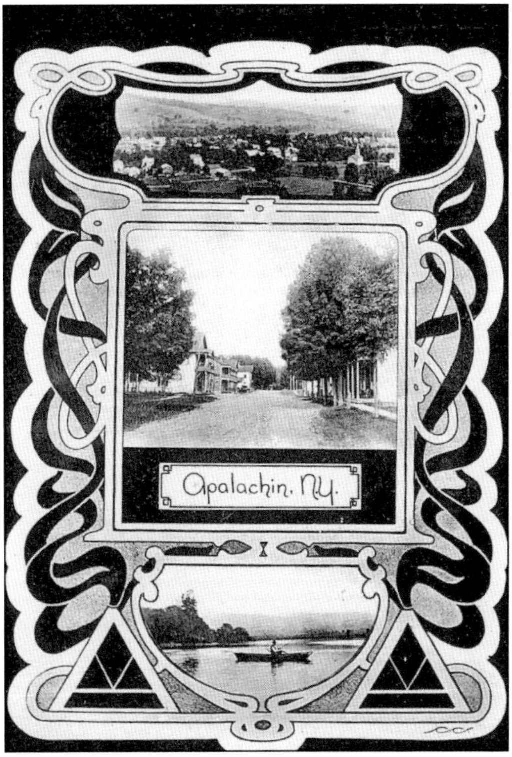

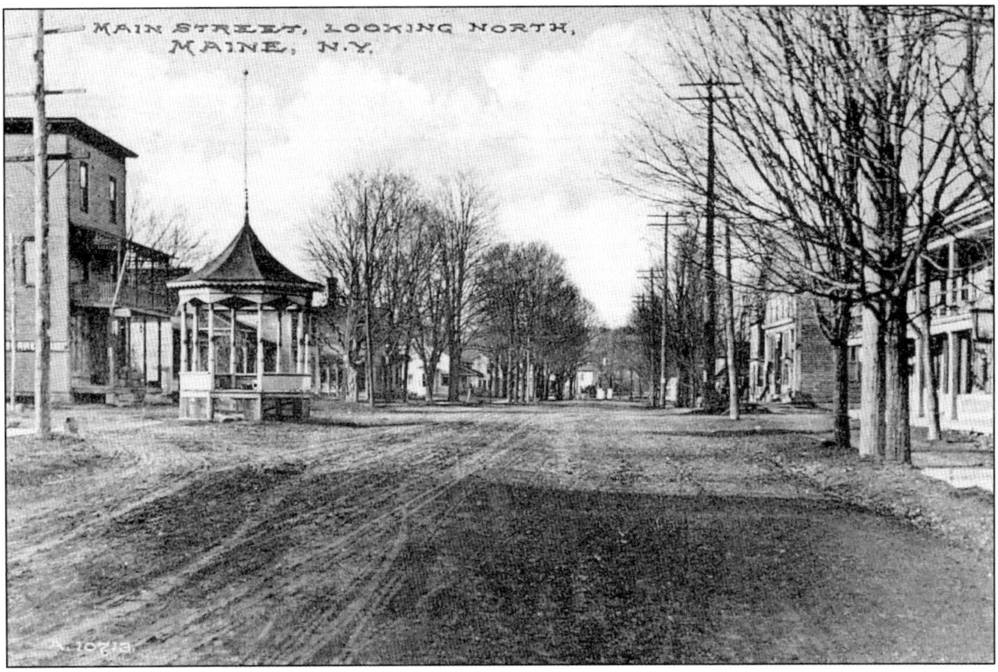

An 1852 *Union News* article stated, "The town of Maine is not only known for the industry and intelligence of its people but for being a strong temperance community. . . . Also in its favor is the world record for growing large potato. . . . One delivered to this office weighed almost four pounds!" The photograph shows a Main Street of long ago.

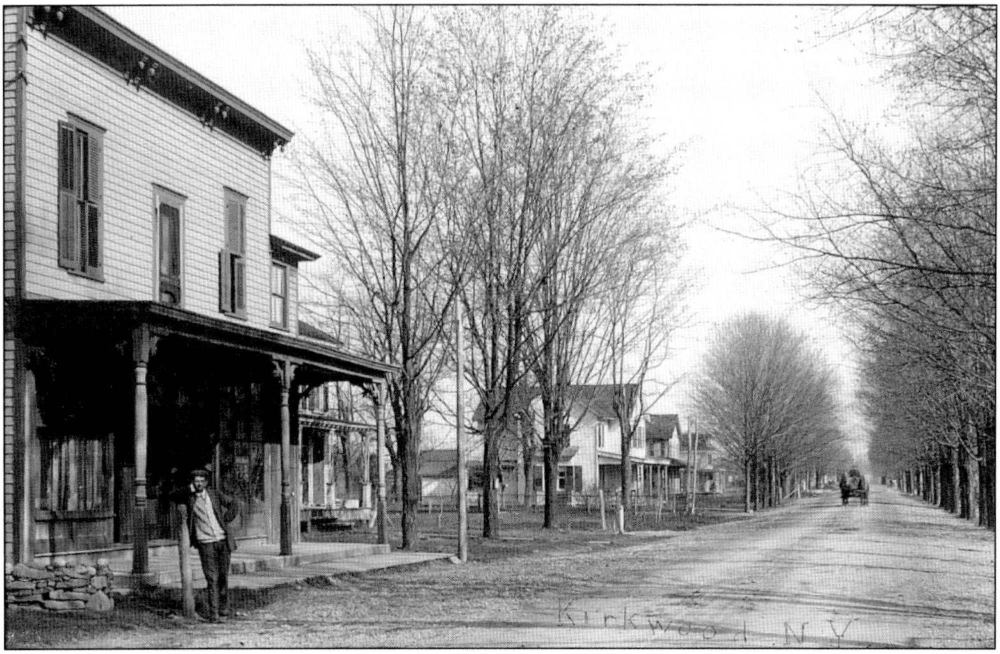

Inspecting a quaint street scene of the town of Kirkwood, an elderly gentleman remembered an event in 1806 and published these sentiments in 1880: "A day predicted to be the end of the world brought the gathering obscuration & veiled the entire disc of the sun at its utmost, cattle, foul & birds sought their nocturnal abodes, and I ran for home as the world darkened." All survived, and so has Kirkwood, a town since 1859.

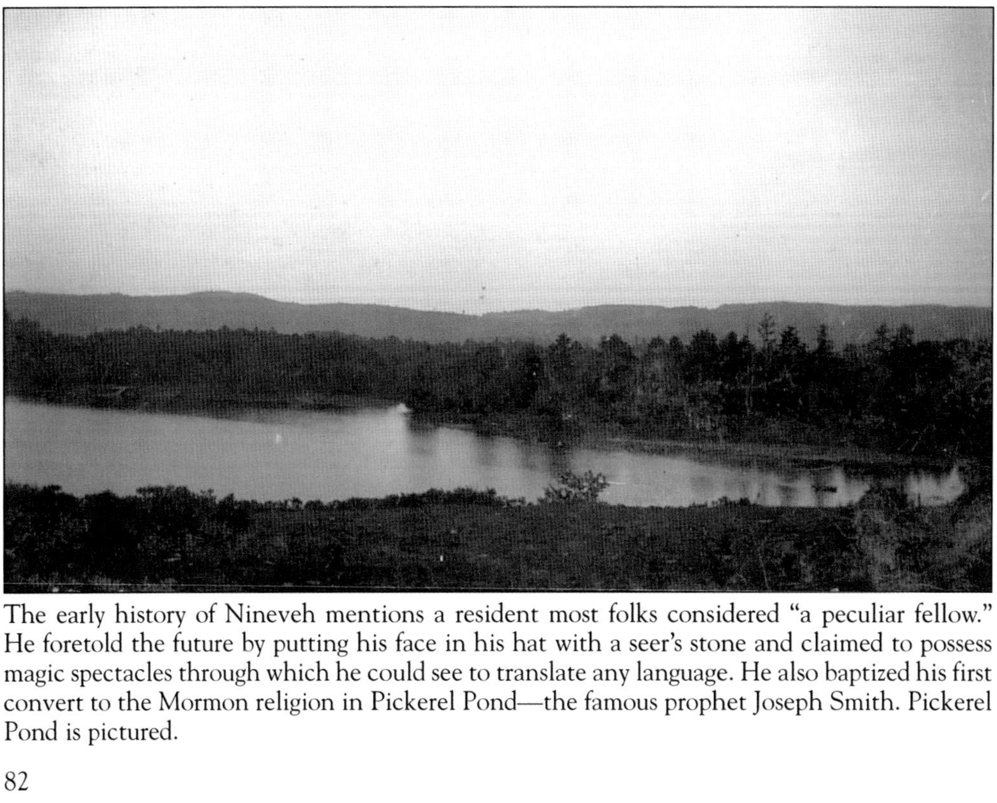

The early history of Nineveh mentions a resident most folks considered "a peculiar fellow." He foretold the future by putting his face in his hat with a seer's stone and claimed to possess magic spectacles through which he could see to translate any language. He also baptized his first convert to the Mormon religion in Pickerel Pond—the famous prophet Joseph Smith. Pickerel Pond is pictured.

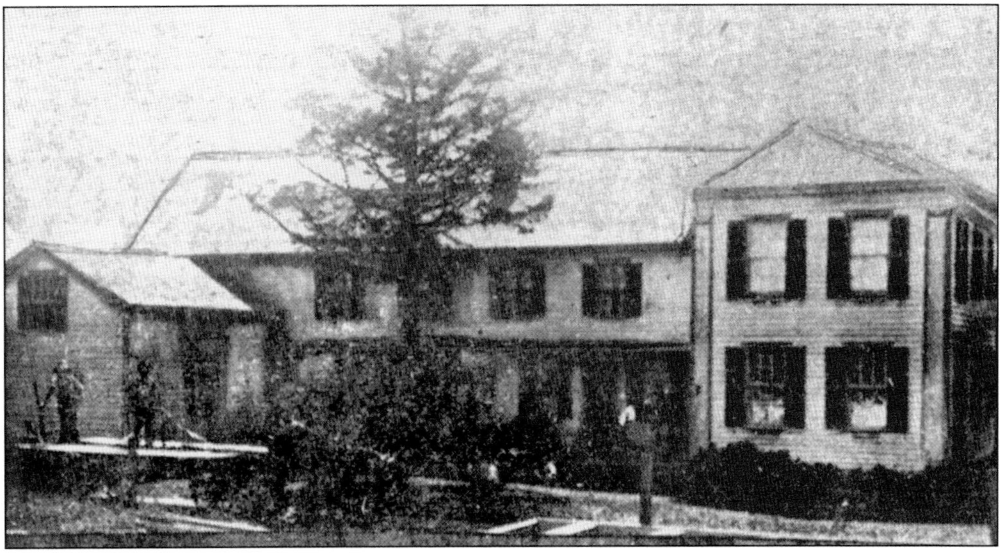

Union Endicott High School was built in 1915 on Main Street in Endicott. Before 1900, an 18-room farmhouse occupied part of this site. However, there was a more ancient settler on the same location. When the foundation of the school was excavated, the skeletons of three people were discovered—a man, woman, and a youth whose bones were partially burned. The remains predated any known settlement in the area, and the history of these people remains a mystery to this day. The photograph above shows the farmhouse; the one below shows the high school.

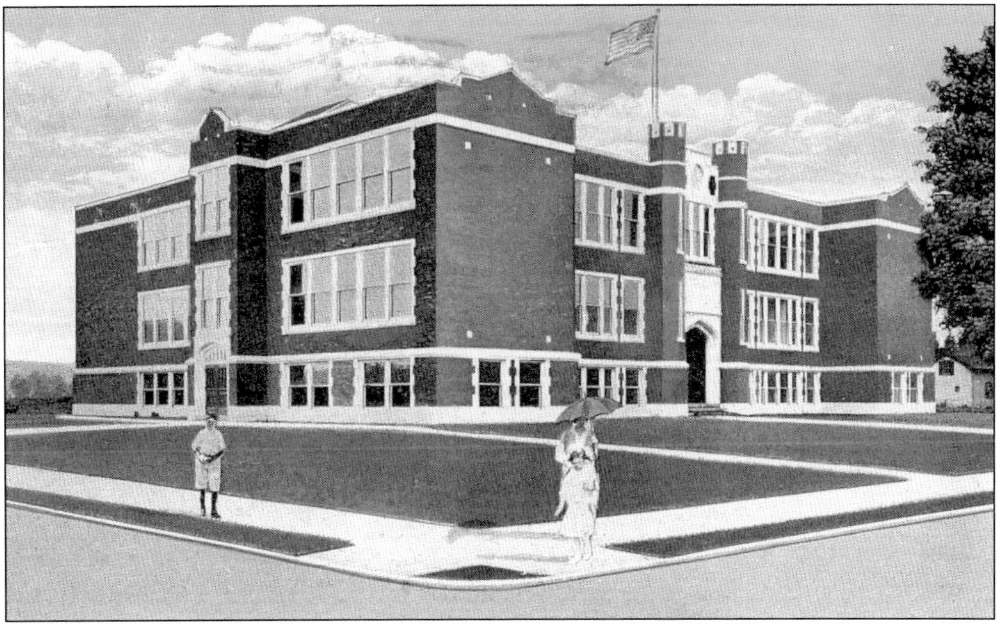

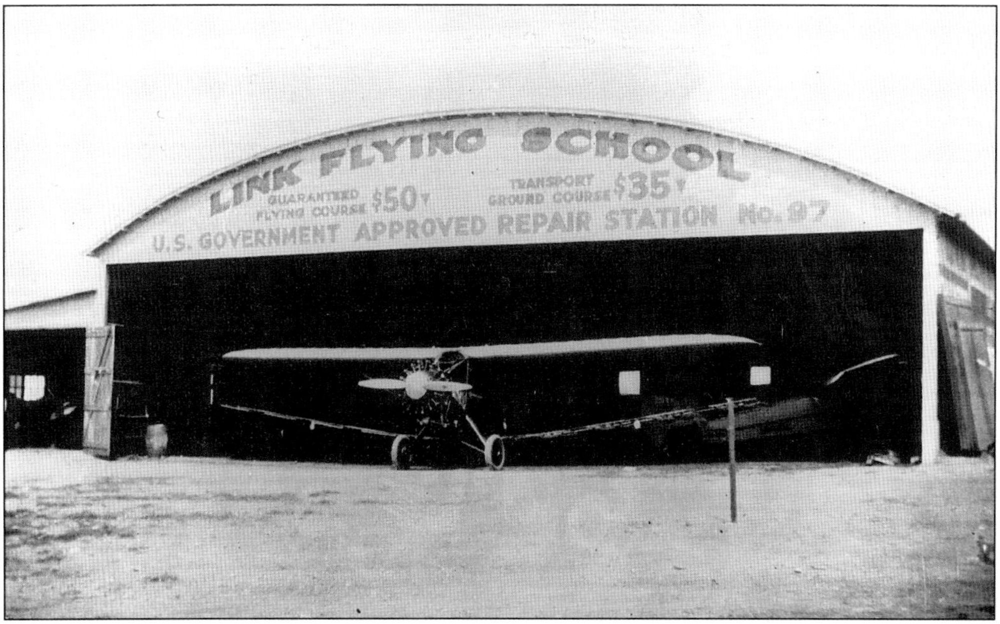

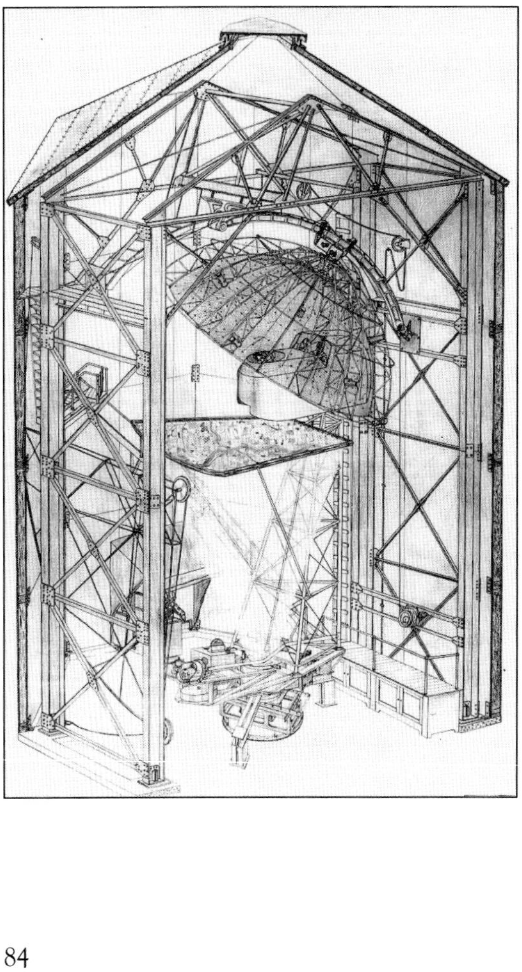

Conquering the air through ground-based flight training began in Binghamton. Edwin A. Link focused world attention on Broome County with his invention of a pilot-training device. Link's earliest simulator was fashioned with bellows from his father's organ factory in 1928. In the early 1930s, there was little military interest in his "Blue Box" aeronautical device, so Link promoted the machine at carnivals and fairs, charging 25¢ a ride. World War II proved the value of safe, efficient pilot training and turned Link Aviation into a corporate giant that dominated the simulation industry for decades. American and allied governments ordered more than 10,000 trainers that produced over 500,000 pilots. The diagram is of the 1941 Celestial trainer for teaching navigation by the stars, one of the most important military secrets of World War II. It was described as a shifting, star-studded umbrella that simulated the passage of time, latitude, and longitude. Training was conducted in a silolike structure at the Link Aviation Hillcrest plant.

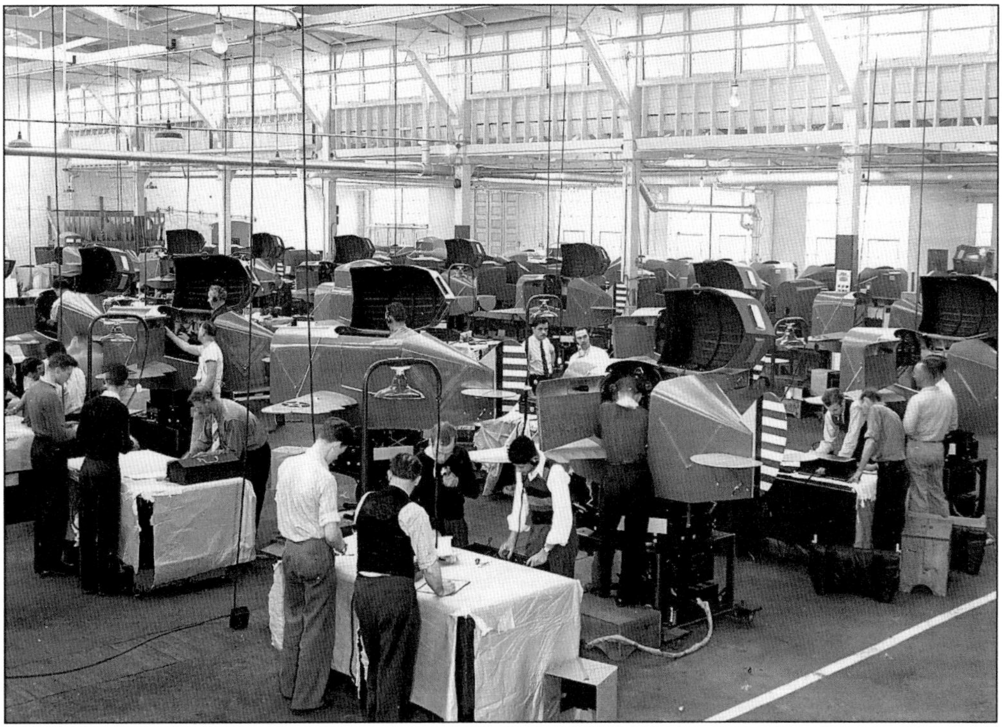

The Link Aviation factory photograph shows the Brandywine Creek site during World War II production. Ed Link is seated in the trainer below. Link's inventions carried the corporation into the space age, with simulators for the Apollo astronauts' moon-landing expedition, and into the uncharted domain of undersea exploration.

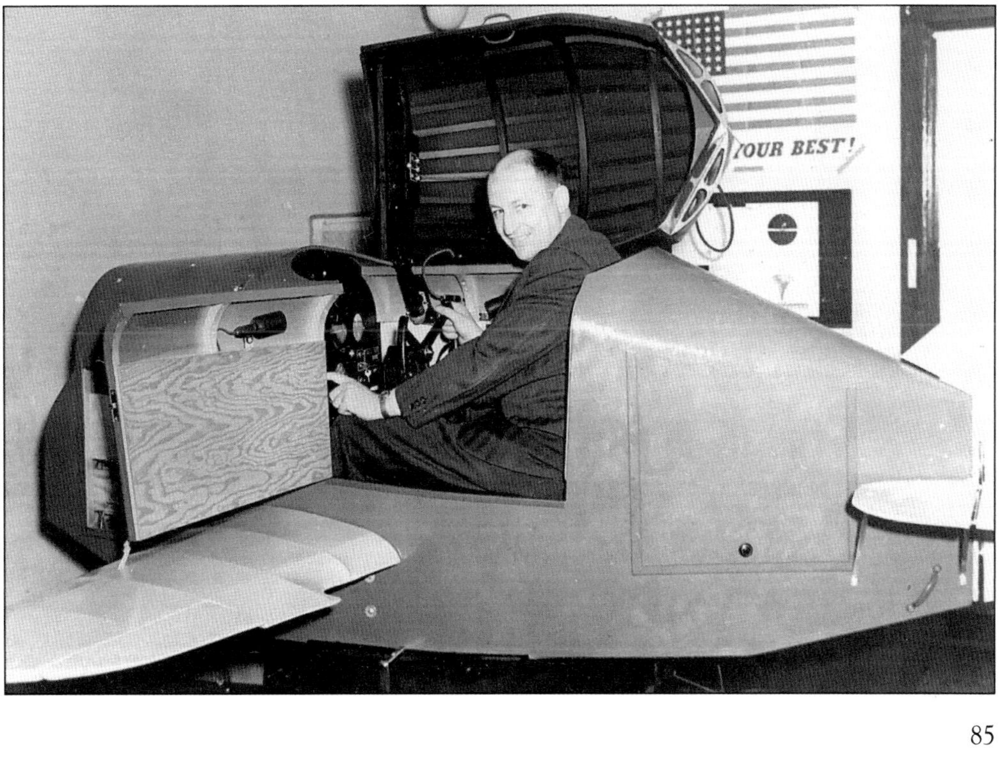

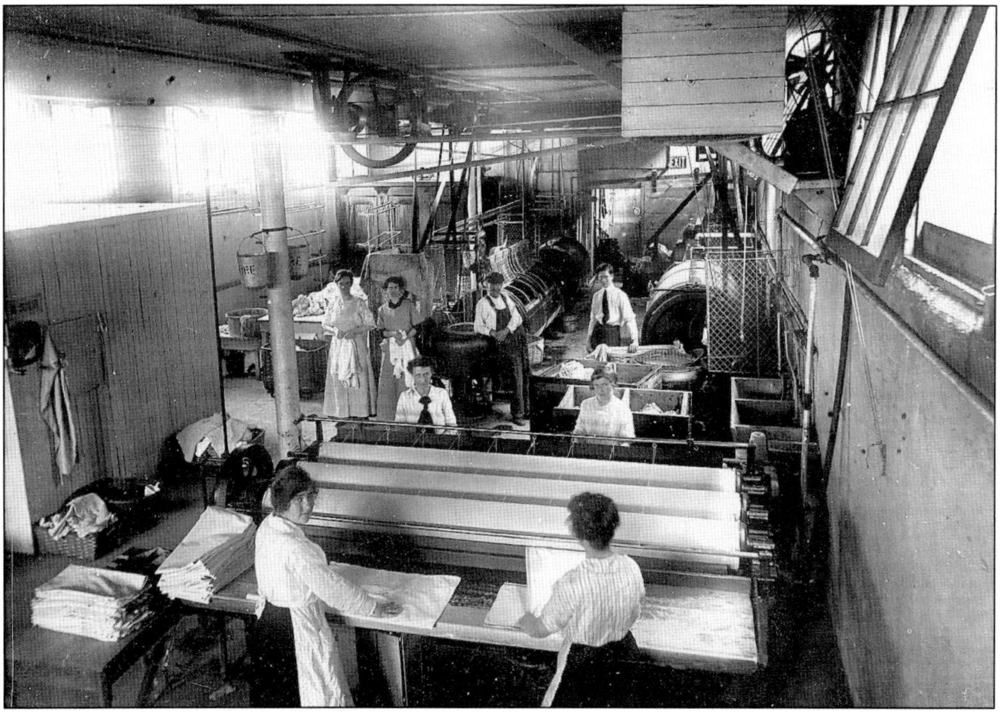

Here for your viewing pleasure is reality in 1916. The Davis-Sweeny Laundry was located at 346 Chenango Street in Binghamton. Teams of women used heavy flatirons and enormous mangles to eradicate wrinkles. Although large tumble washers were used for most of the laundry, all delicate items were cleaned by hand. Note the fire safety devices located on the pole in the photograph above: tin buckets.

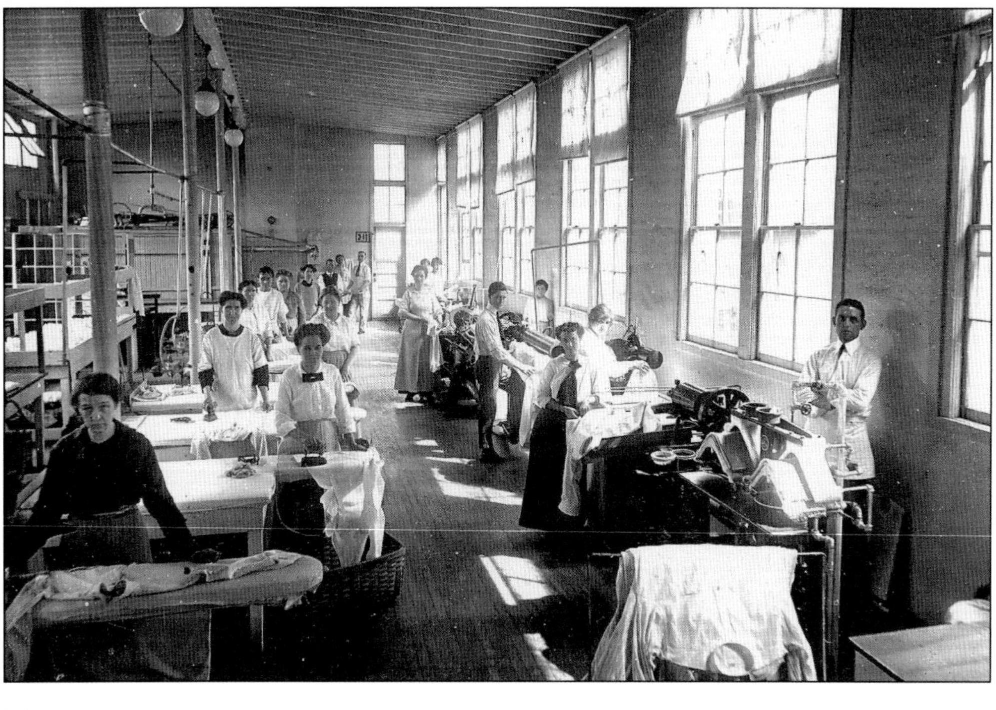

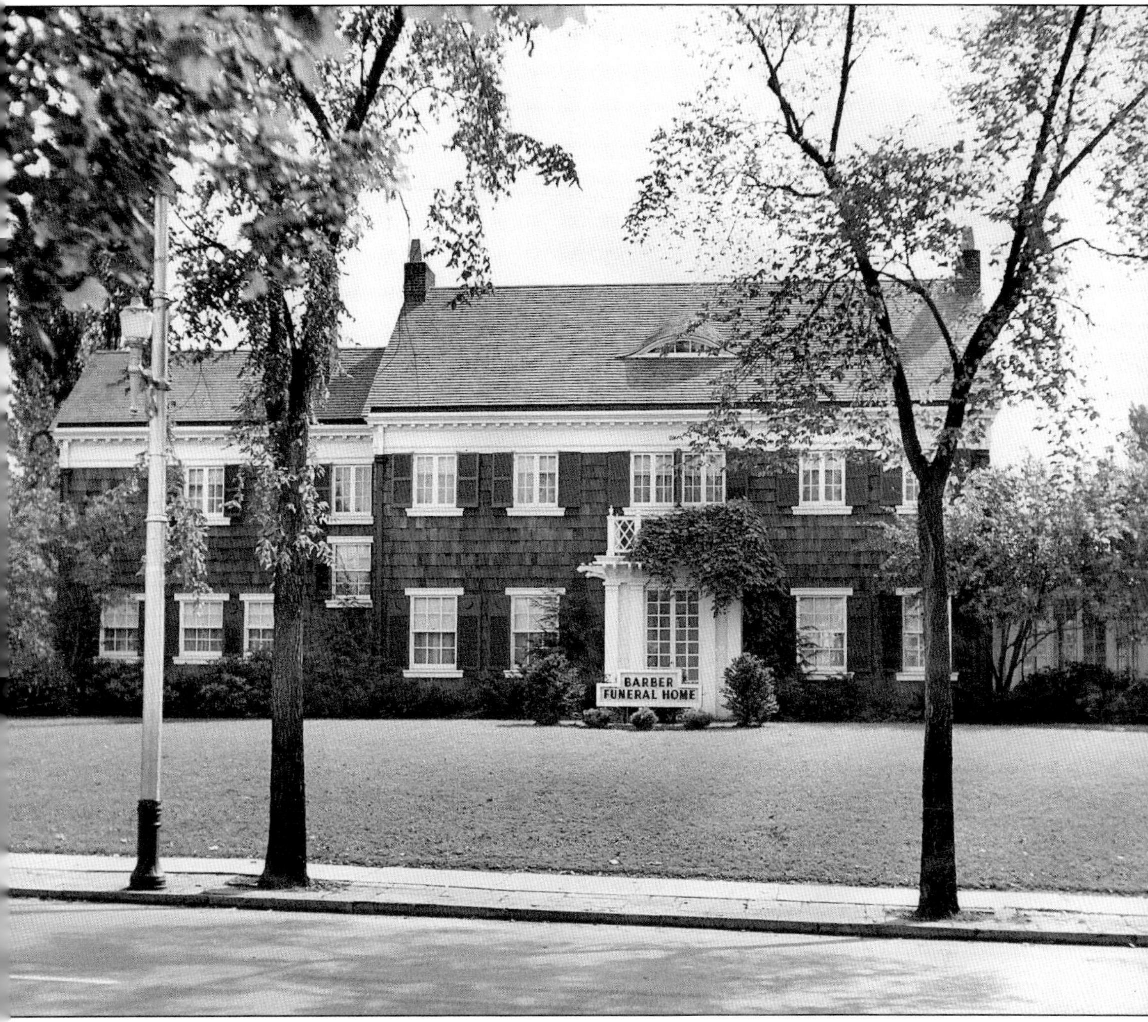

Harry L. Johnson was the youngest of the four Johnson brothers. George F. Johnson deemed it necessary for one of the four to live in Johnson City, enter into the life of the village, and keep in touch with workers. Harry L. was general manager of the Johnson City factories and maintained this position until his death. His home was built *c.* 1912 with extensive gardens and a greenhouse. During World War I, "Mrs. Harry" dug up her gardens and lawn to plant potatoes. She also used the third floor of their home for groups of women making bandages for the Red Cross war effort. Harry L. worked tirelessly with war activities and, in 1921, suffered a nervous breakdown. He died later that year of "apoplexy, worry, and overwork of the brain that wore out his system." Eventually, his widow sold the house to Mr. Barber for use as a funeral home, with a promise that the building would remain as intact as possible. The Barber family has run this Johnson City funeral home for three generations and treasures the Johnson legacy.

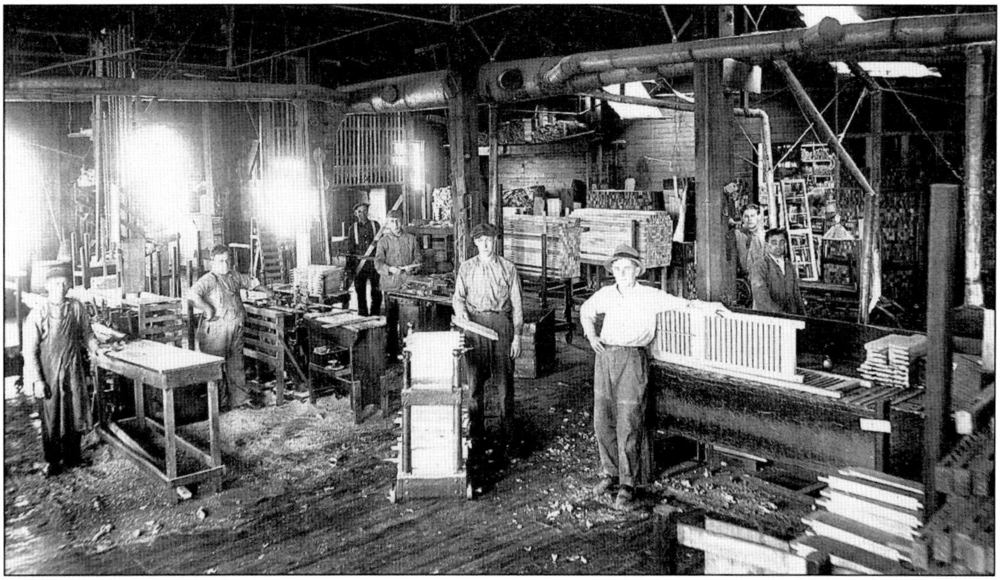

Bartlett and Company Lumber and Millwork was established in 1850 and was still a strong presence in Binghamton in 1916, when these photographs were taken. Located at 45 Collier Street, the company specialized in " 'odd work' such as mantels, bookcases, carvings, doors and stairs made to order at short notice from any kind of rare or common wood. Estimates, suggestions and samples always available to the very welcome visitor to our yards and factory. Our work is about as good as can be obtained yet our prices are no higher than any competitor."

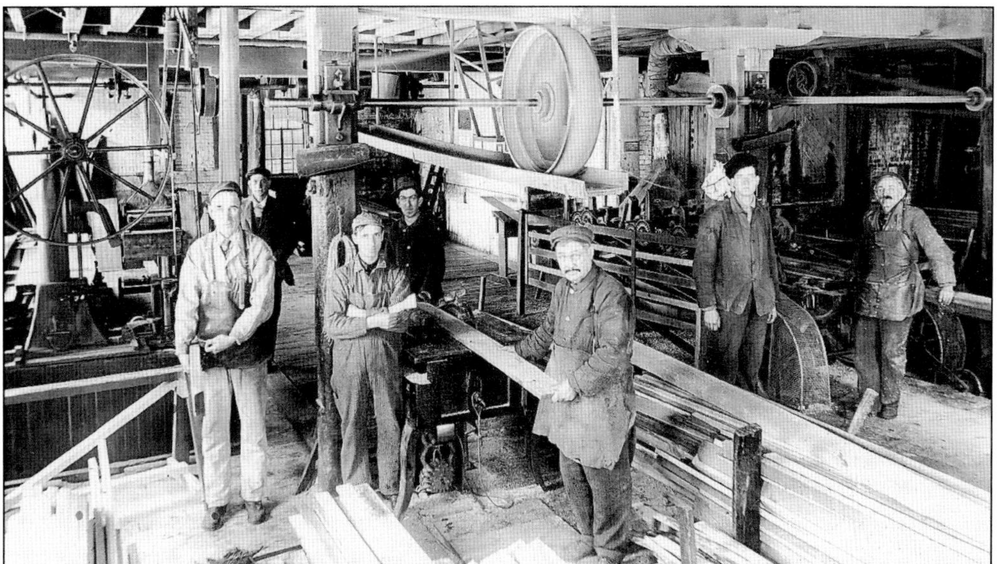

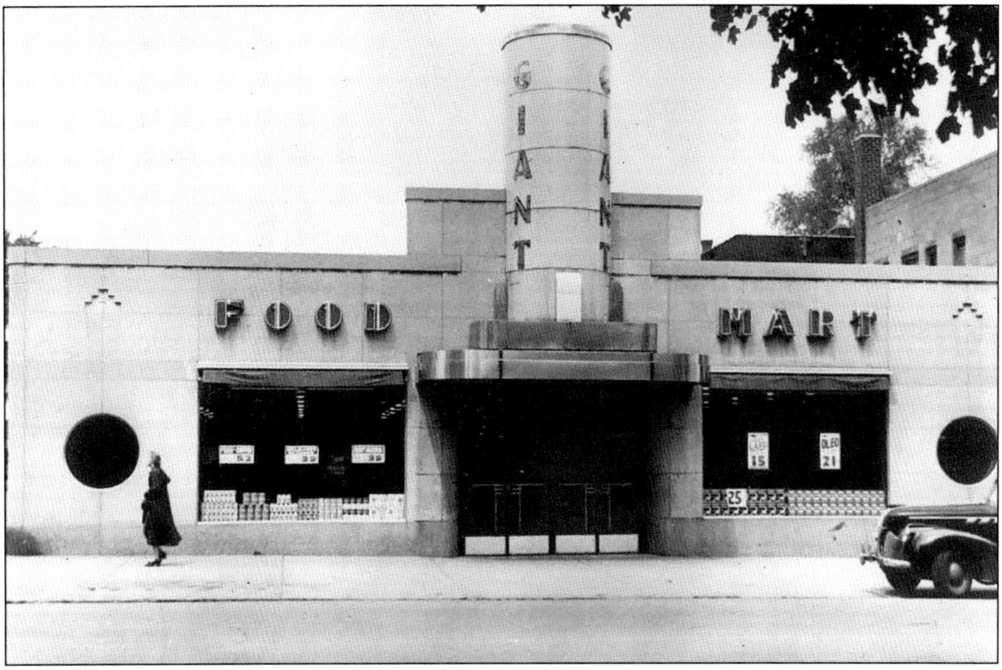

The Akel family brought supermarket shopping to Broome County in 1933. Regardless of the severe economic conditions of the era, the progressive style of food merchandising was an instant success. As part of the National Cash Register exhibit in the 1939 New York World's Fair, the art deco design of the Giant market, at 56–58 Main Street in Binghamton, was selected for special architectural recognition.

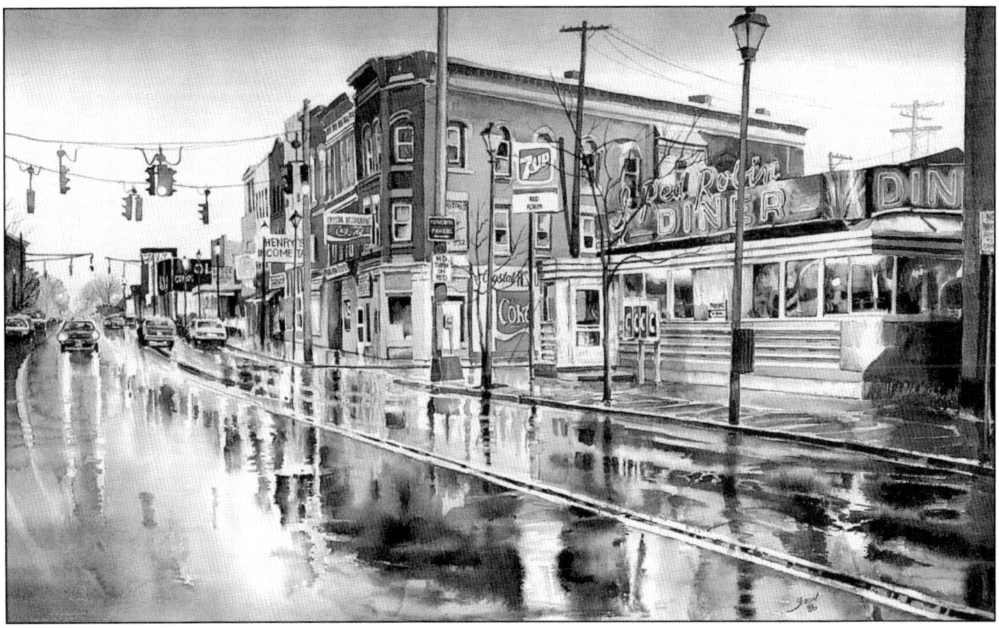

The art deco design of the 1930s extended to a modern interpretation of the neighborhood restaurant. The Red Robin Diner remains a landmark to the deco era. In 1959, it was moved from Binghamton to its current site on Main Street in Johnson City. This rendering of the building is a watercolor painting by Cheryl Stein.

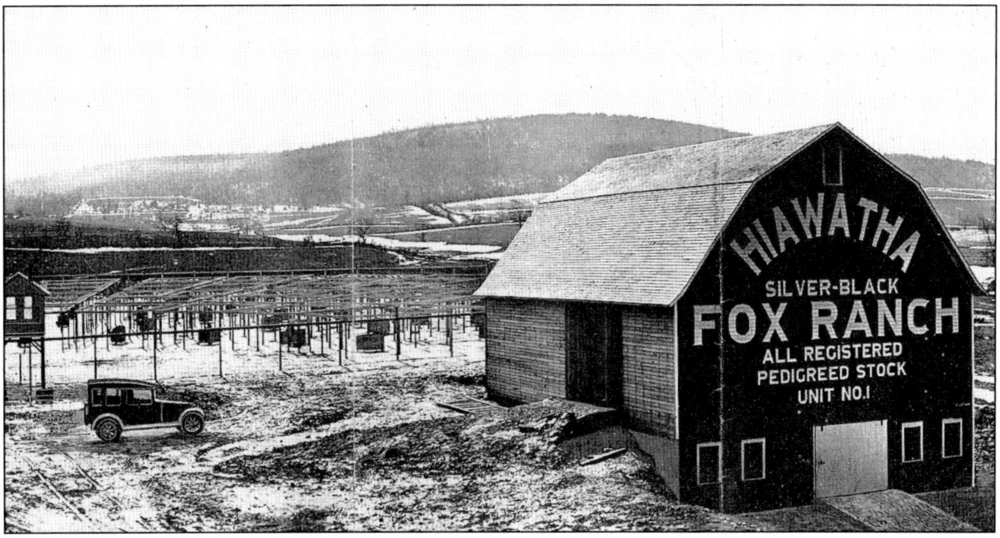

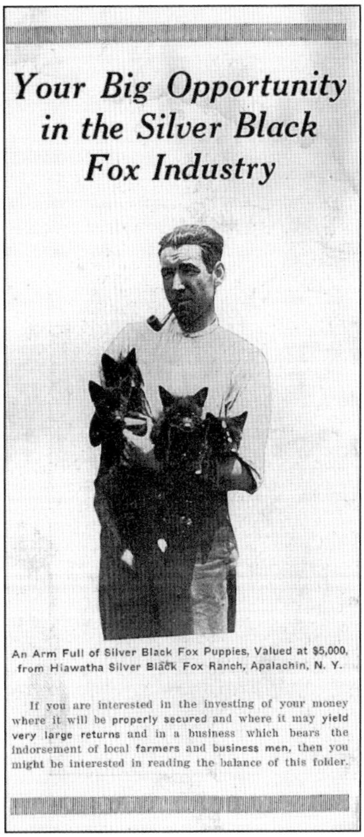

A law was passed in 1837 offering a bounty on foxes. To protect livestock from this mighty, menacing mammal, 25¢ per body would be paid. By 1920, there were few wild foxes left to meet the needs of fashion, so the Hiawatha Silver Black Fox Ranch of Binghamton opened for business in Apalachin. It was considered one of the finest fox-breeding ranches ever built. Sixty pair of award-winning pedigreed foxes were set to work propagating, each pair in its own wood hutch guarded by a high fence and a watchtower manned both day and night. Although the fox ranch went out of business, the large farmhouse survives today as a restaurant and gift shop.

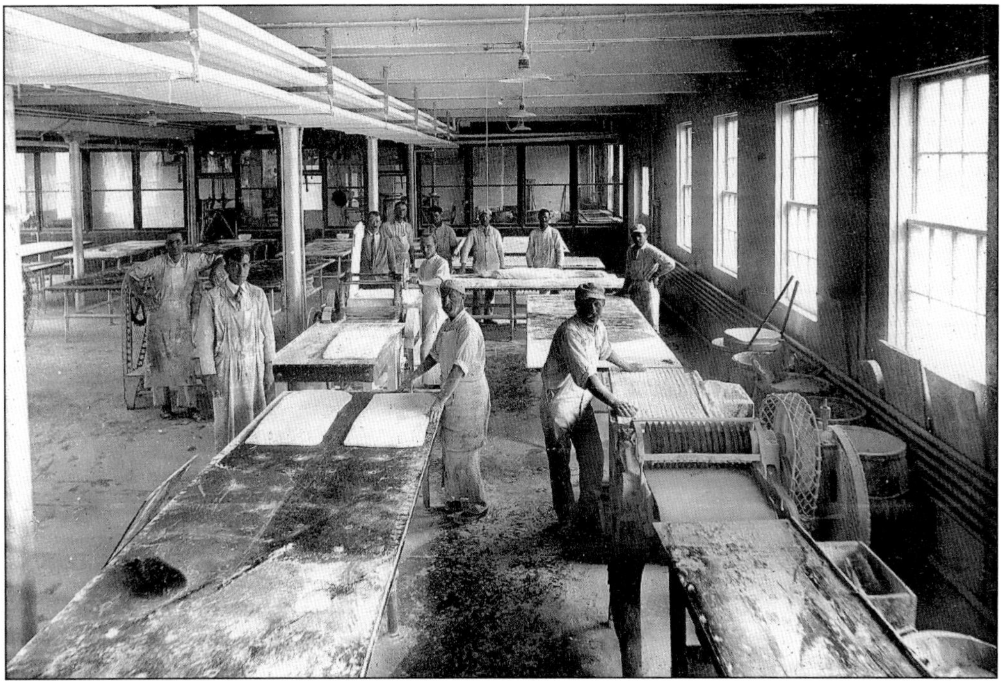

The E.F. Hopton Candy Company formed in 1923. The name changed to the Ideal Carmel Company and then changed again to the Fair Play Carmel Company in 1924. Located on the corner of Grand Avenue and Willow Streets in Johnson City, the company produced popular candy that was shipped throughout the United States. The Fair Play name derived from an Endicott Johnson slogan depicting Broome County as the Fair Play Valley. The top floor of the building housed a two-ton tank full of corn syrup used in creating treats such as B-B Bats, Kits, and Carmel Pops. When the company closed its doors in 1990s, the building became a mosque.

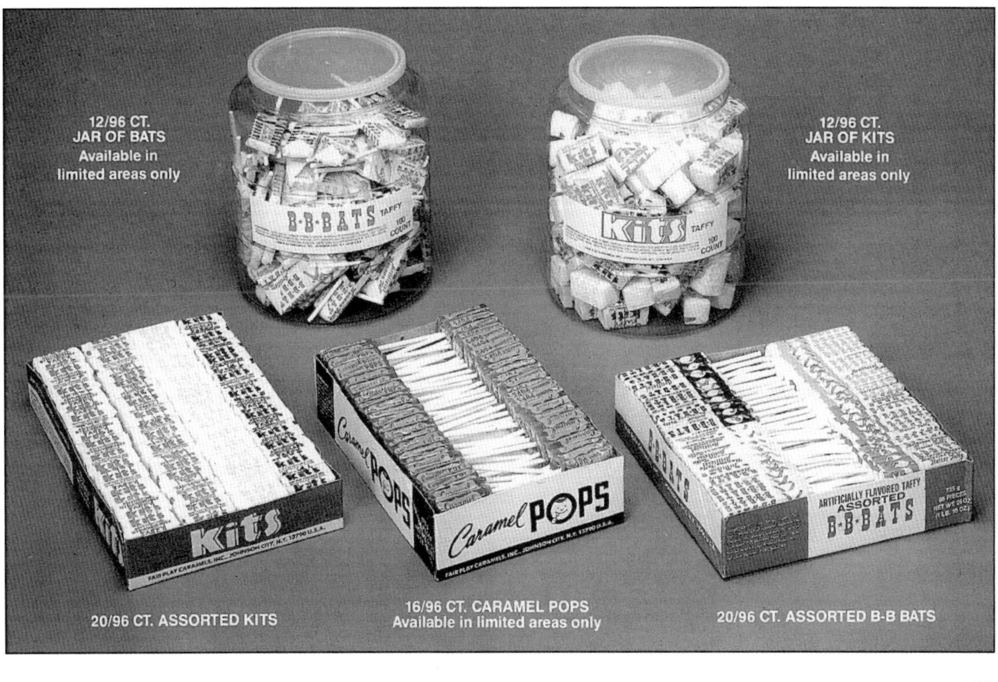

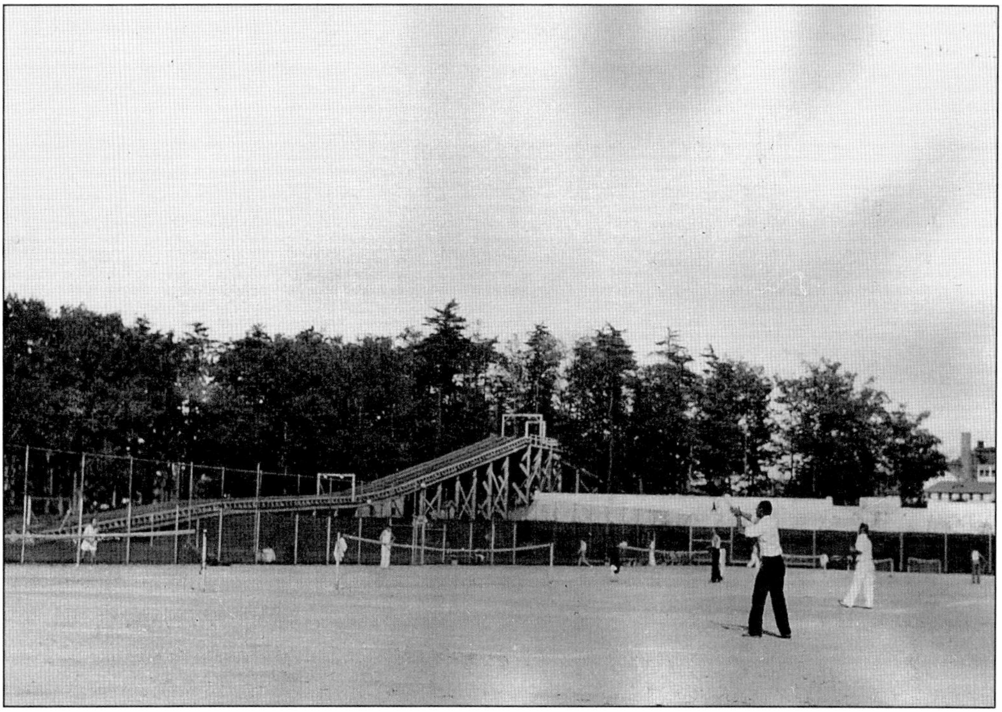

During the 1920s and 1930s, this huge toboggan slide was a dream come true, especially for Depression-era children. Large wooden toboggans with leather seats were provided free. The lines were often long but worth the wait, as four to five riders at a time could slide down the long ramp. This, of course, was in the days before insurance companies and lawsuits gained overwhelming control of society.

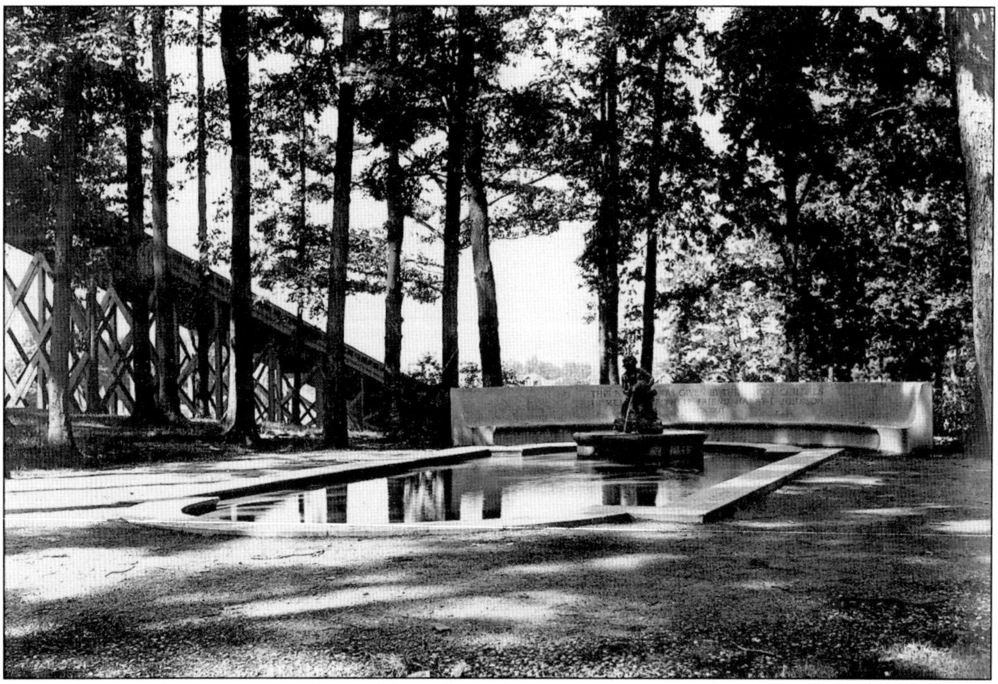

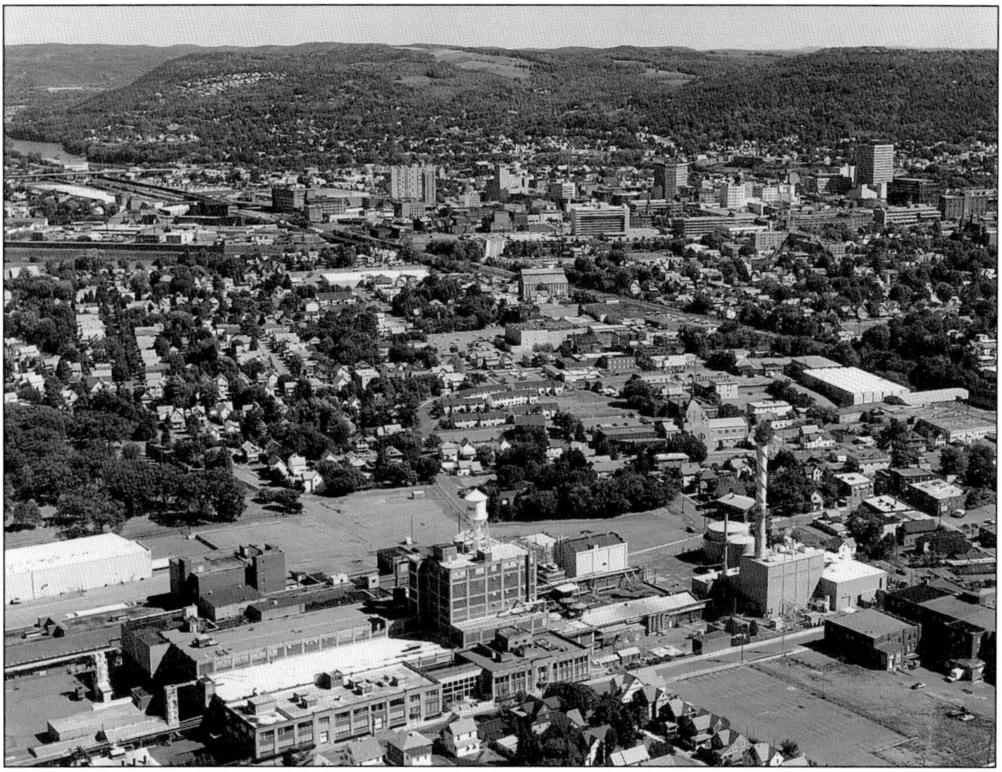

Anthony and Scoville combined their names and talents in creating the Ansco Company in 1854. Ansco manufactured photographic supplies and cameras in Broome County beginning in 1903. A major factor in choosing the Triple Cities was the abundance of water in the river valley. Ten wells were drilled on the property. More than 3.5 million gallons of water were used daily in producing photography products and effectively draining the swampy land nearby. Homes were built in the surrounding area, but when the company shut down, the water table rose to its natural level and neighboring families began experiencing water in their basements. This was a soggy example of nature reasserting its dominance of the land. The photographs (both taken by Ed Aswad) show acres of active Ansco factory buildings and the current vacant land.

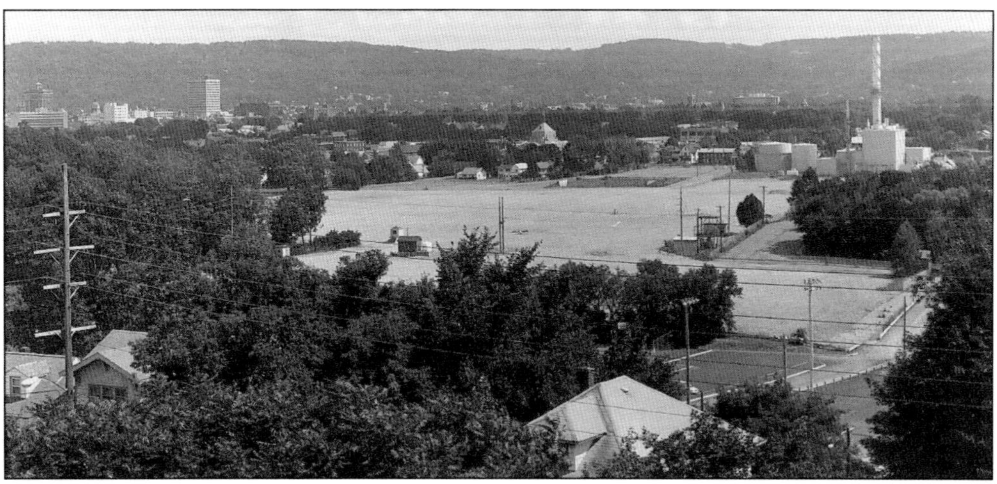

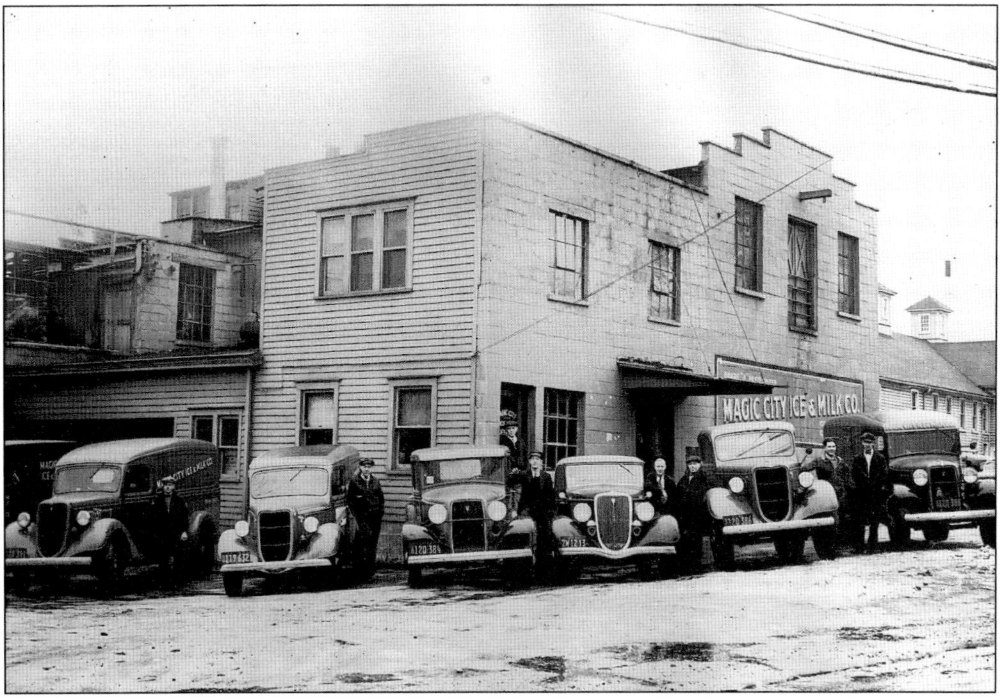

The Magic City Ice and Milk Company began operations on North Street in Endicott in the 1920s. It continued in business for many years, delivering milk to the customers' doorsteps. All milk and cream was packaged in glass bottles, such as those being filled in the factory pictured below. The firm was eventually absorbed by Crowley's Milk Company.

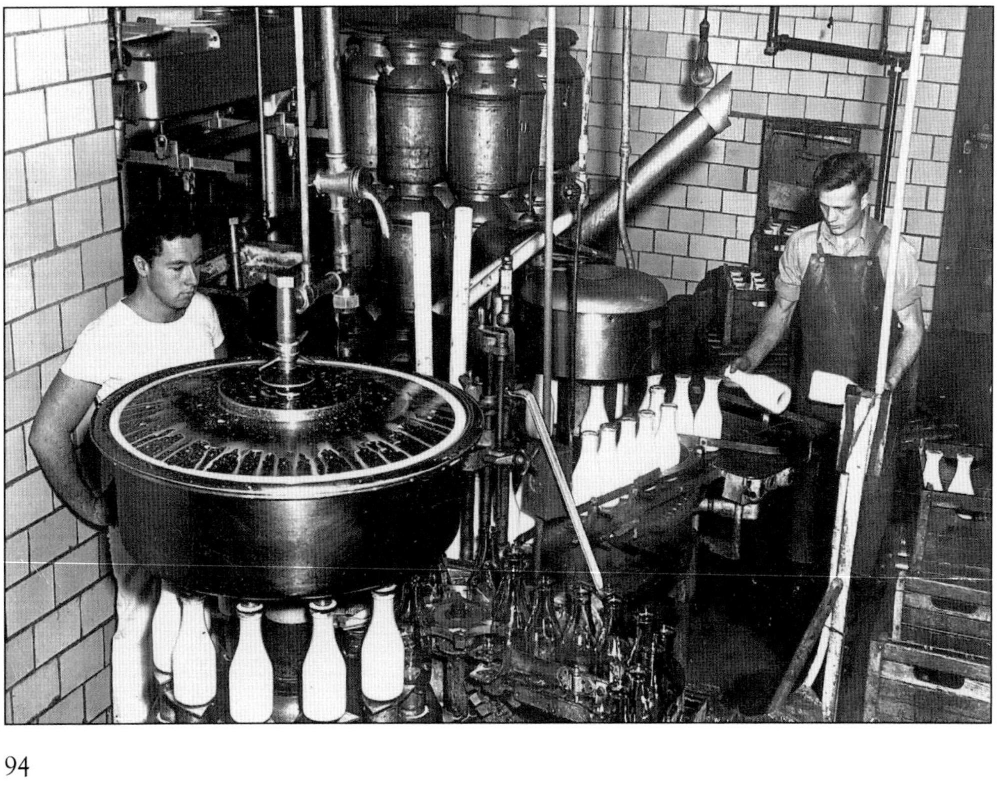

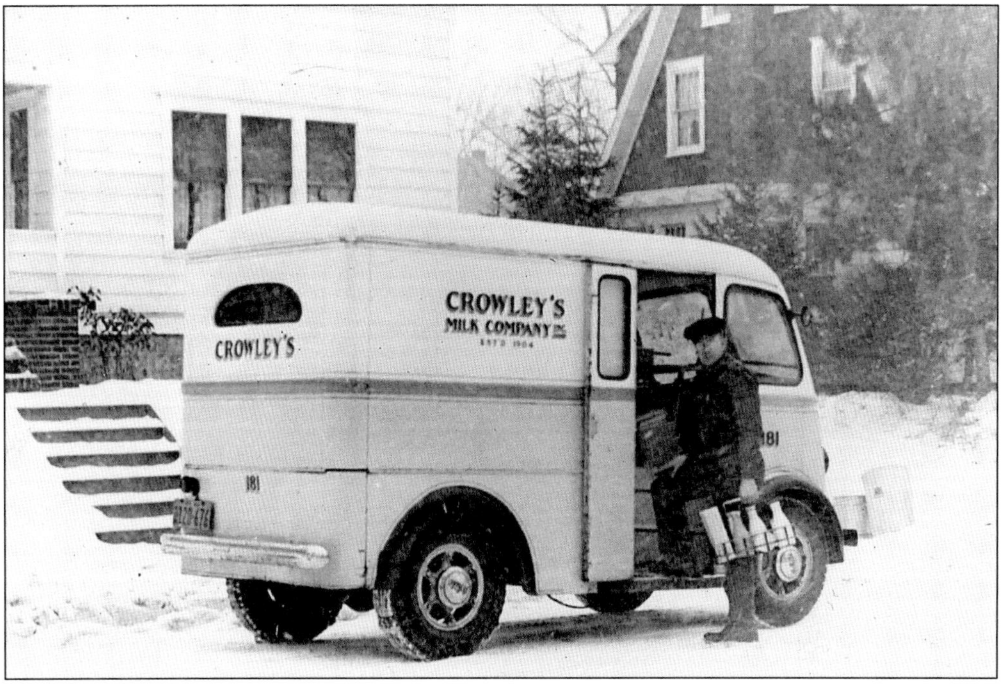

Crowley's Milk Company, established in 1904, has produced dairy products for decades from its plant on Conklin Avenue in Binghamton. Often, the first sounds of morning were the clanking milk bottles delivered to the front steps. During winter months, if the milk was not brought into the house quickly, the cream at the top of the bottle would freeze and expand through the lid, producing a treat for neighborhood felines.

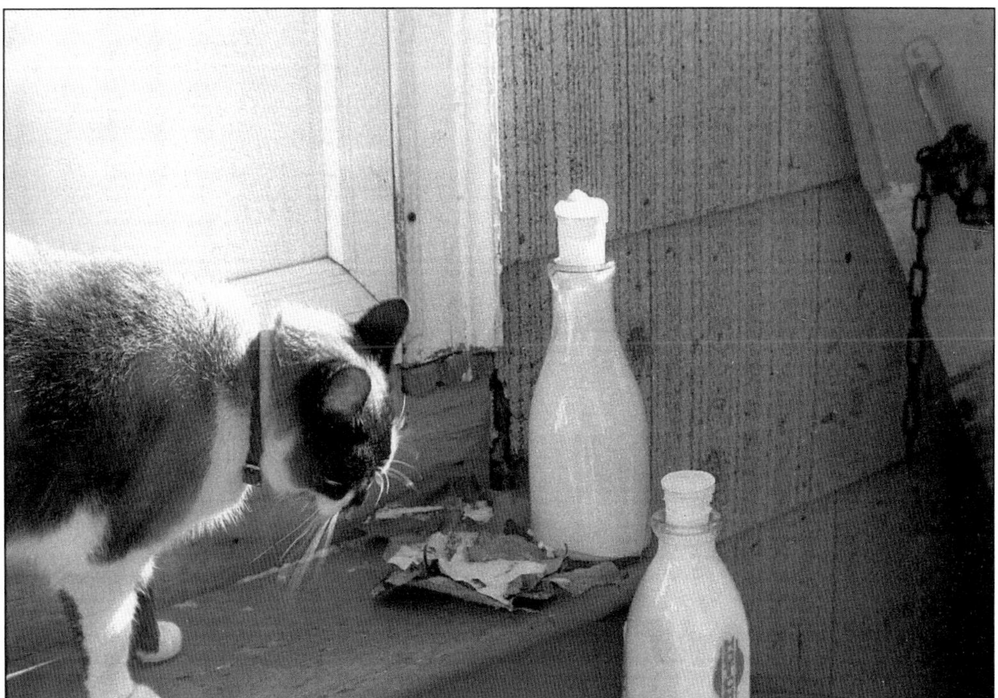

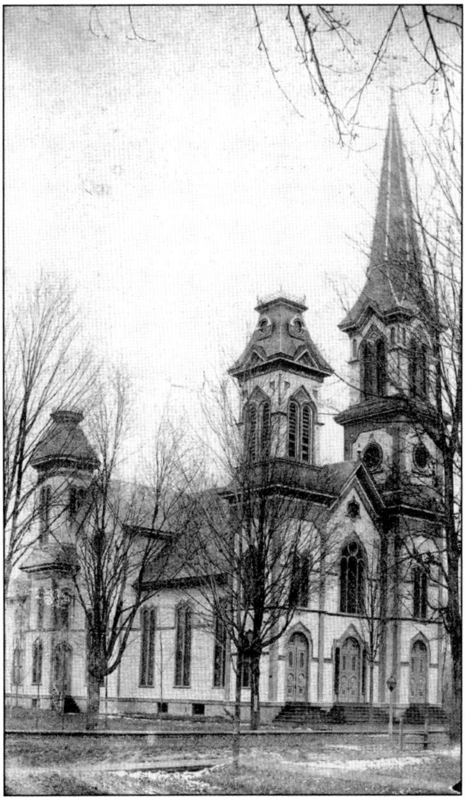

The Union Presbyterian Church began as the Dutch Reformed Church in 1791 on land now part of the Riverside Cemetery. Lack of funds and a malaria outbreak caused the abandonment of this church, but, in 1819, it reopened as the First Presbyterian Society. By 1871, the society was prosperous enough to build a new church at Main and Liberty Streets in Union. In 1906, lightning struck this building, completely destroying it. The oldest congregation in the valley did not become discouraged; the members got to work, and a new stone structure was built in 1907. It stands today as an inspiration to survival.

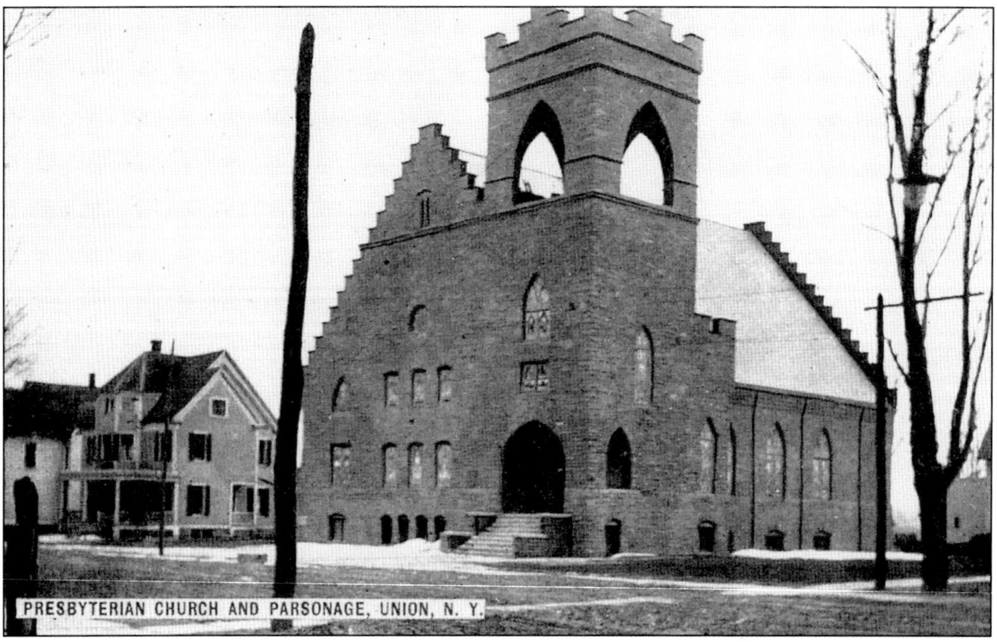

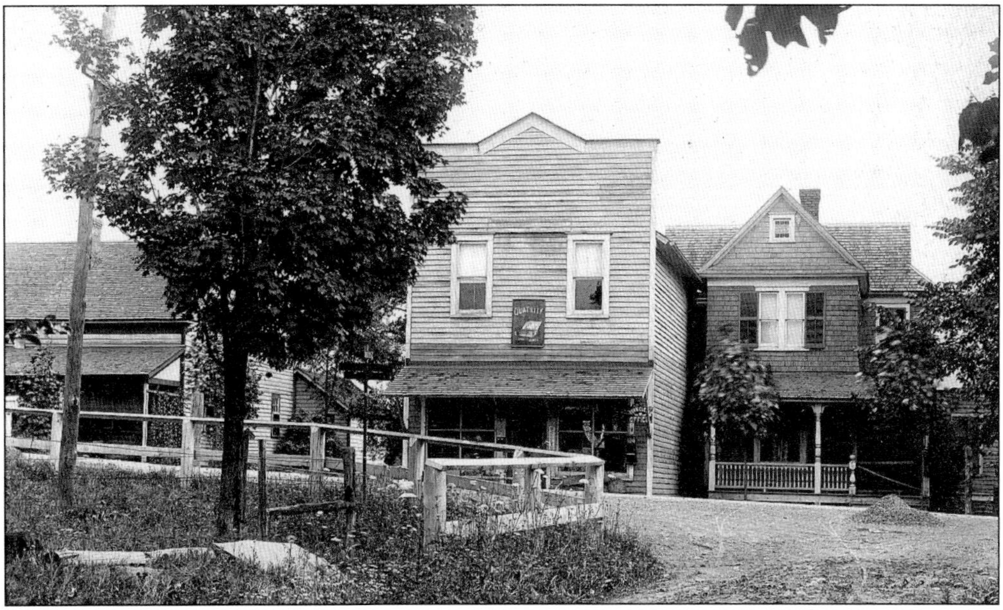

Conklin was formed in 1824. The photograph above is a rare view of the intersection of Conklin Road and Conklin Forks Road. The building in the center is the Town of Conklin Clerk's Office *c.* 1900. A new town hall is being constructed on Conklin Road, and the "Castle" previously used will be turned into a repository for historical exhibits.

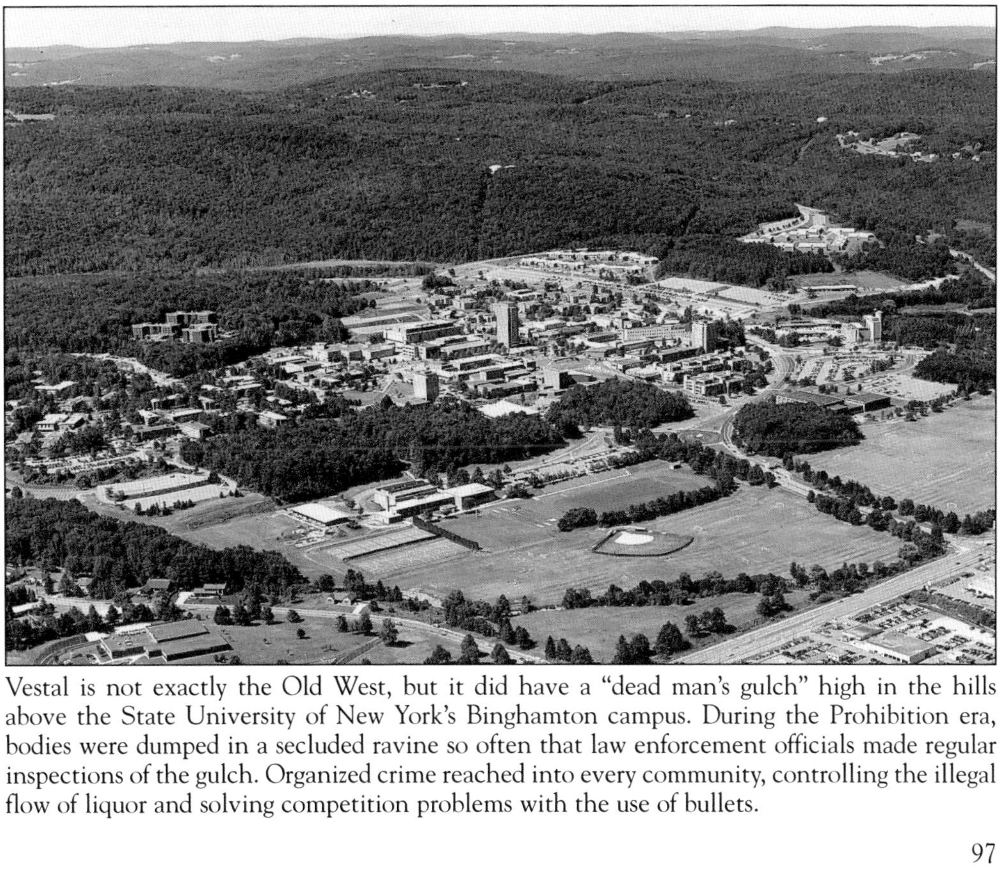

Vestal is not exactly the Old West, but it did have a "dead man's gulch" high in the hills above the State University of New York's Binghamton campus. During the Prohibition era, bodies were dumped in a secluded ravine so often that law enforcement officials made regular inspections of the gulch. Organized crime reached into every community, controlling the illegal flow of liquor and solving competition problems with the use of bullets.

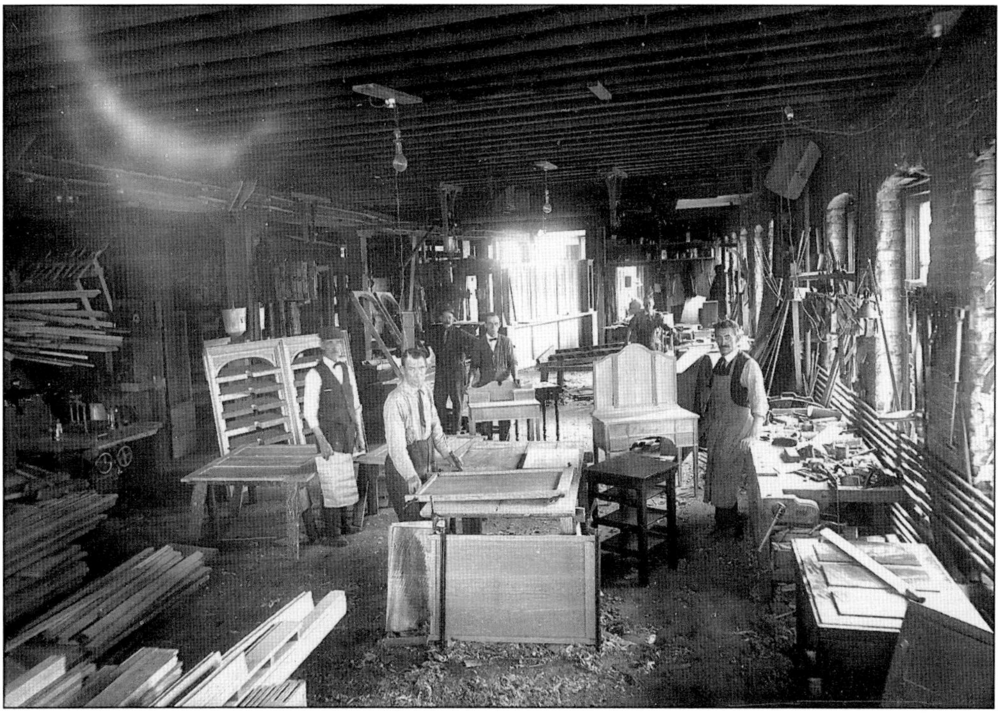

Gibbs Carpentry Shop was in business in 1916, producing a wide range of special order and standard carpentry items. Quality woodworking and attention to every detail made the shop successful with contractors and homeowners.

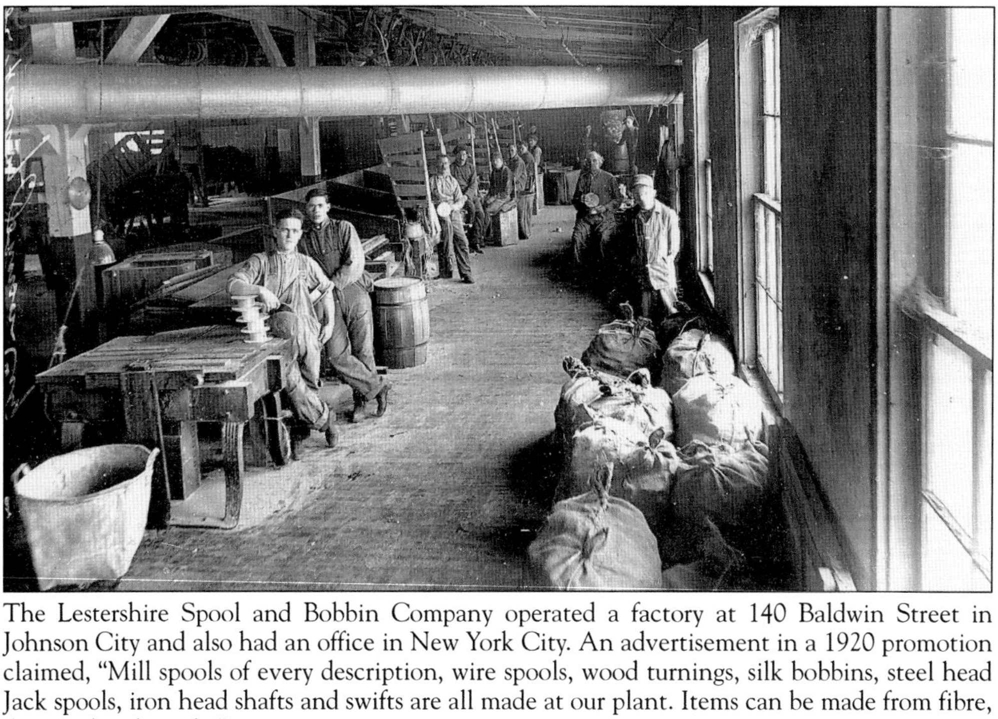

The Lestershire Spool and Bobbin Company operated a factory at 140 Baldwin Street in Johnson City and also had an office in New York City. An advertisement in a 1920 promotion claimed, "Mill spools of every description, wire spools, wood turnings, silk bobbins, steel head Jack spools, iron head shafts and swifts are all made at our plant. Items can be made from fibre, dogwood and maple."

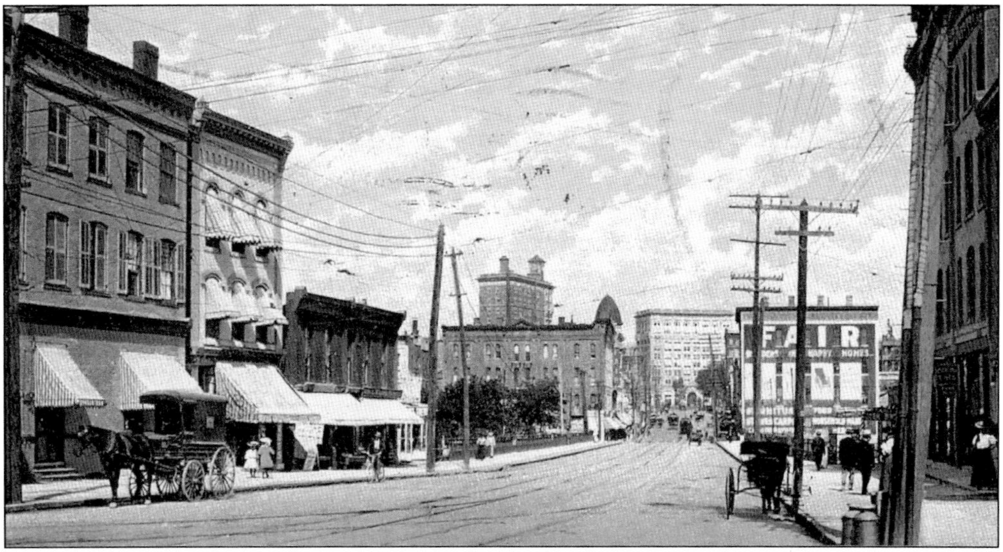

More than a century separates the times these photographs were taken of Court Street in Binghamton. The building on the corner of Front and Main Streets has been torn down, the horses and wagons have passed into time, and traffic lights have replaced the trolley tracks, but perhaps some things never change. Note the milk cans still waiting on the corner; the delivery truck is somewhat late. (Courtesy of Ed Aswad.)

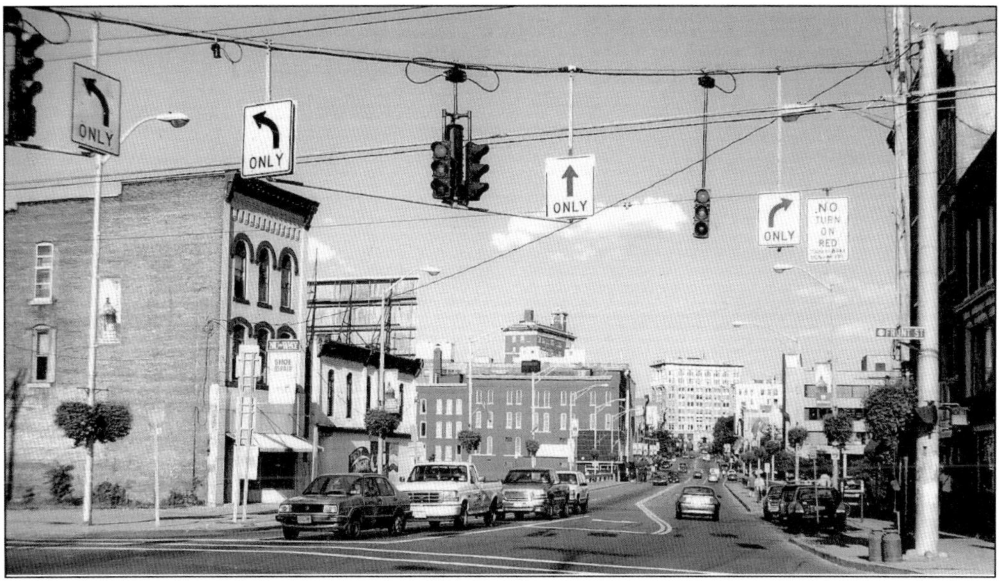

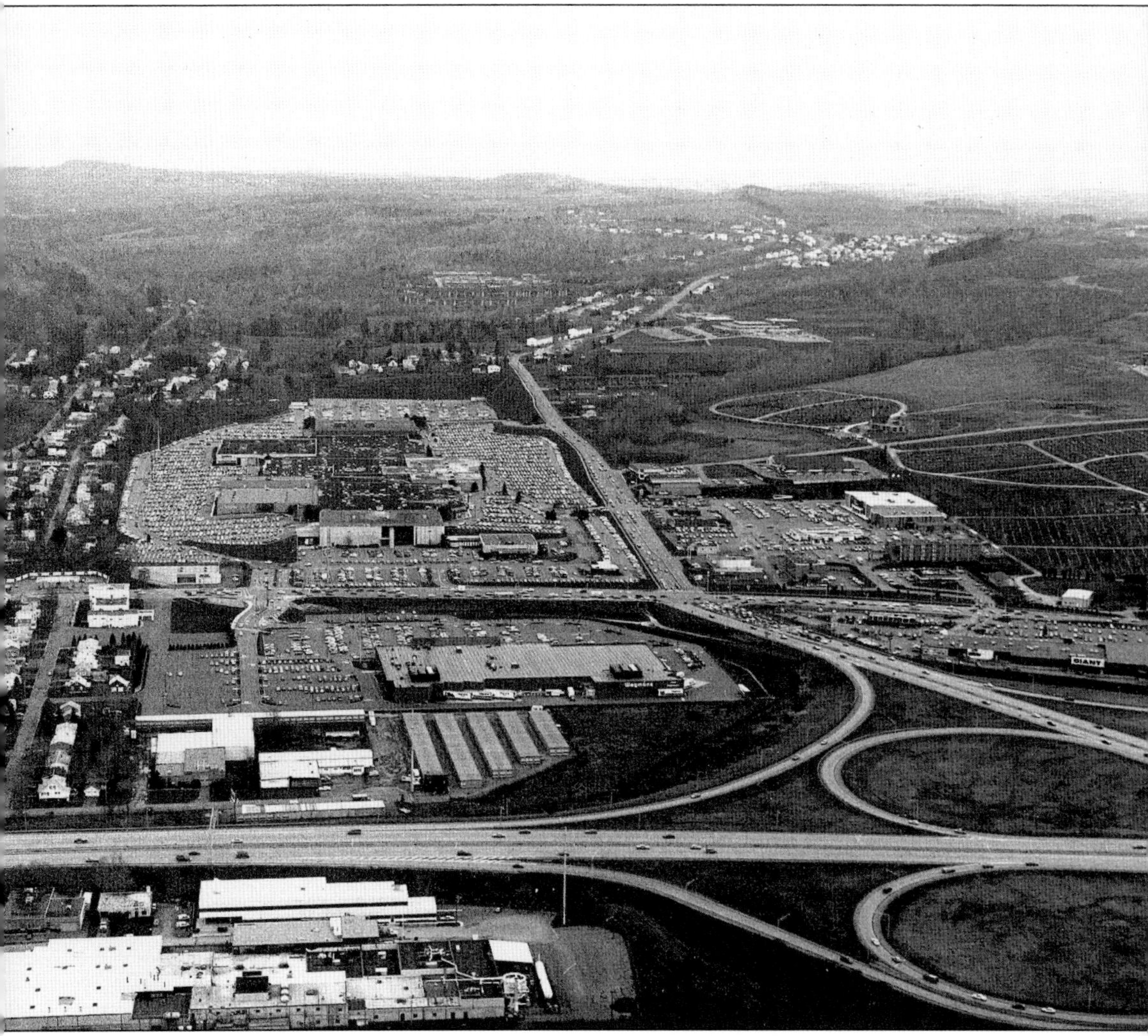

Simon Bigler was the owner of the first steam sawmill in this portion of New York. Located in Oakdale, Bigler and the mill played an important role in winning the Civil War. Bigler was awarded a government contract to provide a 60-foot-long solid piece of white oak for the frame of the Union fighting ship the *Monitor*. A special conveyance was constructed to transport the beam from the mill to the canal in Binghamton, and from there it was taken to a shipyard in New York City. On Mach 9, 1862, the *Monitor* went to sea, battling with and causing the retreat of the previously invincible ironclad the *Merrimac* (renamed the *Virginia*). After the war, to prove the superiority of American timber, "Bigler sent a single piece of pine six feet thick and twenty feet long, hewn from the base of a giant tree, to the London Exposition." Years later, the Bigler mill burned to the ground and was not rebuilt. The Oakdale Mall now occupies the mill site that provided pine, oak, and hickory used in building America.

Three

WAR

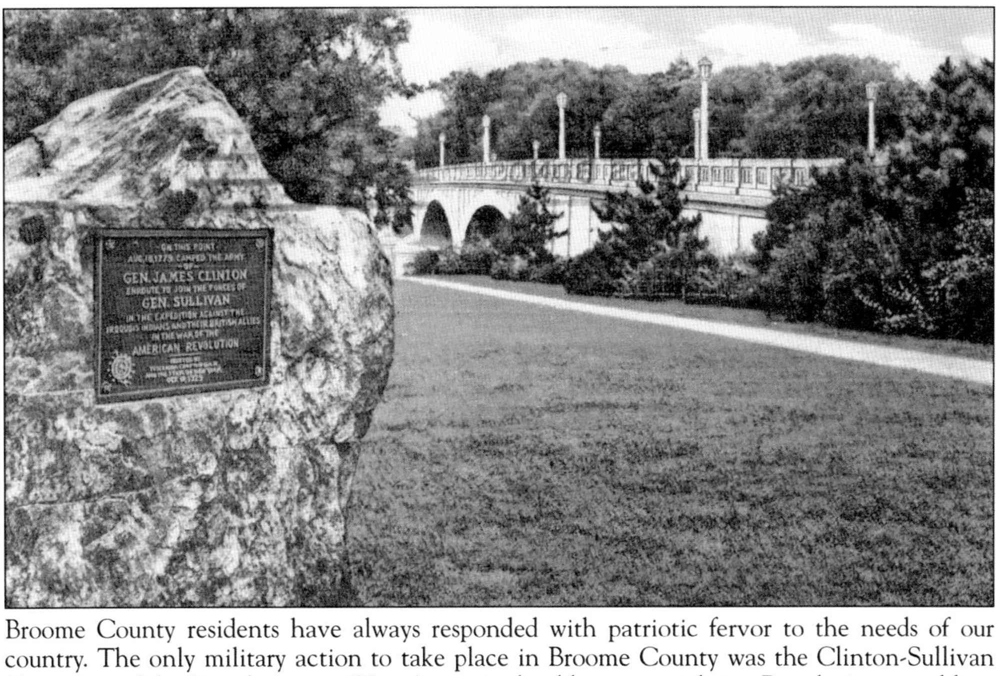

Broome County residents have always responded with patriotic fervor to the needs of our country. The only military action to take place in Broome County was the Clinton-Sullivan Campaign of the Revolutionary War. A granite boulder memorializing Revolutionary soldiers is located in Chenango Point Park near Memorial Bridge at the junction of the Susquehanna and Chenango Rivers in Binghamton.

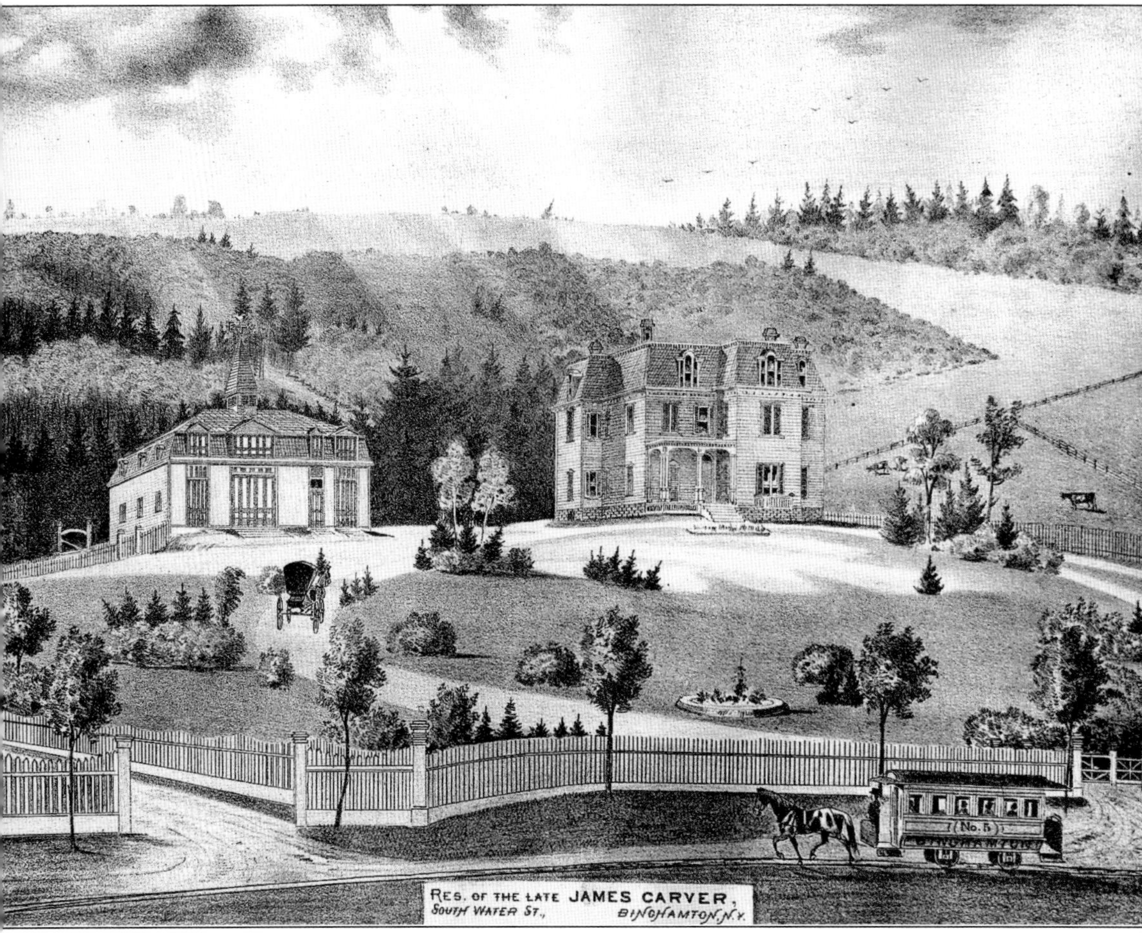

James Carver owned a large farm on South Water Street in the 1860s. It was located just outside the city of Binghamton on what is now called Conklin Avenue. As seen in the engraving from an 1876 atlas, both the three-story home and barn were large and elaborate. Carver was said to be a member of the local Liberty Men—abolitionists. He fought for his beliefs, joining Union forces in the Civil War in 1864. By 1874, his vast properties were listed for sale, and he died from "softening of the brain." The site sold several times and was empty for a few years before being purchased by Dr. S. Andral Kilmer and turned into a "cancertorium" in the 1920s.

The barn was irresistible to small boys in the neighborhood, my uncle Ralph among them. One day while exploring the deserted barn, Ralph ran against a supposedly sound wall, and a secret door opened to reveal a narrow stairway to a windowless room. Small bundles of work clothes were piled in one corner. A chair and a sturdy trunk were the only other contents, but the trunk was filled with Civil War–era letters and notes from J. Carver and family, a forgotten legacy. Many letters contained references to helping slaves reach safety. Ralph and his friends carefully replaced the items, removing nothing from a hidden room that was part of the Underground Railroad system. In 1926, the estate was sold to the city of Binghamton, and Benjamin Franklin School was constructed. The old buildings were torn down and buried with memories of freedom.

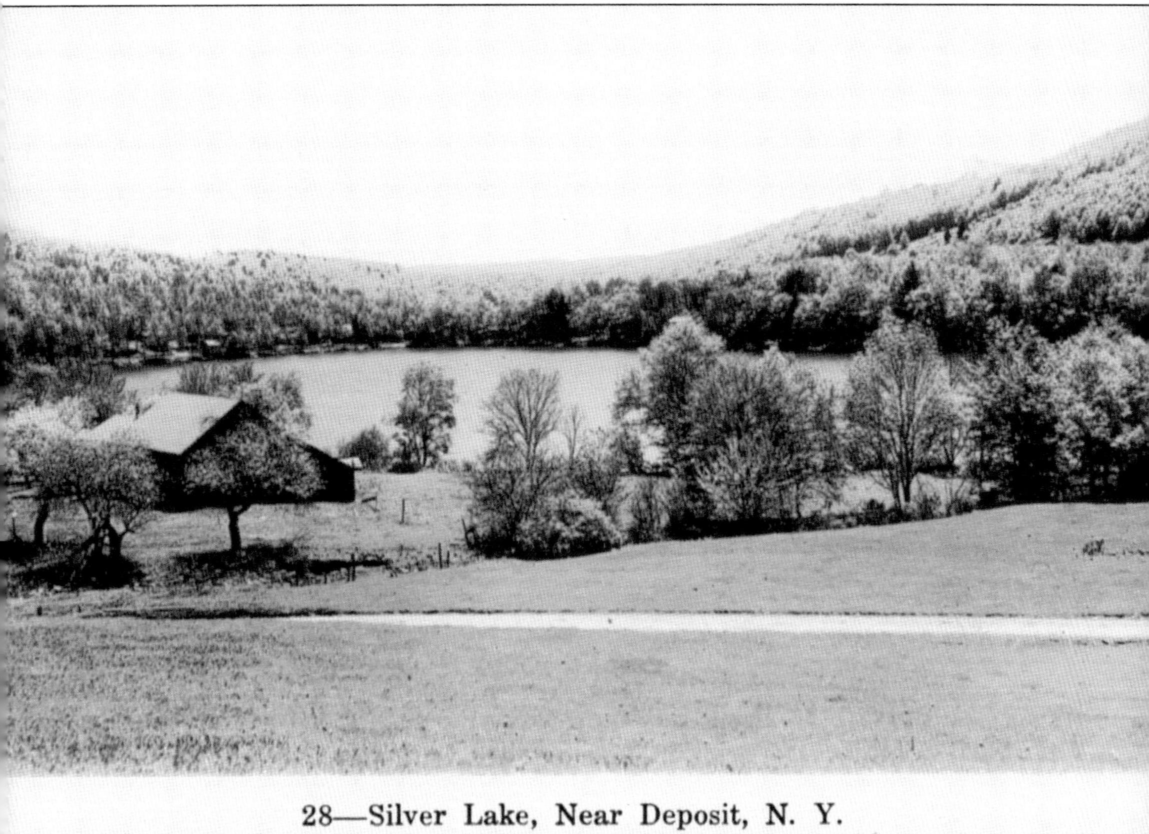

28—Silver Lake, Near Deposit, N. Y.

This Civil War letter dated June 1862 from a Silver Lake man to a friend at home describes images of war:

> Since I inlisted [sic] we have marched night and day. . . . They have marched us like you know what through rain and mud. . . . We have went about 400 miles but not all by foot. Rail cars part of the way and some by boat. They say the rebels are but a few miles away but so far we are guarding bridges and railroads. I have got my old fiddle with me but not much time to dance. . . . Lots of pretty girls when we do get to town. You and the folks at Silver Lake probably got spring work done. Not much plowing done here this spring and I am feared some of the farmers in Fredericksburg will starve next winter, perhaps before as no planting can be done. We got six rebels this morning who had nothing to eat for a week and nothing to fight with, but guess some of them have guns in Richmond, our next destination.

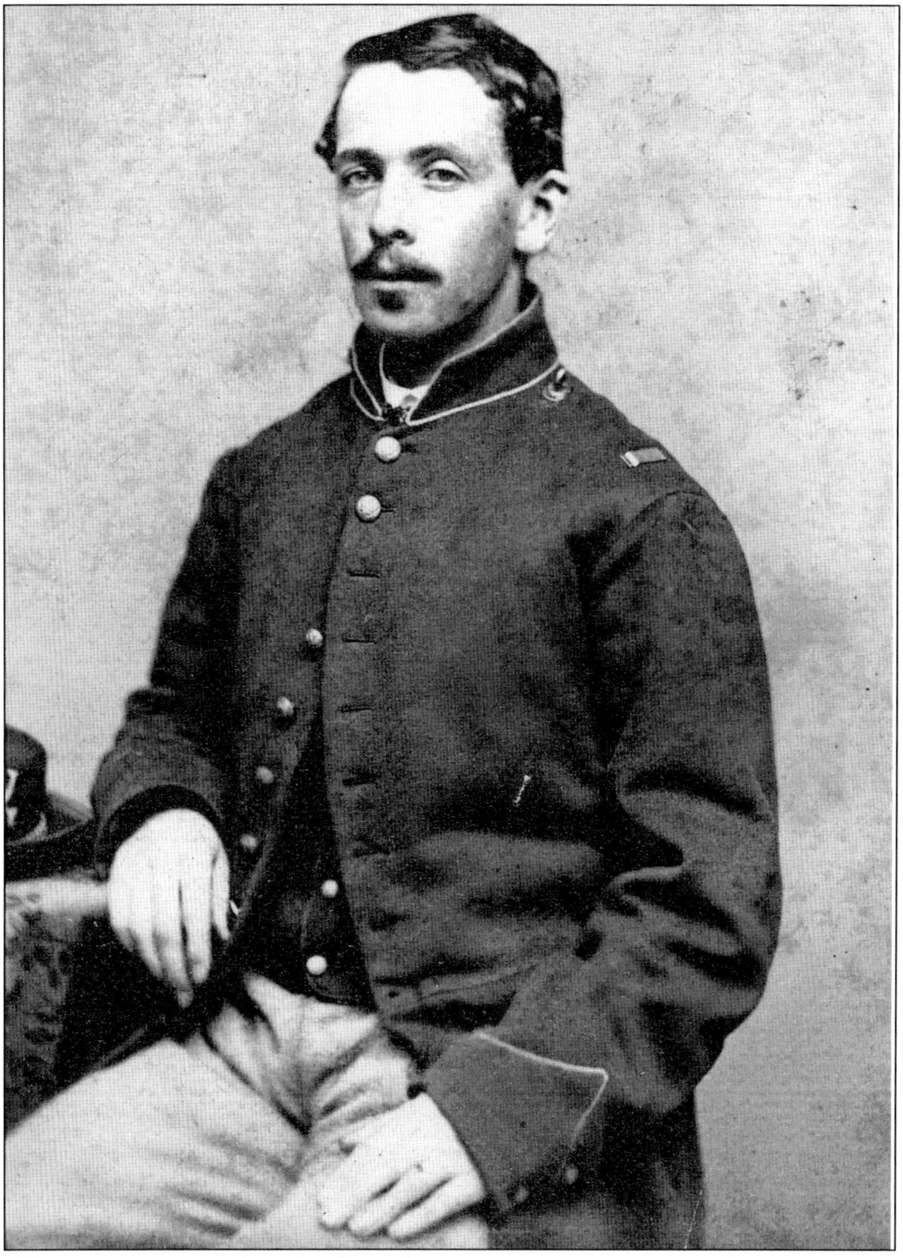

The following are excerpts from Civil War letters to Broome County residents:

> 1864—I expect we will join the regiment soon, . . . am sick of being dogged around so much. . . . We can't get enough to eat and what we do get is not fit to eat. . . . Those of us with money find victuals at saloons. There is someone playing the violin in camp & it makes me think of home.
>
> 1865—I am in NC now and it is cold. We came by steamer and our horses was so crowded they fell down & there they lay on top of each other struggling for life. . . . One of them was dead before we got them up and most all of them badly hurt, and now 23 are dead. Those left had to swim 20 rods to get to shore.

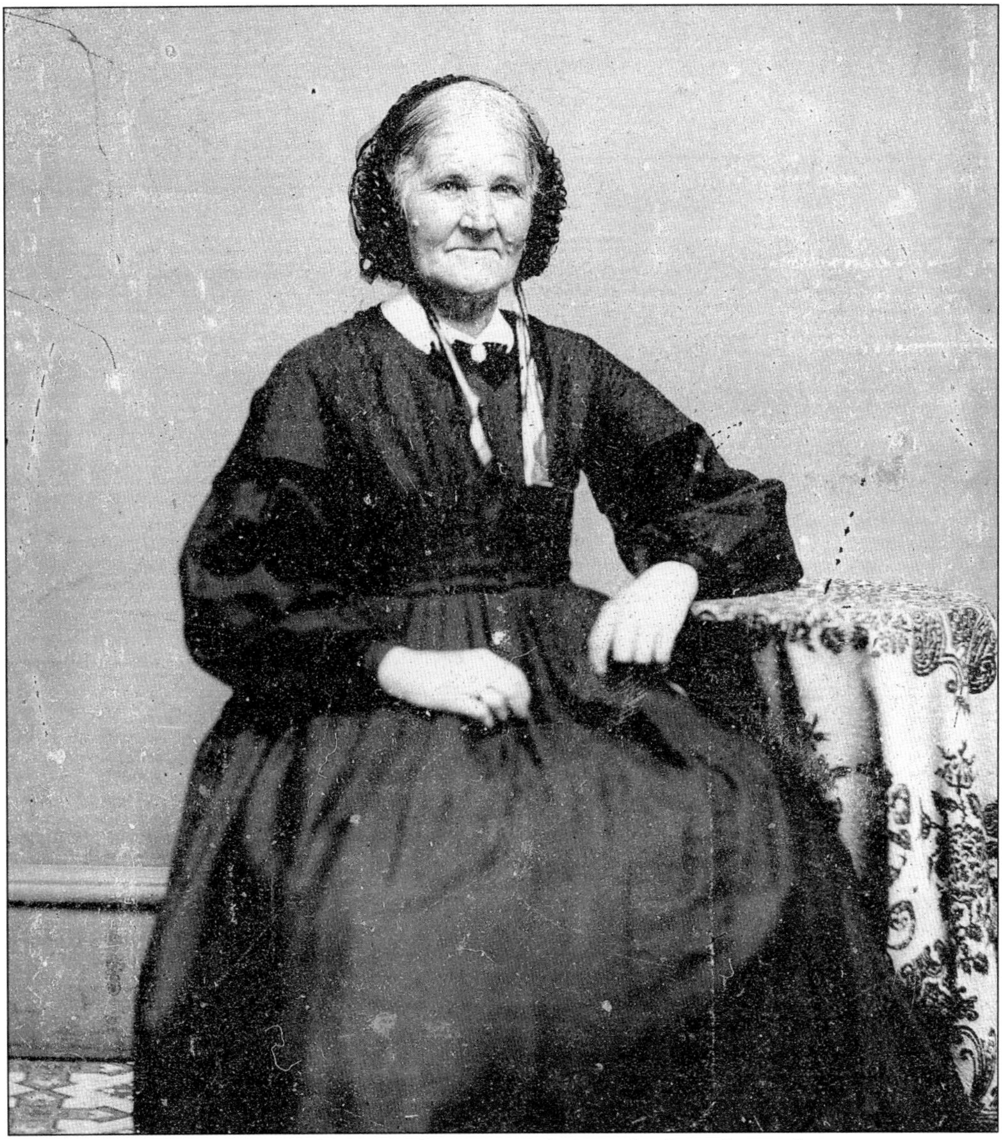

A woman's view of the Civil War is demonstrated through these letters between cousins in Concord and Binghamton:

> 1863—We have had a trying time for many weeks past with the draft and then the fires to trouble us and we are not safe at all. Most of the conscripts felt bad about leaving but put up no resistance. I suppose you have seen the reports of the Jackson riot. We have had terrible fires. . . . Incendiaries are lurking around here. . . . They have burnt houses and barns all lost to fire and that large boarding house close by the gate to Willey burying ground. They have been robbing clothes lines on the other side of the river and have taken whole washings.
> 1864—Sister, Our once proud and happy country is now filled with war & many warriors have perished & many mor [sic] gone to fill their places. If they cannot restore piece [sic] other brave hearts will bleed at home and fighting, . . . and we will fight till this rebellion should have passed away. Eternity is before us."

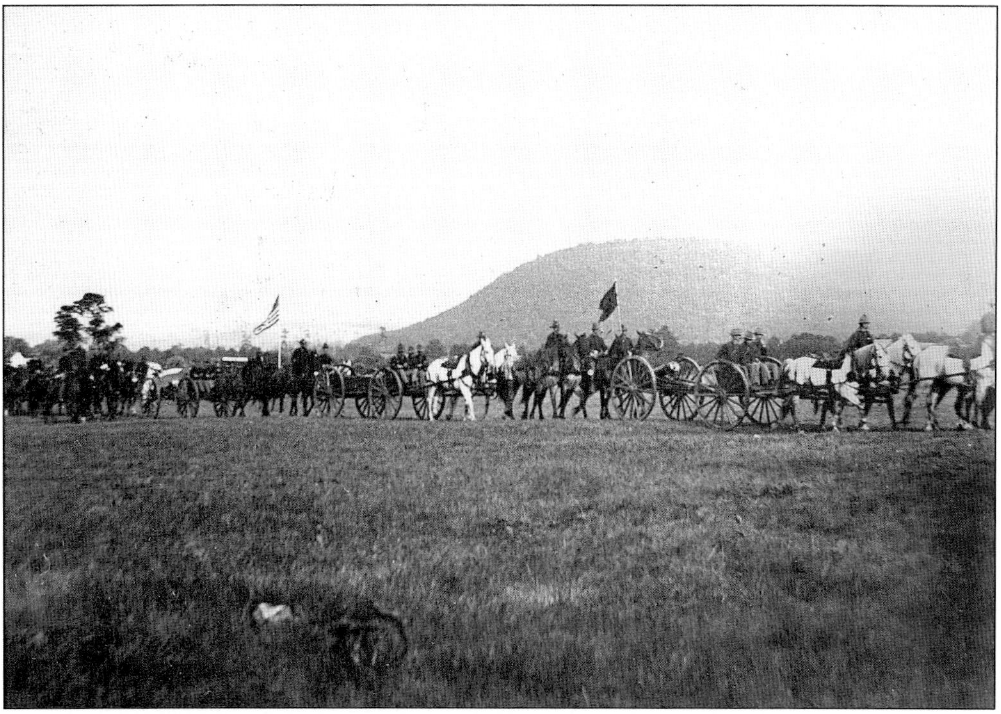

This Civil War letter home was dated 1865: "There is considerable firing this morn from the gun boats. . . . We have a great victory at Fort Fisher for there is the greatest artillery I ever saw. One gun in particular England presented to Jeff Davis is mounted on mahogany wood and it is the nicest piece of artillery there is in the whole Union Army." The photograph shows a post–Civil War local battery.

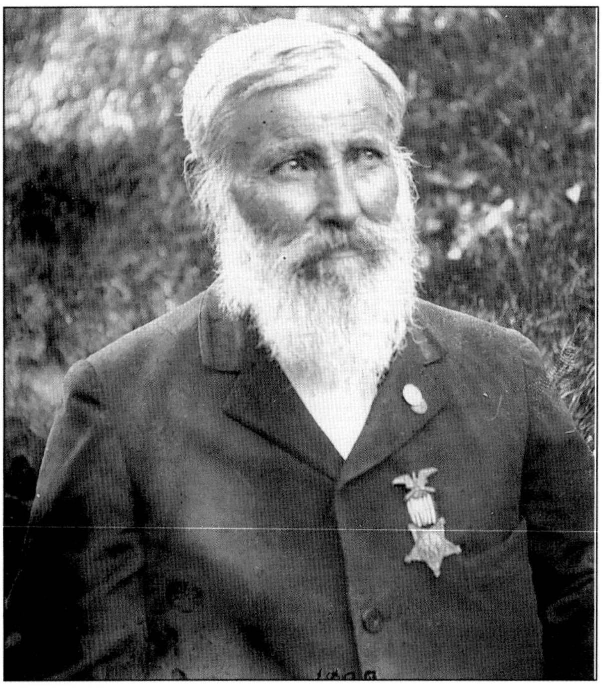

The Grand Army of the Republic was formed in 1866 for Union veterans. Most of the members were Republican and were active in securing the adoption of Decoration Day (Memorial Day) as a national observance to preserve the memory of fallen comrades. Each year a grand national convention was held, until 1949 when only six men attended. This *c.* 1899 photograph shows a man wearing a GAR ribbon of membership.

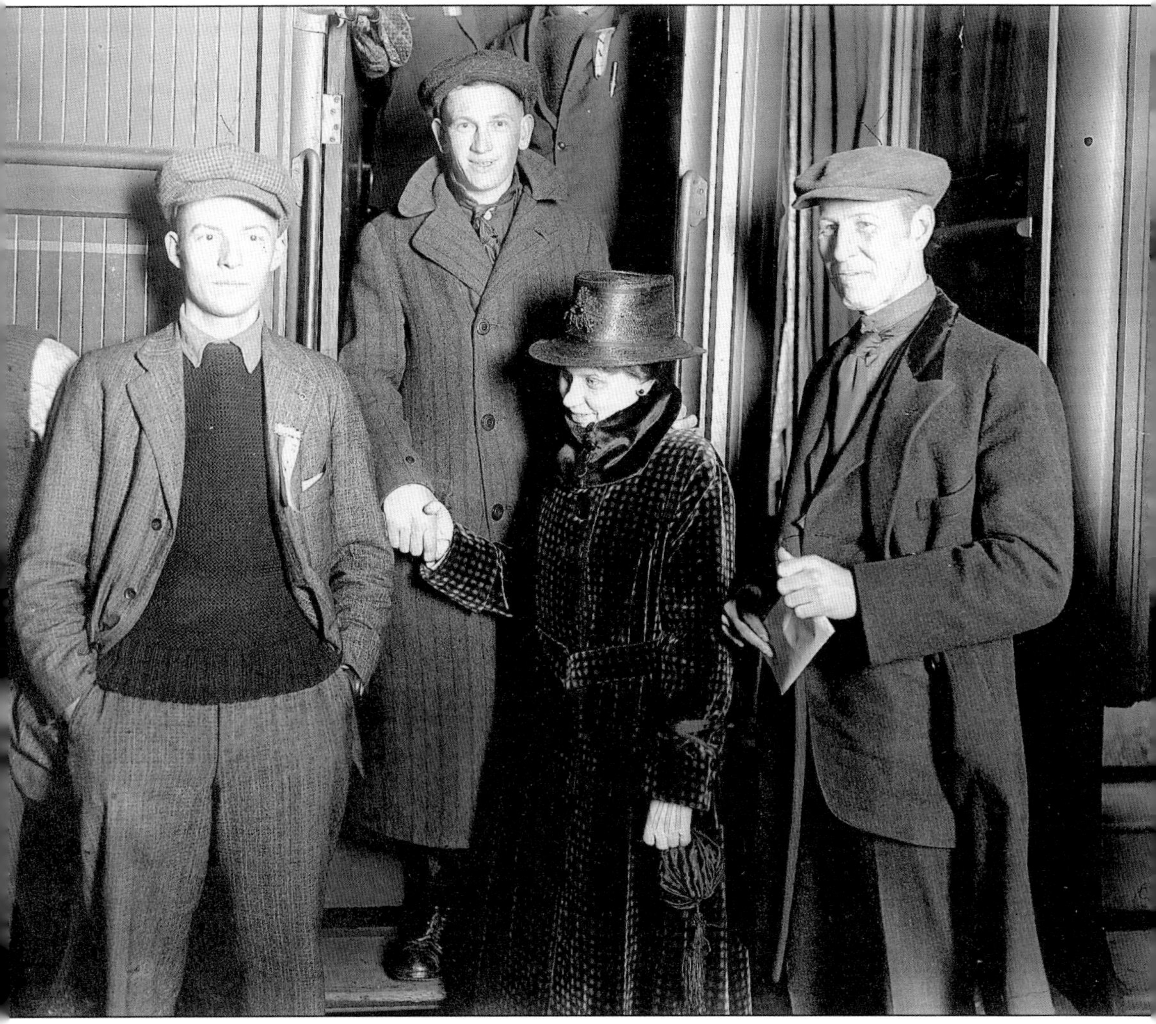

The following are World War I letters home to Broome County, dating from 1914 to 1918:

—Dad, it is good of you and sis to send things when I know you are strapped for cash, but I appreciate the cigars and socks.
—Dear Mother, At last I was able to get away from Brest, that hole in hell & blot on God's creation. Bordeau while drizzly is still a better place. Some 'frog' got my Christmas box from you and I wish him medical distress.
—Folks, hope you are fine these heat less, meatless, wheat less days.
—Folks, I fear in another year I will be useless for anything but war.
—Mom, hope you are making Victory Bread & canning up enough steam to can the Kaiser.
—Dear Son, the first Army Corps along with the British, French and Italians are sure putting a crimp in Heine's tail on the Marne Sector.

This photograph shows a family leave-taking at a troop train in Binghamton at the beginning of the war.

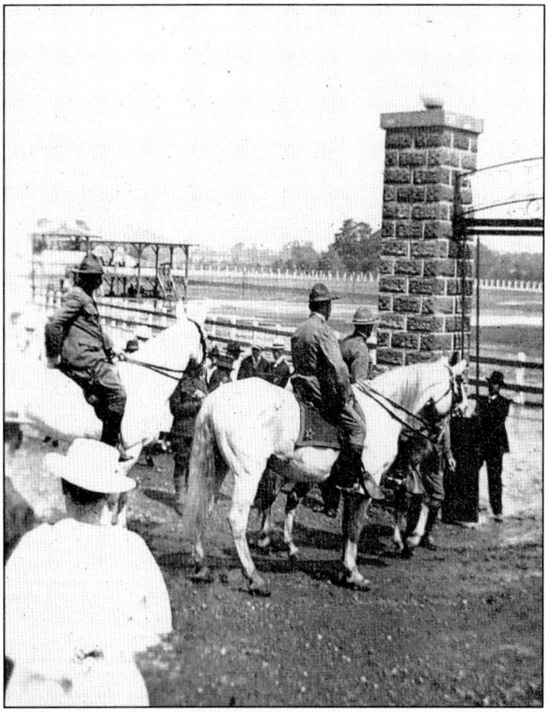

A home defense guard was formed in Broome County during World War I. All arms were furnished by George F. Johnson, and the members were permitted to carry the weapons to their homes. In this photograph, one of the units is practicing at Casino Park in Endicott in 1916.

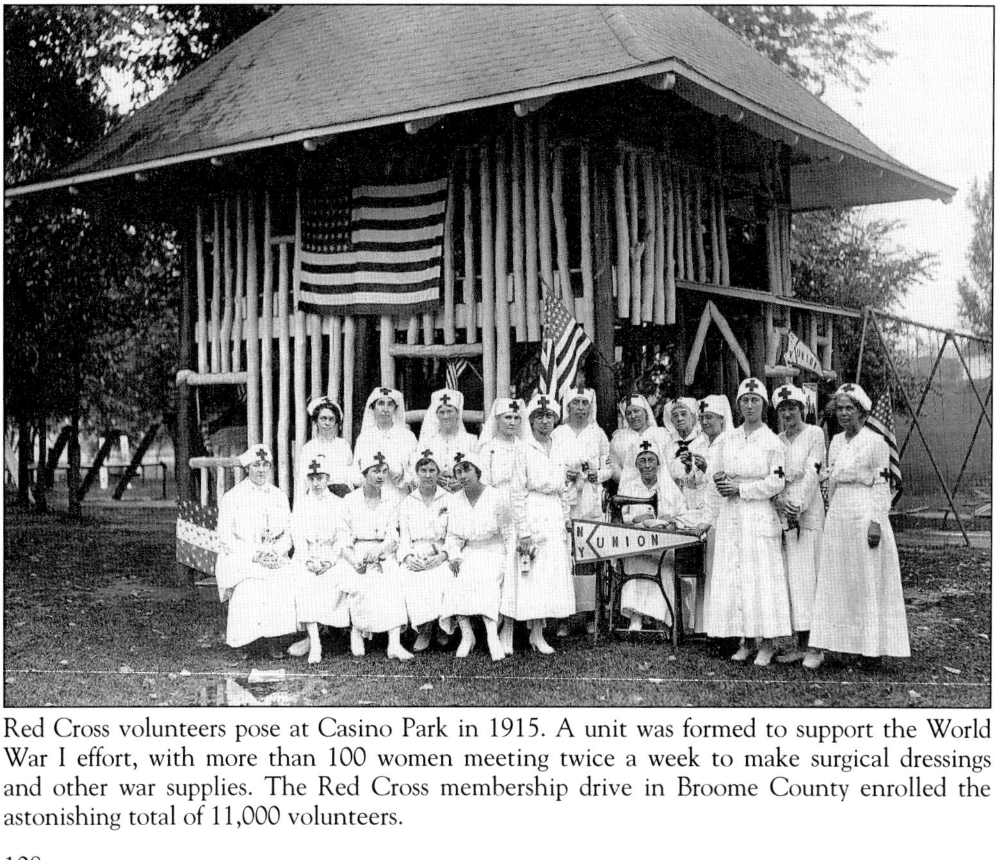

Red Cross volunteers pose at Casino Park in 1915. A unit was formed to support the World War I effort, with more than 100 women meeting twice a week to make surgical dressings and other war supplies. The Red Cross membership drive in Broome County enrolled the astonishing total of 11,000 volunteers.

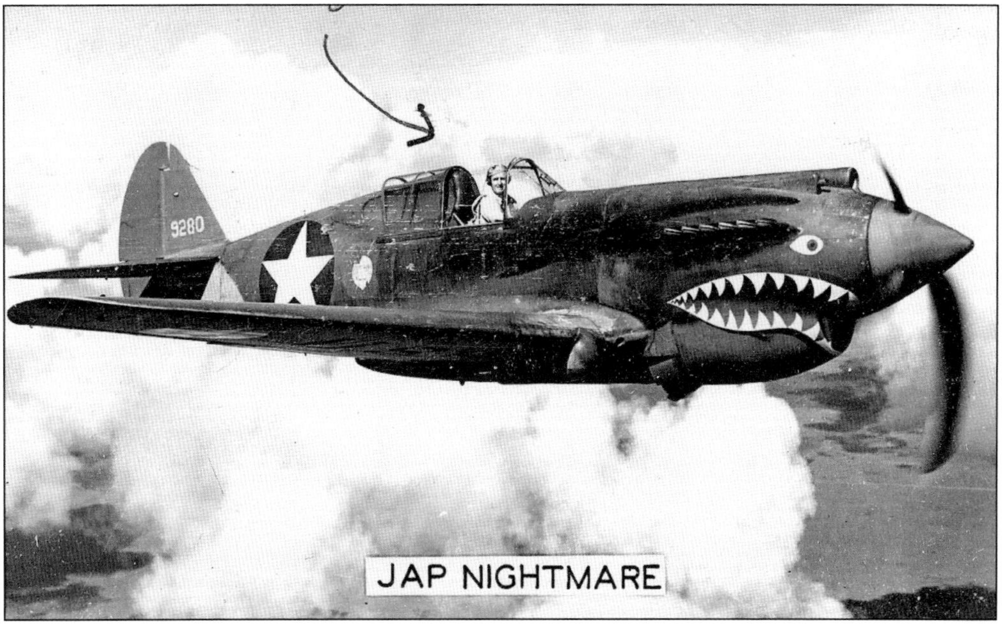

Typical of the patriotism shown by Americans during World War II is this postcard sent home in 1943 by a potential pilot. The booklet below was published by the military as the Great War ended. It included information about what a soldier could expect before being mustered out of the armed forces and advised that occupation duty was important for making the world safe from future wars.

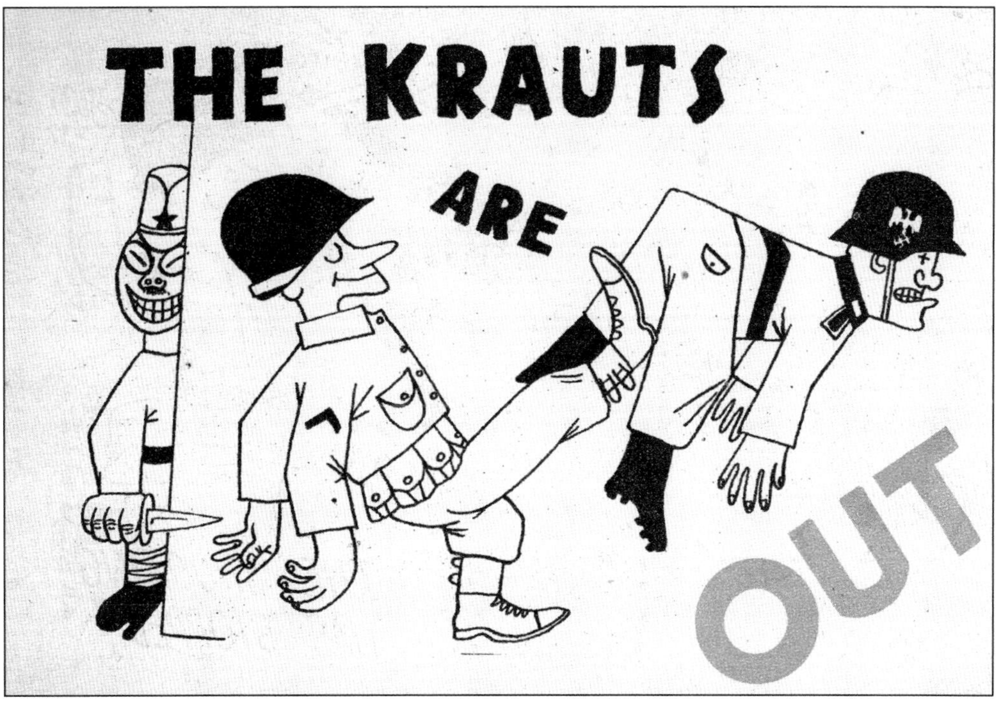

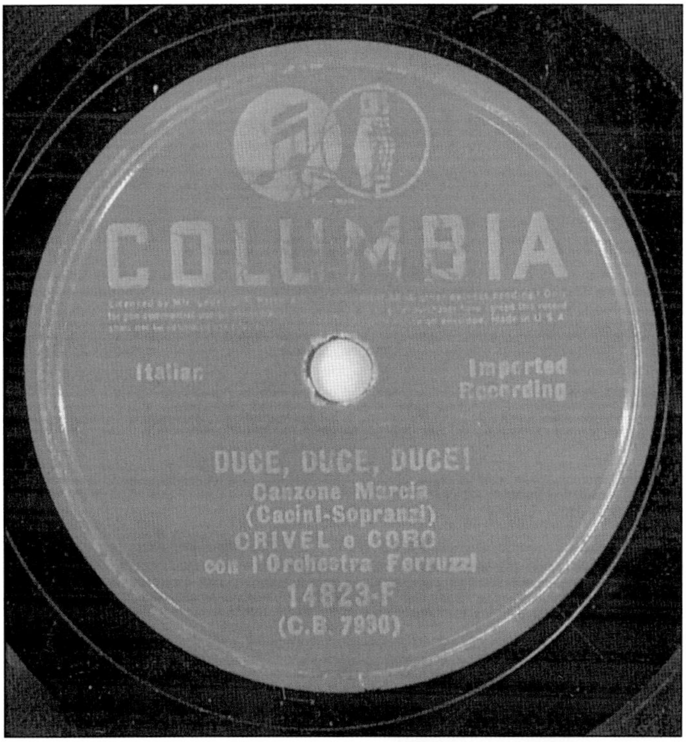

A local Italian family was sent this record in 1940 from relatives in Italy. Although the American parents were embarrassed to own the record, their children loved marching to the lively music, not realizing that the title *Duce, Duce, Duce* (leader) was a tribute to the fascist dictator of Italy, Benito Mussolini.

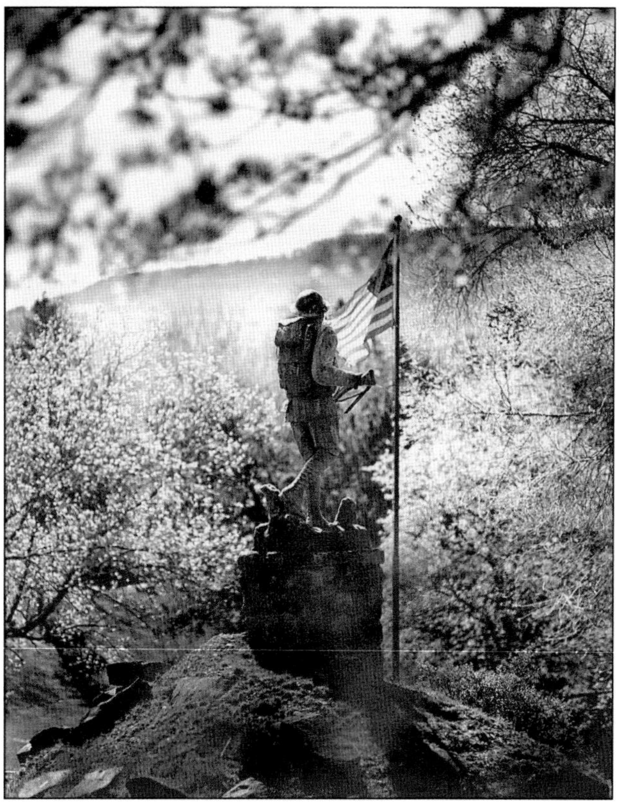

The historian Wilkinson in 1840 wrote, "The local hillsides do not rise high enough to be considered sublime, but are comforting." Nowhere is this truer than in Vestal Hills Memorial Park. A powerful monument reigns over the valley of memories, a tribute to those who served the United States during military actions.

Four

Legends, Lore, and Loonies

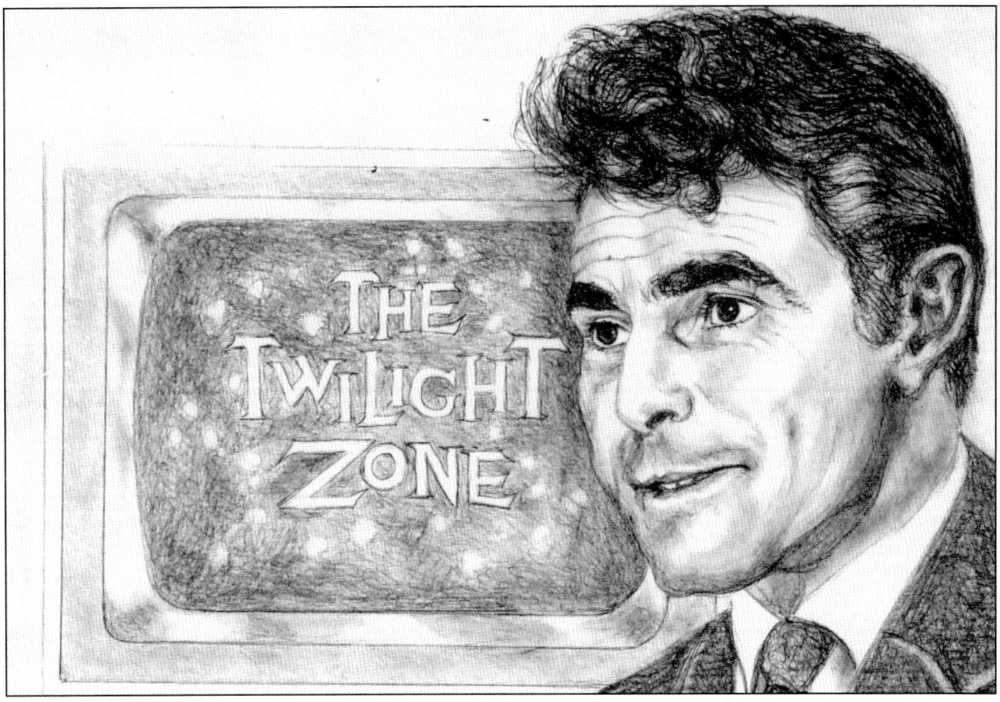

Time weaves some very strange threads into the fabric of life. No one knew this better than Rod Serling, the nationally-known writer and television personality. Serling considered Binghamton his hometown, so, in honor of the master of the genre of bizarre, we present legends, lore, and almost true stories of Broome County and the surrounding areas. This drawing was created by artist Robert Keller for the Rod Serling Foundation.

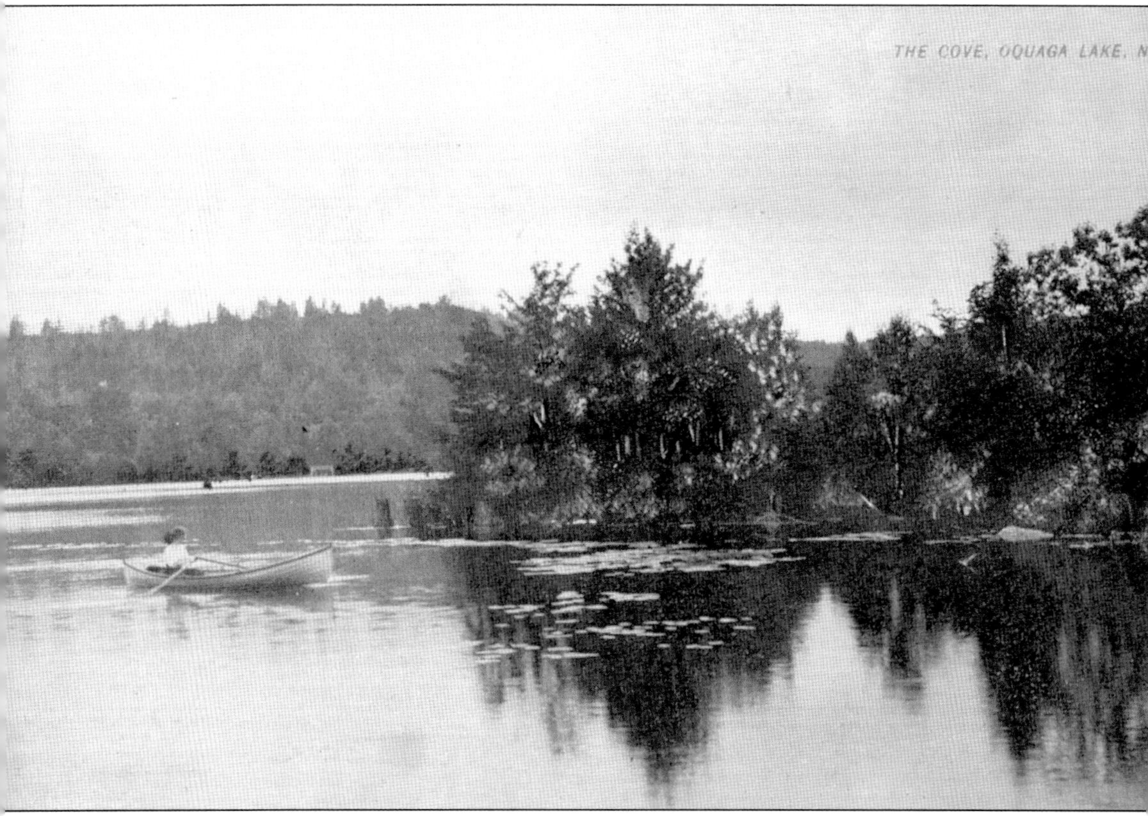

The following tale was told by an octogenarian who was present when the Oquaga Monster was caught. During World War II, food shortages and rationing were prevalent. Local people augmented food supplies by fishing in Oquaga Lake. Parts of the icy depths reach 180 feet, but in other areas traditional methods of measurement have failed to locate the bottom. On an overcast day in 1942, a regular fisherman tried his luck over one of the deepest frigid pools, where he hooked and landed what became quietly known as the Oquaga Monster. Described as six feet long and prehistoric looking, it "resembled neither fish or eel, or any other water varmint and was able to live for quite some time outside the water." Everyone who saw the creature agreed it was in the best interests of the community not to let the existence of a beast become widely known. No one wanted to take a chance on eating the thing, so the "monster" was carried into the woods and buried where the remains were never likely to be found.

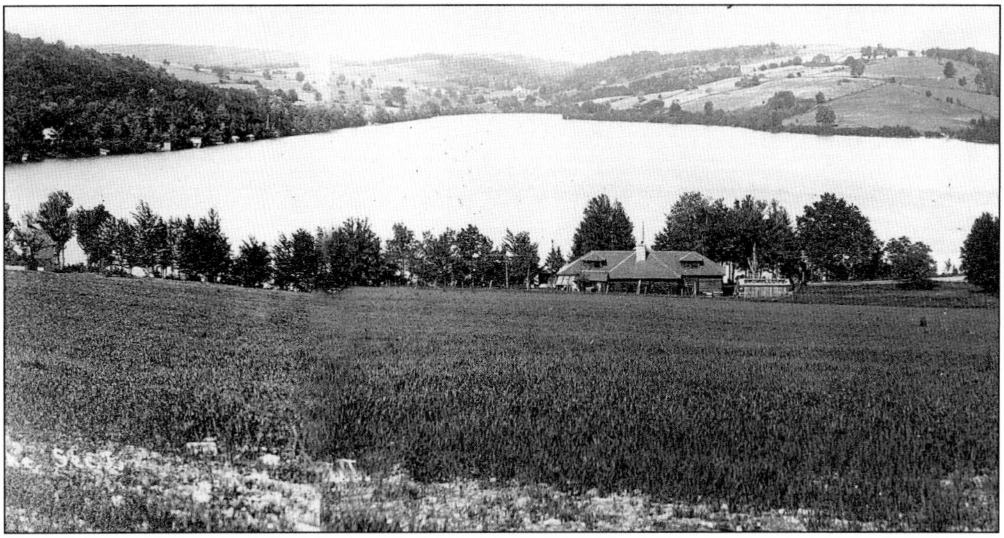

Quaker Lake, once called Derwent Lake, has attracted many Broome residents who own or rent cottages in the area. Over the years, sightings of a surfing sea serpent have prompted an occasional monster watch party. The creature, affectionately named "Old Basketball Head," has rarely cooperated with photograph opportunities but has a reputation for possessing a benign personality, as far as sea monsters go.

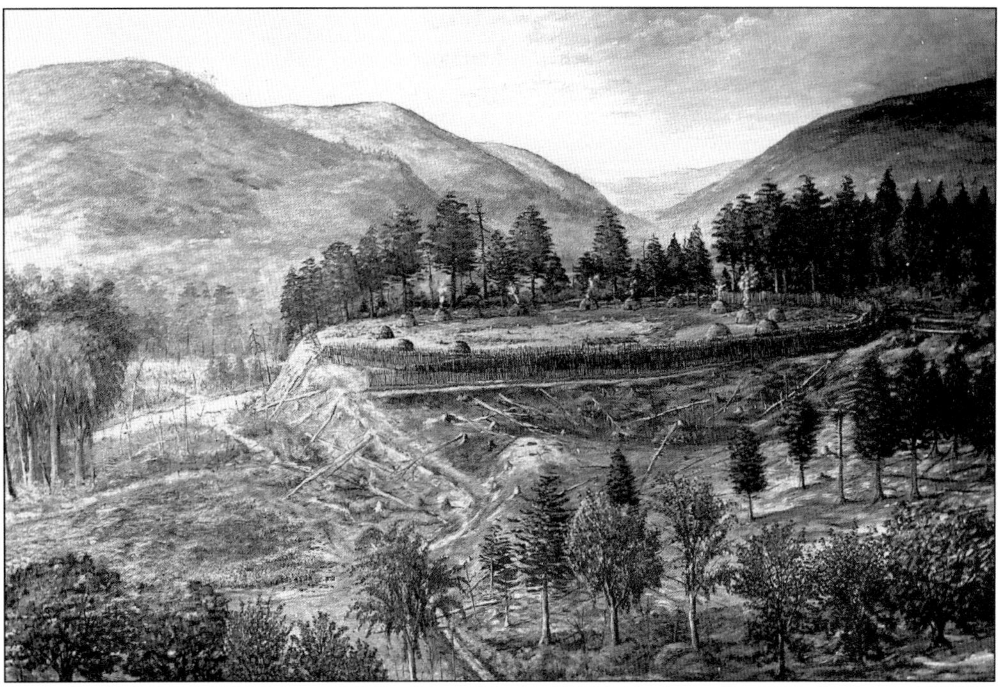

Castle Creek may have a lost treasure cave once belonging to early Native American inhabitants. A 1900 newspaper reported that "an elderly resident has described a yearly pilgrimage made by Indians to their ancestral lands, Castle Farm. They would conduct ceremonies, and occasionally blindfold a trusted white man and escort him to a sacred cave with walls covered in gold. Visits continued through the 1870s." The photograph is of a Foster Disinger painting of the locale.

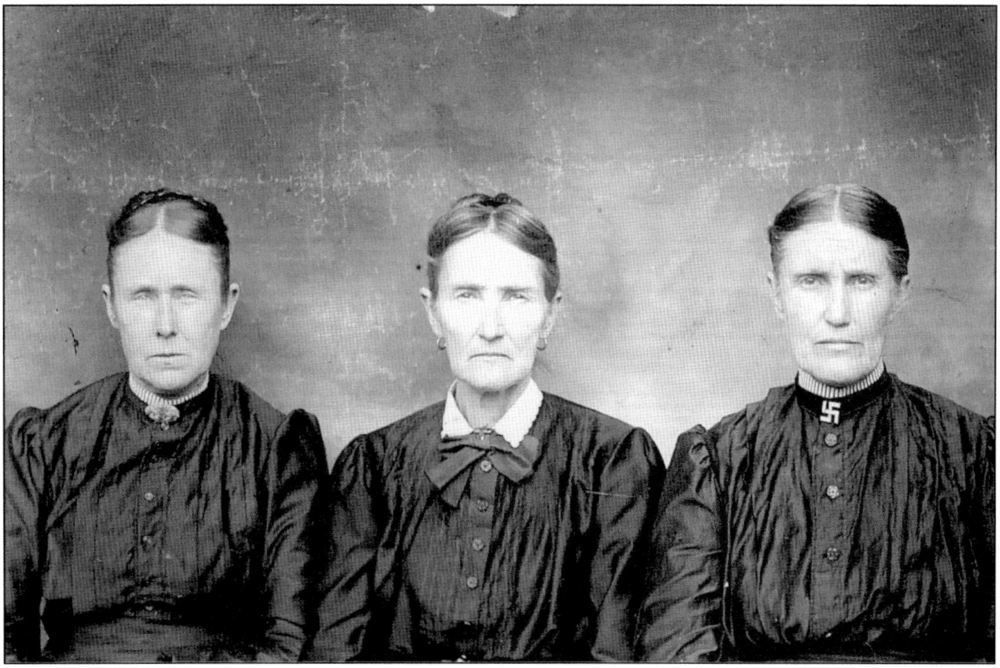

The photograph of three women was taken in 1890 and was carefully preserved with the postcard below. Perhaps an embarrassed descendant wished to explain why his relative was wearing a broach molded in the form of a swastika, although the image was created long before it became associated with war and death. The ancient symbol has been seen for more than 2,000 years in astronomy, art, and as a good luck charm in dozens of cultures. One theory of the origin of the shape is its resemblance to the four seasonal positions of the Big Dipper. The postcard below was used in 1907. Both items were from a Binghamton family.

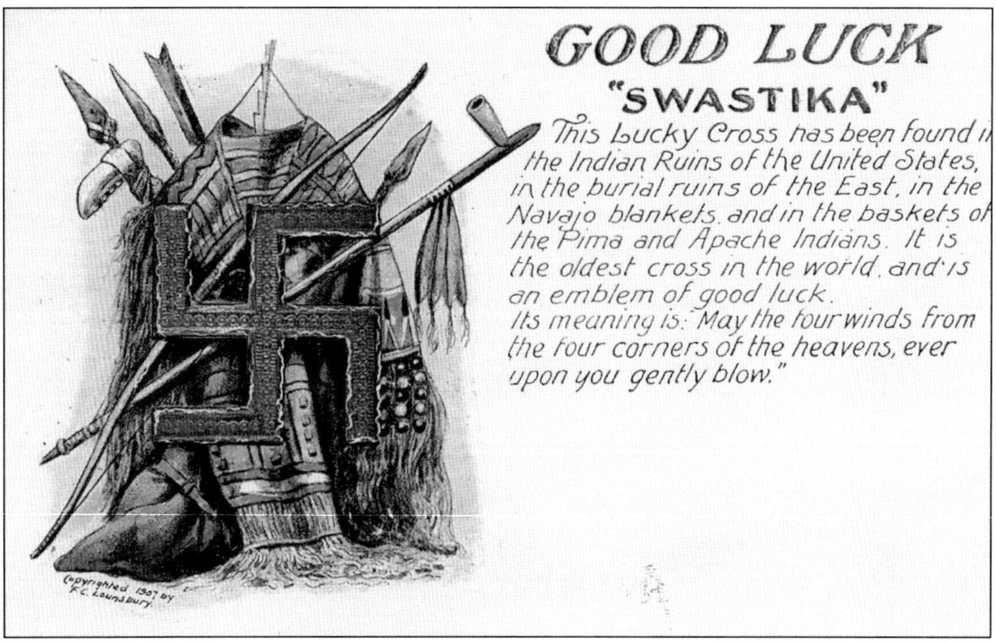

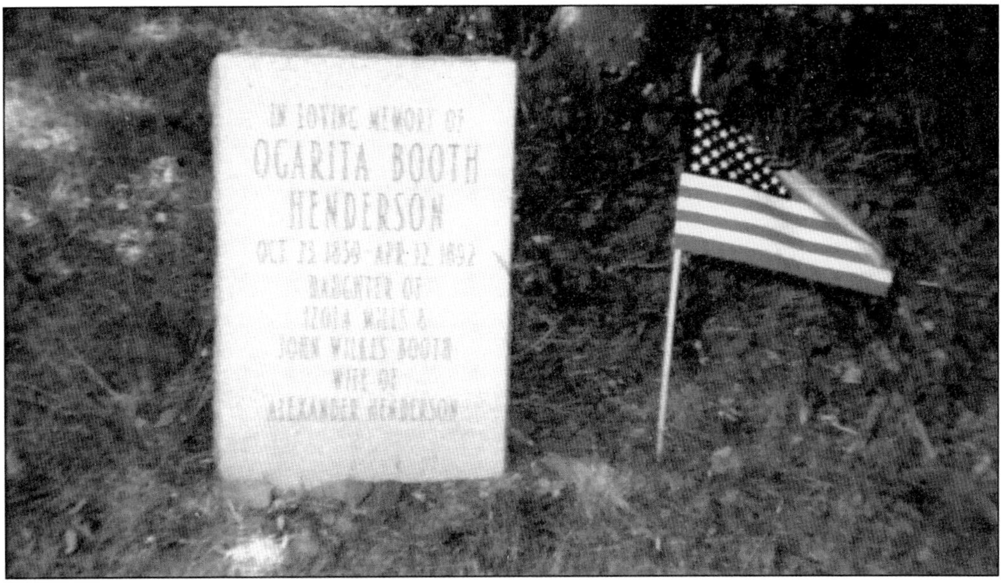

In Glenwood Cemetery on Mount Prospect is a new headstone designating a grave as the final resting place of Ogarita Booth Henderson, a traveling actress who died in 1892 while performing in Binghamton. The stone was erected by Ogarita Henderson's descendants, claiming she was the legitimate daughter of John Wilkes Booth, assassin of Pres. Abraham Lincoln. Many historians disagree with the words carved in granite, believing Booth never married.

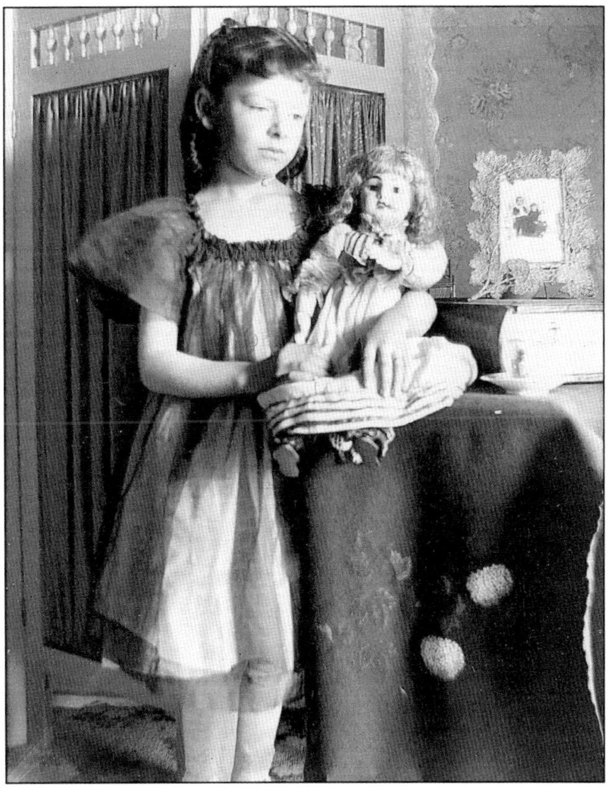

This report was published in a local newspaper: "In 1898 a gentleman living on Chenango Street had a severe 'attack of nervous prostration' late one night while making a necessary trip to the back yard. His distress was caused by a frightening whack on the leg by a creature emitting a fearful squawk. The man claimed a rattlesnake of huge proportions made him faint. Later the culprit was discovered to be his small daughters rubber doll left on the path. The true facts have made him sicker and his recovery from embarrassment is doubtful."

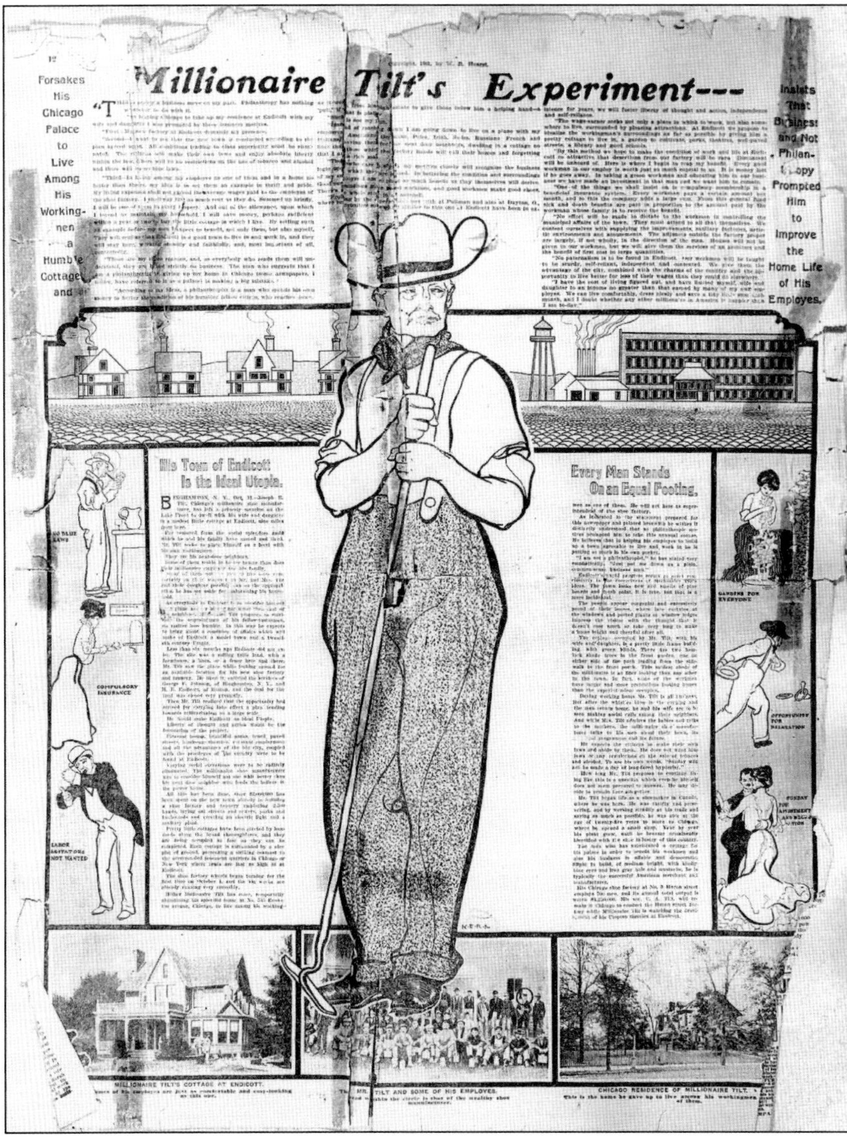

The "Magic City" of Endicott was built in 1901 by the Endicott Johnson Shoe Company. New factories and a modern utopian atmosphere were created. At the same time in Chicago, a full-page article in a newspaper owned by William Randolph Hearst reported that "millionaire J.E. Tilt was moving from his mansion in Chicago to a simple workers cottage in Endicott. . . to be closer to workers he managed at the EJ shoe plant." Tilt planned to live in perfect social equality, envisioning a "square deal town" where fairness would rule. The truth was buried deep and no one has been able to find mention of Tilt in local records until now. If this story were a hoax, even the *Binghamton Globe* fell prey. On July 6, 1901, the newspaper ran a story of millionaire Joseph E. Tilt moving to Endicott. Tilt did exist and for a short while lived in Endicott. In July 1901, the *Lestershire Press* wrote a lengthy article about Tilt, including a physical description. A story in the same paper in November 1901 describes his abrupt severing of connections with Endicott Johnson. A rift between George F. Johnson and Tilt is hinted. When Tilt vacated the Endicott home, C. Fred Johnson moved into the house and into the position of general manager of EJ.

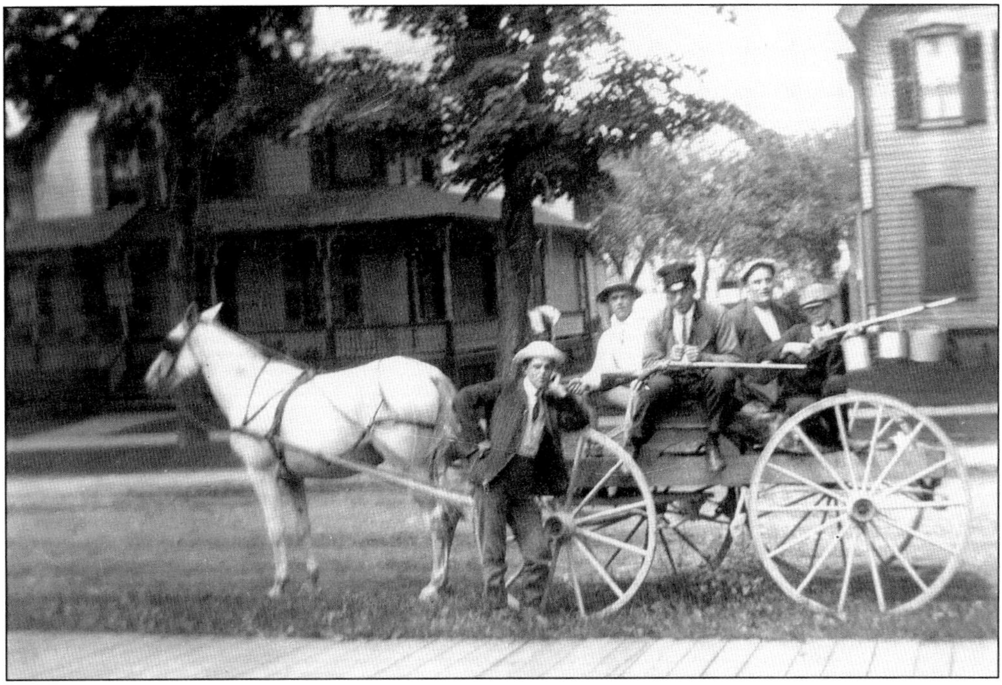

The picture shows Broome County men on their way to demonstrate marksmanship of a shooting phenomenon. As reported in 1876, "It is not generally known that an orange hit in the exact center by a rifle ball will completely vanish at once from sight. Such, however is the fact, and expert shooting through the center scatters the orange into such infinitesimal pieces as to be invisible."

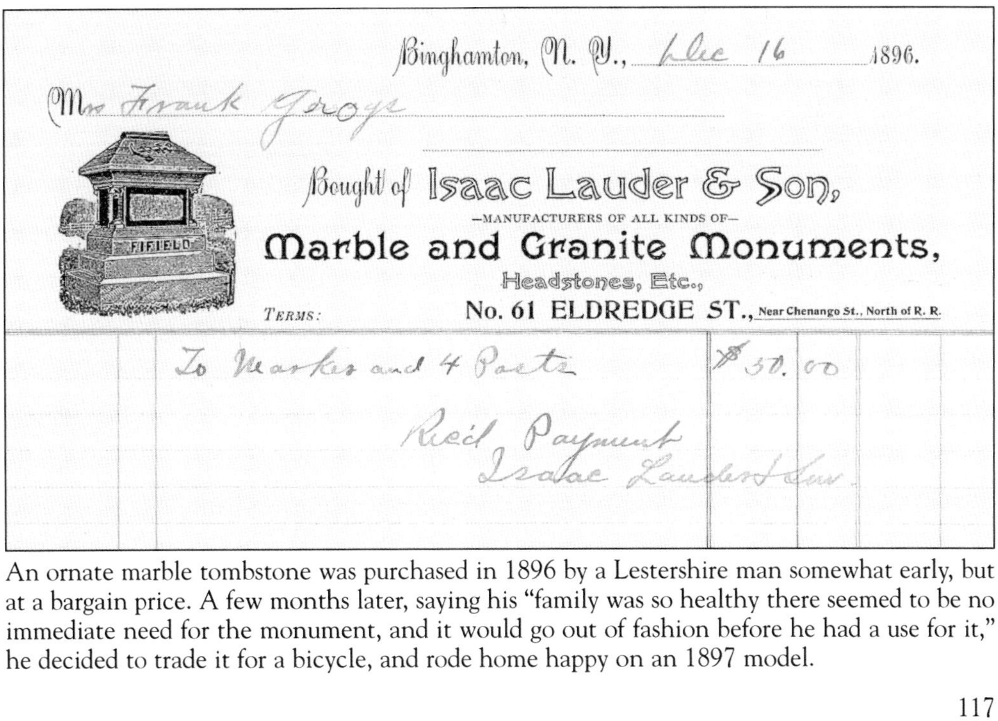

Binghamton, N. Y., Dec 16 1896.

Mrs Frank Gross

Bought of Isaac Lauder & Son,

—MANUFACTURERS OF ALL KINDS OF—

Marble and Granite Monuments,

Headstones, Etc.,

TERMS: No. 61 ELDREDGE ST., Near Chenango St., North of R. R.

	To Marker and 4 Posts	$30.	00	
	Rec'd Payment Isaac Lauder & Son			

An ornate marble tombstone was purchased in 1896 by a Lestershire man somewhat early, but at a bargain price. A few months later, saying his "family was so healthy there seemed to be no immediate need for the monument, and it would go out of fashion before he had a use for it," he decided to trade it for a bicycle, and rode home happy on an 1897 model.

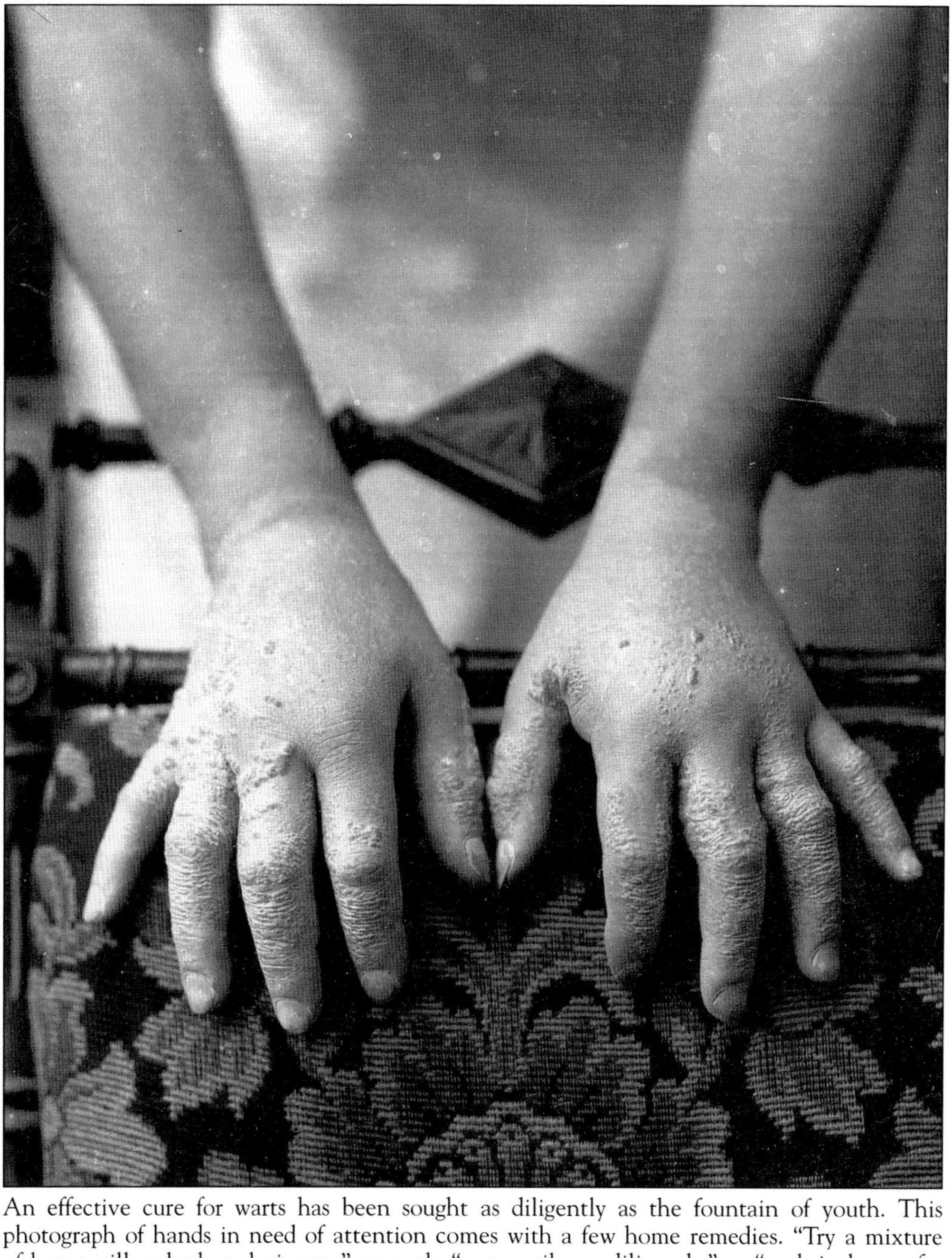

An effective cure for warts has been sought as diligently as the fountain of youth. This photograph of hands in need of attention comes with a few home remedies. "Try a mixture of burnt willow bark and vinegar," or apply "castor oil . . . diligently," or "soak in bacon fat till it rots" (presumably just the afflicted part), or "marigold flower juice could work," or try "banana peels held to the blight for two days," or "use the juice of green bean leaves." All treatments claimed to remove any vexation but in this case were used without success. The most interesting suggestion was dated 1874: "To rid oneself from hard horny protuberances touch the offending part on the tip twice a day or more with a clean quill dipped into aquafortis. After a few applications it will turn brown and fall off." Hopefully this recipe was only for warts. The picture was captured on a glass negative *c*. 1900.

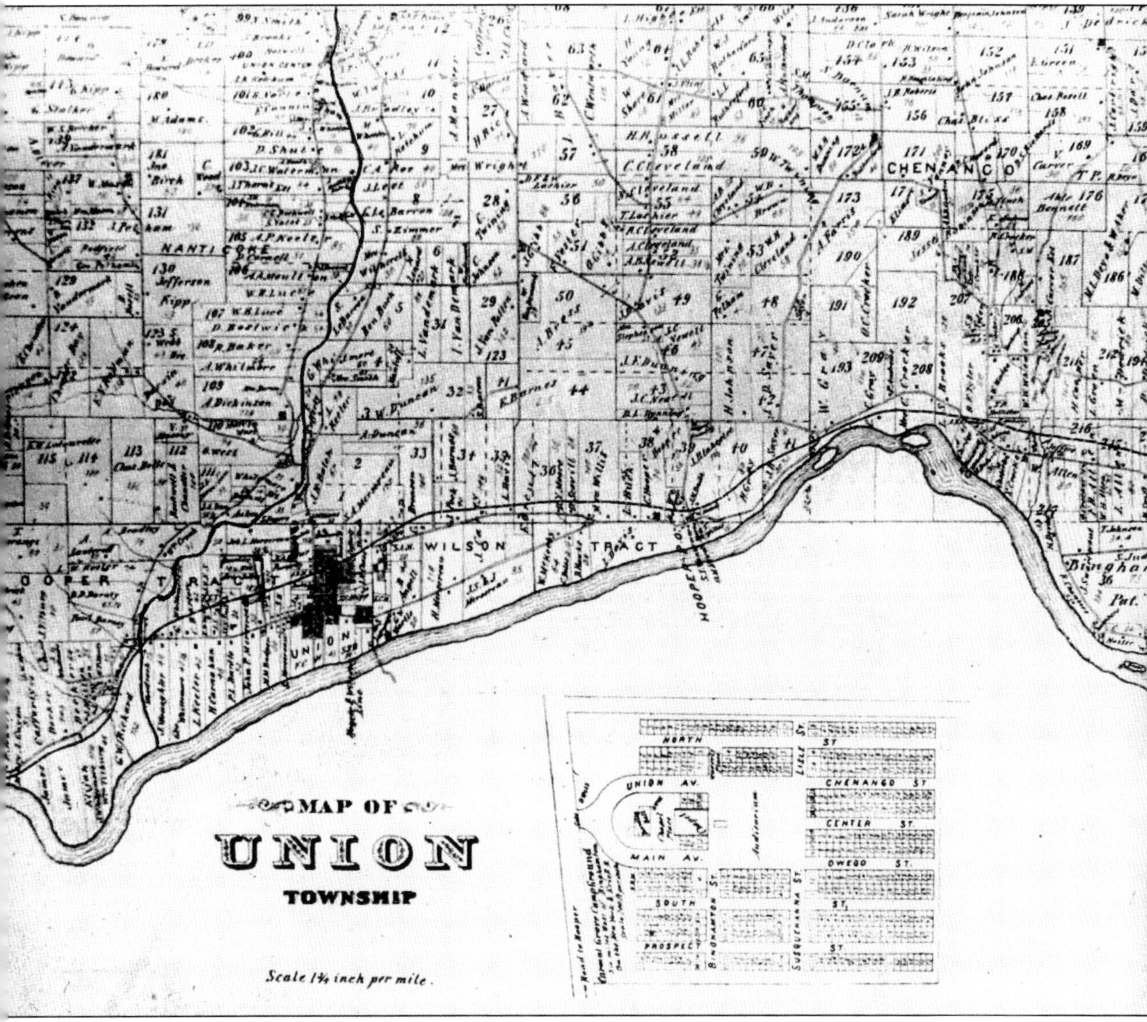

"Discovers lost treasure cave," read the *Union News* of 1876, followed by this article:

> A man supposedly sane and sober reported that on a squirrel hunt he chased the critter until it disappeared suddenly. Upon searching around he found a small steel ring attached to a stone slab in the ground. Being curious he opened the hidden door and followed a flight of stone steps into the dark earth—he ran home for a lantern and continued the search. The only inhabitant was a mummified figure seated on an ornate chair wearing a large amount of jewelry. Gold pieces in odd shapes with queer inscriptions were also found in abundance. The foul cave air made him dizzy. . . . He staggered outside, fainted then dragged himself home. Upon recovery he plans to find the treasure spot again, . . . sure it was not more than 200 feet from the bridge on the bank of Nanticoke Creek . . . just below the sawmill.
>
> He never found the cave again, and if anyone is interested in following the treasure trail along the creek noted on this map, there were at least seven sawmills bordering the creek.

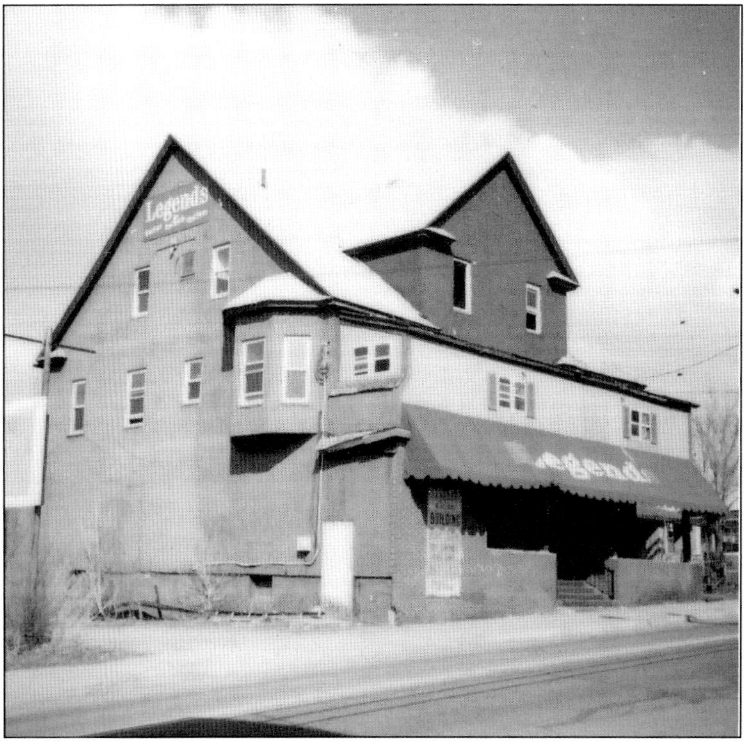

Prohibition did not put taverns out of business—operations just went underground, sometimes literally. A man whose father once owned this building on Oak Hill Avenue tells of finding an underground room in the backyard years after Prohibition had ended, still equipped with tables and hooch waiting for a speakeasy to open. He claims a tunnel system under Endicott had been extensive in order to thwart the "feds." This site is now a parking lot.

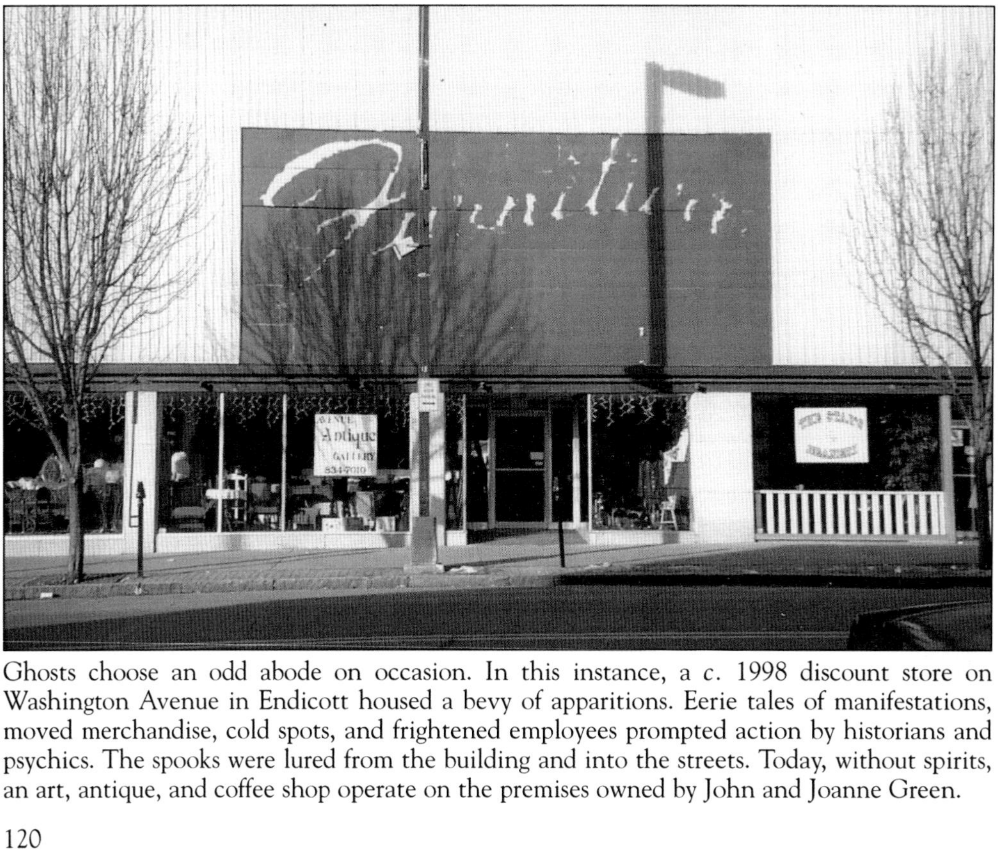

Ghosts choose an odd abode on occasion. In this instance, a c. 1998 discount store on Washington Avenue in Endicott housed a bevy of apparitions. Eerie tales of manifestations, moved merchandise, cold spots, and frightened employees prompted action by historians and psychics. The spooks were lured from the building and into the streets. Today, without spirits, an art, antique, and coffee shop operate on the premises owned by John and Joanne Green.

Throughout the 1890s, German immigrants maintained a tradition of creating a life-size wax effigy of a dead child to be viewed during the funeral instead of the corpse. The image was garbed in clothes of the deceased, with strands of human hair incorporated into the folk art doll. It was displayed at the wake and then left at the graveside. The picture shows a *c.* 1898 doll that survived the elements.

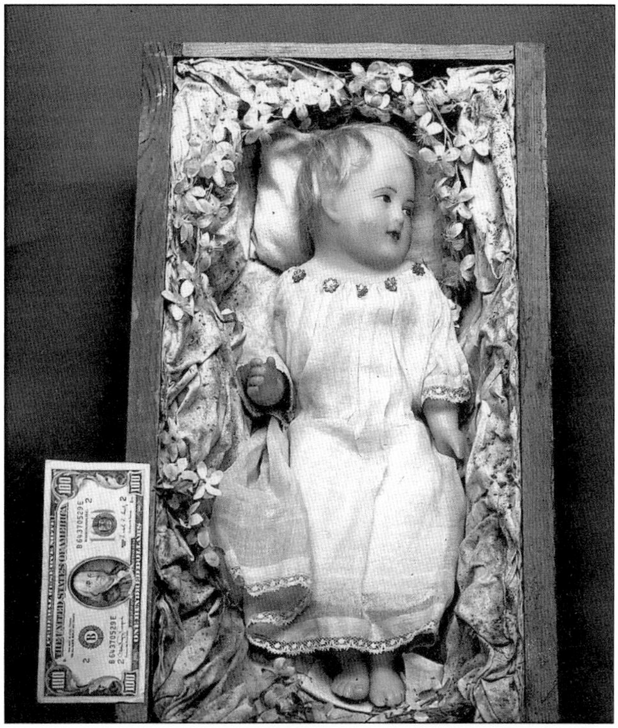

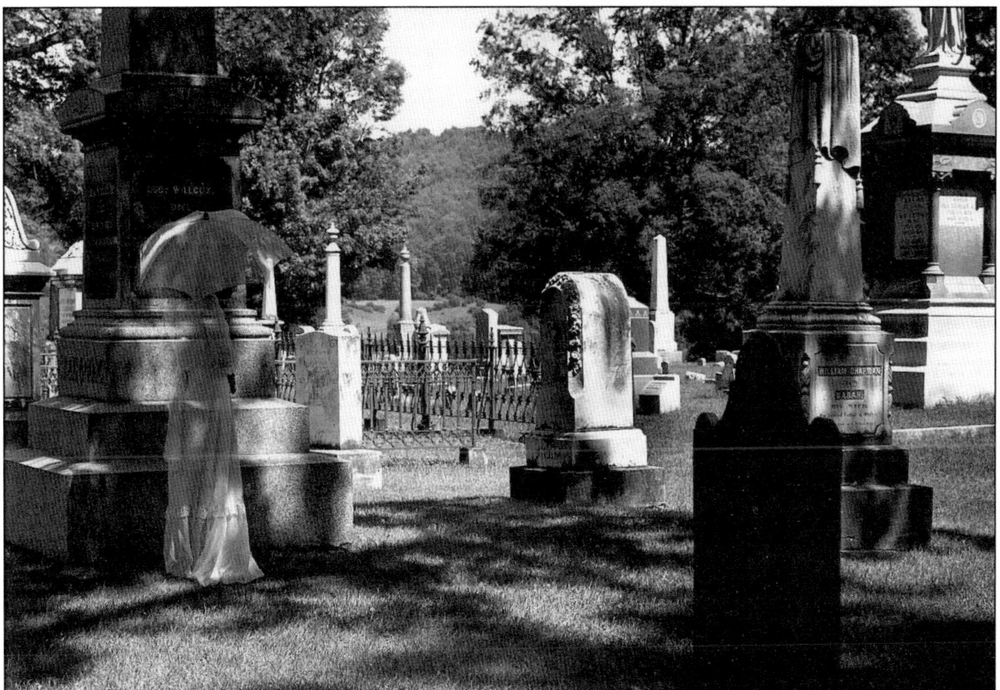

Cemeteries are repositories for memories and sometimes for the wit of a photographer. Proving you cannot always believe what you see, this ghostly image may have been created by the authors. It is appropriately entitled "I Was and Perhaps I Am."

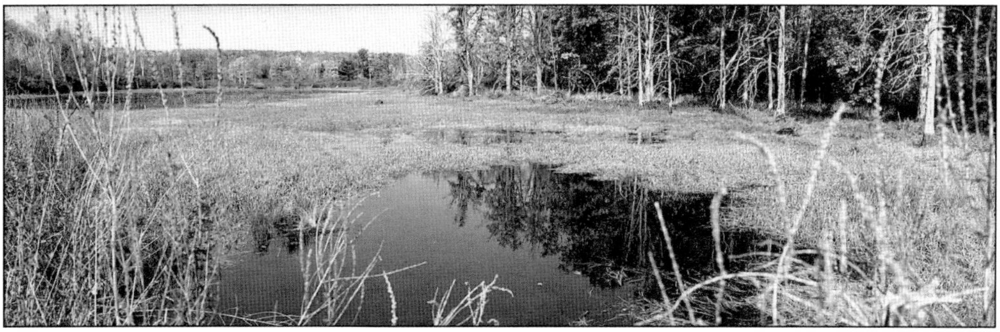

Boland, or Cutler, Pond is located where archeological evidence suggests early occupation by Native Americans; therefore, this story is within the realm of the possible. An elderly gentleman related a tale originally told by his father: "He cut ice for decades at the old pond. One year the water level was terrible low. When the ice blocks were pulled free Dad claimed to see the remnants of a village, . . . foundations and items well preserved."

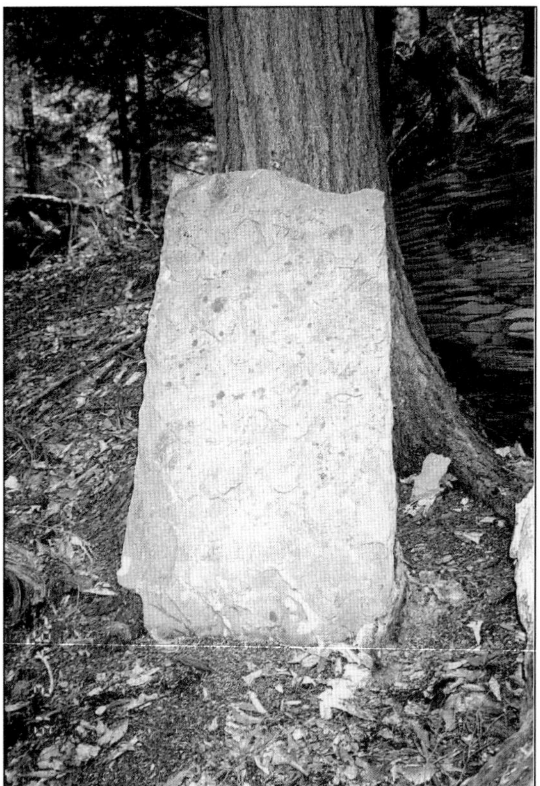

In 1721, on a remote forested hillside in Vestal far from any road, William Platt was buried. A massive slab of native stone, pulled from the surrounding craggy cliffs, leans against a towering fir tree. Crudely carved letters on the marker are the lasting memorial for a man who may be the earliest Caucasian burial in Broome County. The saga of Platt's existence and death were interred with his bones.

In 1867, "excitement was caused by a cosmetic aid! False ears made of flesh colored India rubber [are available] for ladies with over large auditory apparatus! [They are] to be placed in front of real ears, which are drawn back & concealed under the hair." In 1868, a law passed in England that would soon reach America: "All women of whatever age who betray into matrimony any male by virtue of scents, paints, cosmetics, artificial teeth or hair, bolstered hips, high heeled shoes or Spanish wool stuffing, shall incur the penalty of the law against witchcraft and like misdemeanors. . . . Any marriage commenced under these circumstances shall be void." Men also watched their appearance. After this article appeared in the local paper, heavily bearded men congratulated themselves on their foresight in growing a "coat of protection": "Science now claims that full beards are a defense against bronchitis and sore throat. Also, fully fuzzy features prevent colds and most morbid dispositions." The photographs depict local people in the era in which this information was printed.

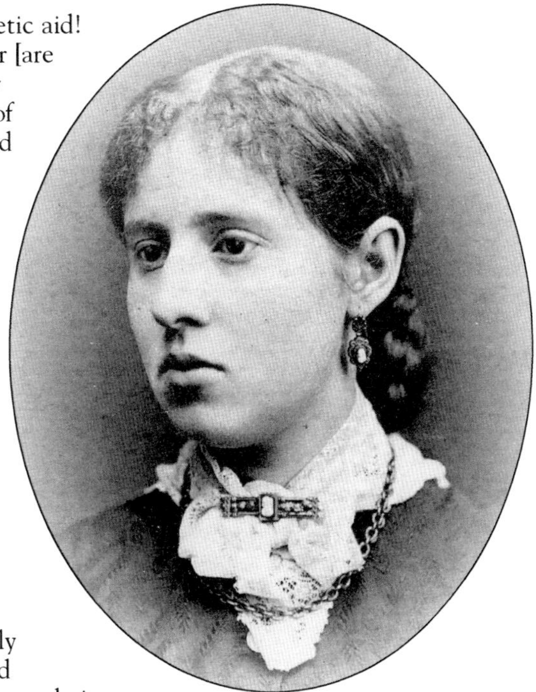

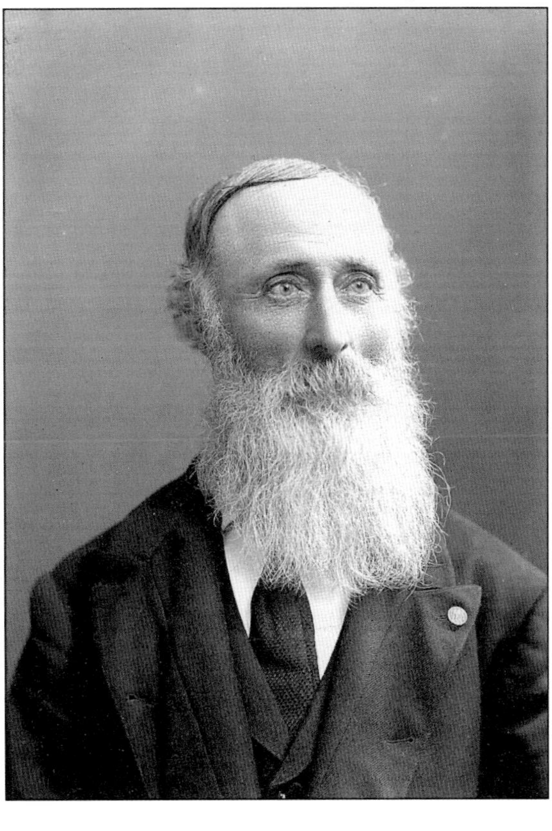

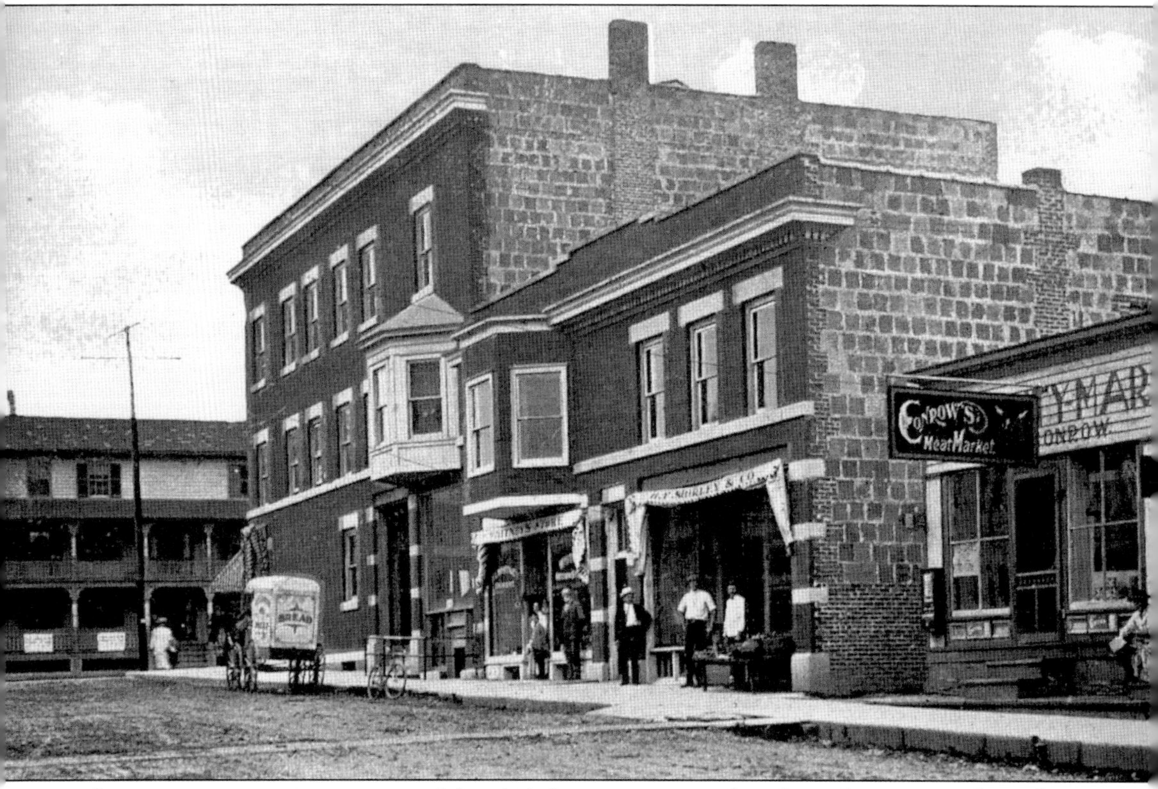

In years past, justice was served by slightly more personal and quicker means than those applied today:

> 1859—Crowd gathers on Exchange Street in Union for the purpose of a tar and feather party for a promiscuous lady. Local sheriff saves her from this fate by putting her on a westbound train and extracting a promise to never return. [News account.]
> 1876—For three months some miscreant has been seizing hold of ladies and using insulting and threatening language on Nanticoke Street. Ladies are afraid to stroll without an escort. Neighbors advocate a coat of tar and feathers as a souvenir of the ruffians misdeeds as soon as he is caught. [News account.]
> 1906—The Greek who keeps the candy store pounded his wife again last night and some men in the neighborhood took him and tarred and feathered him. The latest spring suit for a bully. [Personal letter sent from an Endicott resident to a Binghamton relative.]

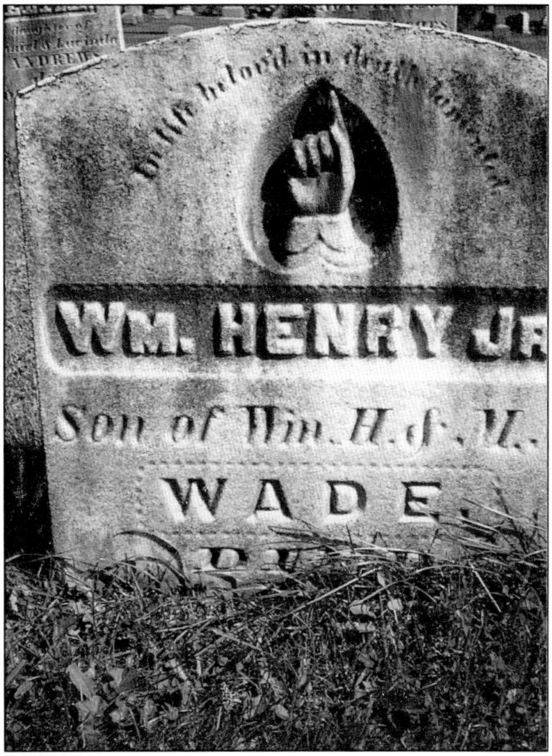

Cemeteries contain history, pathos, and occasionally humor. A gravestone with a carved hand holding one finger pointing upward is considered a symbol of the direction the deceased's soul will be traveling. Such engravings are commonly found on memorial stones of the 1800s. However, in a small country burial ground near the Broome and Tioga County border, an unusual variation can be found. The hand on this fallen stone is pointing downward; any interpretation is left to the observer.

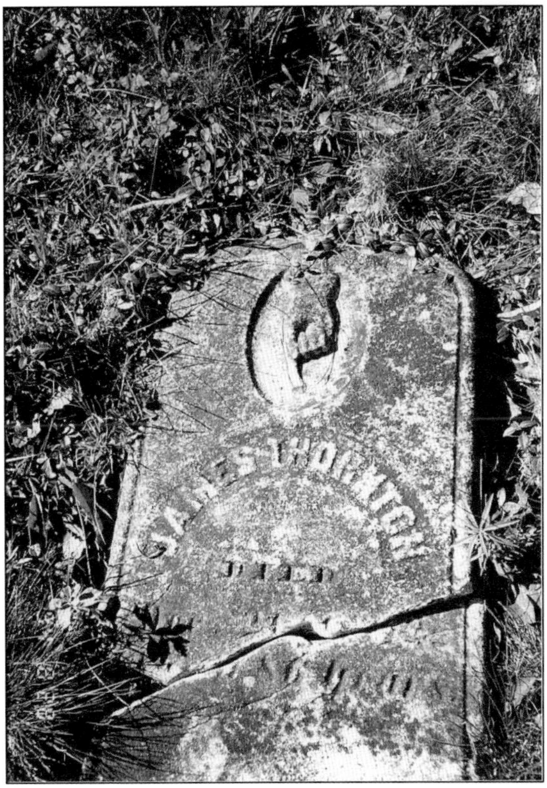

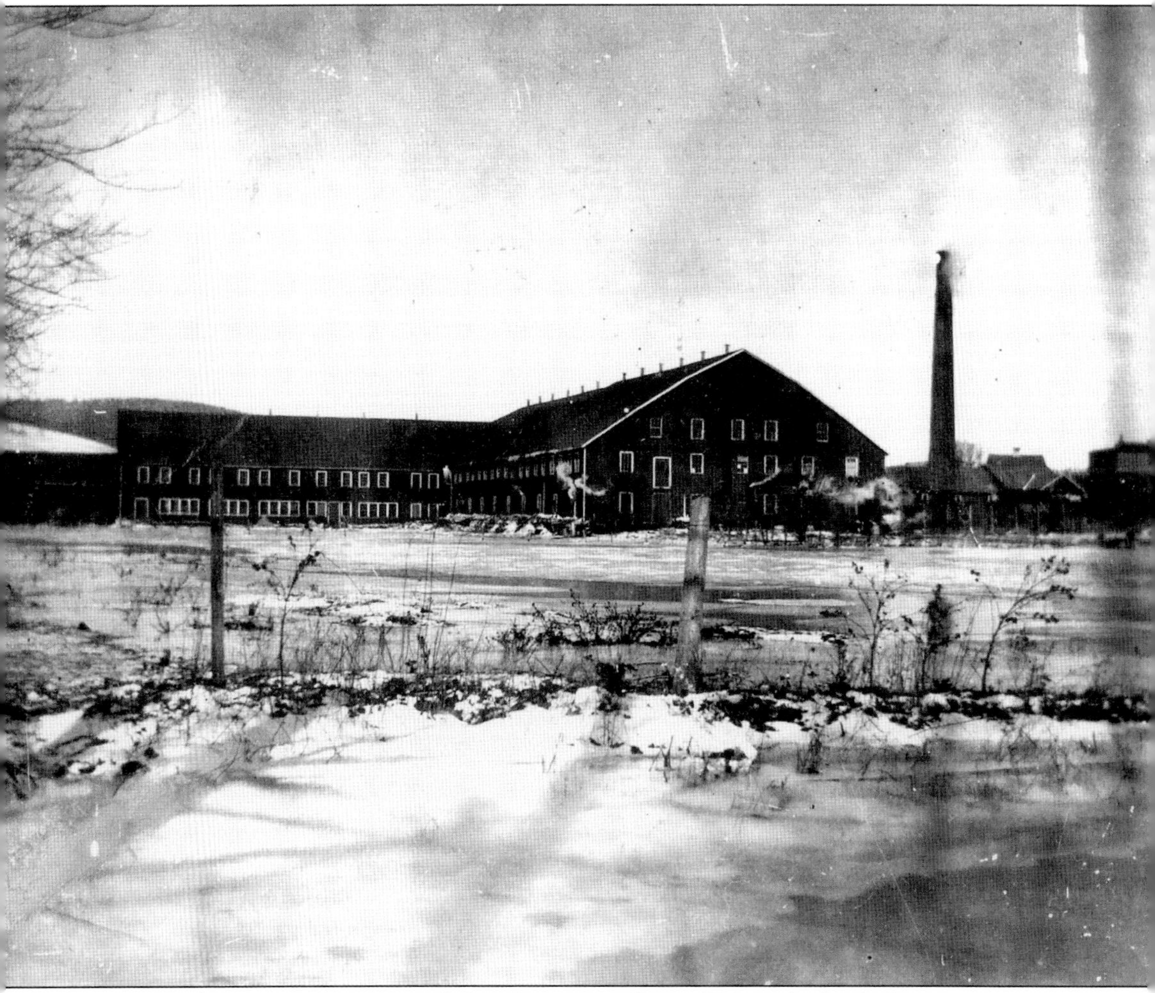

In 1883, the *Union News* reported that the quiet village of Maine had a frightening visitation. Two employees of the Sherwood Tannery were drawing bark in the woods when they were startled by loud noises in the bushes. A huge creature with many of the general characteristics of a man uttered "demonic shrieks" and ran past them into the deep forest. The "Wild Man" was covered with vast amounts of brown hair. The experience was repeated many times over the ensuing months, with scores of people attesting to the veracity of the description. Could it have been a noisy bear, hysteria, or our own version of Big Foot?

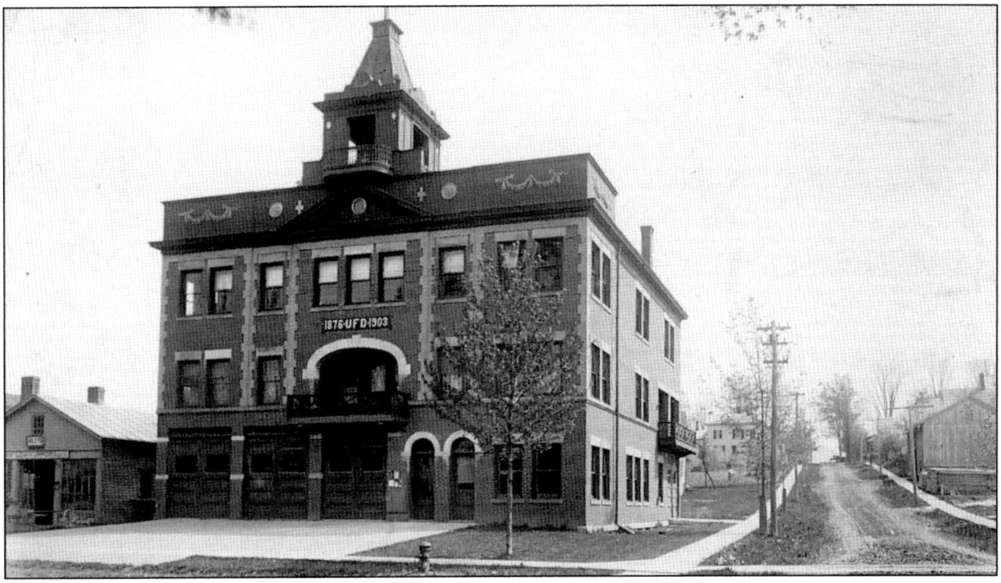

Spook housing must be at a premium. A 19th-century ghost is reported to wander through a modest home that was built in 1935. The shade of a top-hatted man clanks, claws at doors, weeps, causes cold spots, stomps on steps, and bothers pets—all in a quiet neighborhood in West Endicott not far from this fire station and around the corner from a pub where the rowdy spirits usually hang out.

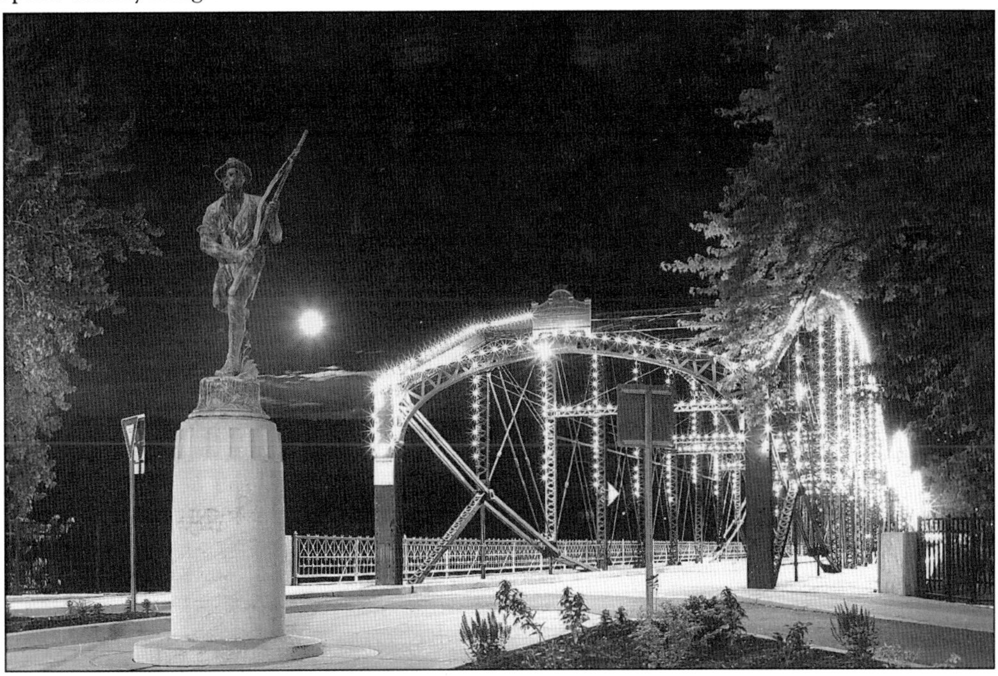

Binghamton's South Washington Street Bridge, built in 1866, is not only a historic structure, but a "Bridge to Betrothal." Outlined in shimmering lights, it is gaining a reputation as a destination for lovers, inspiring proposals of marriage and pledges of devotion. Throughout the seasons, beauty and ambiance make this a walkway to the magic realm of romance. (Photograph by Ed Aswad.)

Bibliography

Binghamton Chamber of Commerce. *The Valley of Opportunity*. Binghamton, New York: Charles W. Baldwin, 1920.

Binghamton Illustrated. Binghamton, New York: H.R. Page and Company, 1890.

Binghamton Past and Present: Its Commerce, Trade and Industries. Binghamton, New York: Evening Herald Company, 1894.

Bothwell, Lawrence. *Broome County Heritage: An Illustrated History*. Woodland Hills, California: Windsor Publications, 1983.

Broome County Centennial souvenir program, 1906.

Combination Atlas Map of Broome County New York. Philadelphia: Everts, Ensign and Everts, 1876.

Eight Hour Day. Endicott Johnson Corporation, 1916.

Hinman, Marjory B. *Courthouse Square: A Social History*. Endicott, New York, 1984.

Lawler, William S., ed. *Binghamton, Its Settlement, Growth and Development*. Century Memorial Publishing Company, 1900.

"Progress of Binghamton and Surrounding Counties." *Binghamton Press* historical supplement, 1904.

Putnam, Dr. Frederick, comp. *A Documentary History of Broome County*. 126 vols. Manuscript collection of the Broome County Public Library History Center.

Sax, Helena A., project ed., and James C. Babbit, historical writing. *Broome County American Revolution Bicentennial Edition*, 1976.

Seward, William Foote, ed. *Binghamton and Broome County New York: A History*. 3 vols. New York: Lewis Historical Publishing Company, 1924.

Smith, Gerald R. *The Valley of Opportunity*. Donning Company and the Broome County Historical Society, 1988.

Smith, H.P., ed. *History of Broome County*. Syracuse, New York: D. Mason and Company, 1885.

Topographical Atlas of Broome County New York. From surveys by S.N and D.G. Beers and Assistants. Philadelphia: Stone and Stewart Publishers, 1866.